# NEW ENGLAND

The American Traveler Series

# NEW ENGLAND

## A Handbook for the Independent Traveler

by

Dana Facaros and Michael Pauls

REGNERY GATEWAY
CHICAGO

First published in Great Britain by MacDonald
& Co. in association with Gentry Books Ltd., 1982


This edition published by Regnery Gateway, Inc.
360 West Superior Street, Chicago, Illinois 60610



ISBN No. 0-89526-857-4

Photoset by PP Graphics Ltd., London

Printed and bound by the Garden City Press Ltd.

To: Mrs Elva Erickson and Mrs Joan Snellenberger, our teachers.

# Acknowledgements

We thank the State Tourist Offices and Chambers of Commerce for their gracious and extensive assistance in preparing this book, and in particular Mr Leonard Panaggio of the Rhode Island Department of Economic Development; the Preservation Society of Newport County; Mr Larry Meehan of the Greater Boston Convention and Tourist Bureau; Ms Edie Shaun-Hammond of the National Park Service in Boston; also, thanks to Alex and Ruth Glaros, who gave us a little vacation with their kind hospitality.

# Contents

## List of Maps

# Introduction

> It is the first American section to be finished, to achieve stability in its conditions of life. It is the first old civilization, the first permanent civilization in America.
>
> Bernard DeVoto

On the map the six states east of the Hudson – Connecticut, Rhode Island, Massachusetts, Vermont, New Hampshire and Maine – are tiny; four New Englands could squeeze into Texas. The soil is mostly poor and rocky, a disappointment to its earliest settlers, and the weather 'irresponsible' – Mark Twain, who lived for many years in Hartford, Connecticut, claimed to note as many as twenty different kinds of weather in a single day. But mention New England to the man on the street, and a glossy, brilliantly tinted calendar picture will spring to his mind, with a white spired Congregational church, a weathered barn or two among the white frame houses, surrounded by fauvist trees of red, yellow and orange beneath a blue sky. He'll populate the scene with long-faced, bony Yankee types, frugal, proud and inventive, made somewhat eccentric by their Puritan heritage and harsh climate, honest drivers of hard bargains, who can't pronounce their r's. Mention New England to a student of American culture, and you'll hear how it is the moral conscience and intellect of the United States, the mother of our public schools, universities, philosophy and democratic principles, the instigator of the Revolution, the Civil War and, in the case of Vermont, the first in the country to declare war on Hitler, a few months before Pearl Harbor. Mention the region to an educated businessman and he'll tell you how the Industrial Revolution in America began beside the rushing rivers and streams of New England, birthplace of the modern factory system and of innumerable inventions from the submarine to condensed milk, and how today New England is the centre of the country's booming electronics industry. Mention New England to a gourmet and your mouth will water with his tales of fresh lobster, scrod, haddock, oysters, Vermont cheese, maple syrup, clambakes, blueberries, cranberries, johnnycake, rum pie, Boston baked beans, brown bread, shore dinners, boiled dinners, Maine potatoes and chicken pie. Suggest New England to your travel agent and get an ear-full of the glories of the majestic White Mountains; the lovely Green Mountains and their ski resorts; the rolling Berkshires and their sophisticated sum-

NEW ENGLAND
0
50
100
mls
Lake Champlain
BURLINGTON
Mt. Mansfield
MONTPELIER
VERMONT
NEW YORK
Green Mountains
BENNINGTON
To Albany
PITTSFIELD
Berkshire Mts.
SPRINGFIELD
Housatonic R.
HARTFORD
CONNECTICUT
NEW HAVEN
BRIDGEPORT
Long Island Sound
Long Island
Connecticut R.
Sunapee Lake
Connecticut R.
Monadnock
Quabbin Res.
MASSACHUSETTS
WORCESTER
LOWELL
Merrimack R.
MANCHESTER
CONCORD
Lake Winnipesaukee
NEW HAMPSHIRE
White Mountains
Mt. Washington
BERLIN
Umbagog Lake
Mooselookmeguntic Lake
Sugarloaf Mountain
Androscoggin R.
Sebago Lake
PORTLAND
PORTSMOUTH
BOSTON
PROVIDENCE
RHODE IS.
NEW LONDON
NEWPORT
Fisher's Is.
Block Is.
NEW BEDFORD
Cape Cod
Provincetown
Martha's Vineyard
Nantucket Is.
Moosehead Lake
Kennebec R.
SKOWHEGAN
AUGUSTA
MAINE
Baxter State Park
Chiputneticook Lake
Penobscot R.
BANGOR
Graham Lake
Acadia National Park
Vinalhaven Is.
St. Croix R.

mertime culture; the wild rockbound coast of Maine; the beaches of Cape Cod and unique beauty of the Cape's islands; the architectural wonderland of Newport; Boston, America's most medieval city; vast wildernesses, lakes and whitewater rivers; quaint towns; covered bridges; the world's most brilliant fall foliage; antique shops and maple sugar houses.

Of all the regions in America, New England is the only one that is finished: it is a civilization that idealizes small-town life and town meetings, icy winters by a woodburning stove, self-sufficiency and hard work. Those who found it incompatible left long ago – they began to leave for the west right after the Revolution – and those who thrive on it settle every year in New England by the thousands, fleeing the social decay of American suburbia, the depressed mid-western Industrial Belt, and the mindless boom-town atmosphere of the South. New England has become for many the symbol of the good days, before McDonalds sold a single hamburger; it does have its cities, to be sure, but until very recently New Englanders didn't know what to do with them, perversely chopping them up with highways and spoiling them with dull or dreadful skyscrapers. If someone wanted to start an anti-New England cult, they could easily publish a calendar with pictures of bleak urban wastelands, or the virulent anti-bussing riots in South Boston, or a Ku Klux Klan rally in Connecticut, or any number of other aberrations. The truth, however, is that New England's small-town heart really does exist in a kind of Norman Rockwell time warp; just pull into any small town café and listen to the locals tell the oldest jokes under the sun.

The hoariest families and traditions in America belong to these six small states, to the extent that in some spots a resident is an 'outlander' if his great-grandfather wasn't born in the same house. Descendants of the Boston Brahmins still live off the interest of trusts established in the heyday of the China trade. Many immigrants from Ireland, Italy, Portugal and Greece (but almost never French Canadians) have become 'more Yankee than the Yankees'. Old country fairs and church suppers, the Harvard-Yale rivalries, the Boston Marathon, the America's Cup – they are all time-honoured traditions by American standards. Our national feast day, Thanksgiving, of course originated in Plymouth; few people, however, know that the Boston descendants of the Pilgrim Fathers meet every October in Waitsboro, Vermont, to defend their pronounciation of tomato ('to-mahto') with bags full of rotten ones, against a hoard of barbaric New Yorkers who pronounce it 'tamayta'. But most importantly for Americans in these days of national numbness, it is comforting to know that New England has retained at least some of its famed nonconformity, the heritage of Thoreau, that it will stand up against things the rest of the country had swallowed whole, like McCarthy and Nixon – a quality probably essential if the democracy is to survive.

## General Information

New England was named by its earliest settlers, not for any resemblance to old England, but to differentiate between New France, New Amsterdam and New Spain. It covers 66,608 square miles in the northeastern corner of the United States, in a region approximately 500 miles by 300 miles, and contains some 12 million people. Despite its small size, its geography varies dramatically, from the White Mountains, the tallest on the East Coast, to the bogs and sand dunes of Cape Cod. Western Connecticut is all but an annexe of New York City, while northern Maine is as wild as any region out west. Some small cities are heavily industrial, while the entire state of Vermont is a rural wonderland.

New England has five very distinct seasons. Winter (December-February) almost always brings piles of snow, Christmas card scenery, cross-country and alpine skiing, while in the cities it is concert and theatre season. March and the first part of April constitute mud season, often grey and dismal with sleeting, adventuresome driving on mountain roads. This is when the maple sap runs, however, and the maple sugar houses throughout the region throw open their doors and have parties on the snow. Spring lasts from April to June; the orchards blossom, wildflowers adorn the roadsides, fishermen and whitewater rafters head for the rivers. Summer is big league tourist season in New England, a time of famous and not-so-famous music festivals, craft shows, antique auctions, summer theatre, sailing, swimming, etc. Fall, however, is New England's favourite season, when the air is brisk and sky its bluest, the season of fall foliage (the peak is in early October), country fairs, the cranberry and other less dramatic harvests.

**Average Temperatures in New England (°F)**

| Jan | Feb | Mar | Apr | May | Jun | Jul | Aug | Sept | Oct | Nov | Dec |
|---|---|---|---|---|---|---|---|---|---|---|---|
| 23 | 25 | 34 | 45 | 58 | 65 | 71 | 70 | 61 | 51 | 40 | 28 |

**Flora and Fauna**

Besides such uniquely American plants as cranberries,

blueberries, and Concord grapes, New England is perhaps most famous for its sugar maples, source of maple syrup and other sticky delicacies. Amazingly enough, this most highly industrialized corner of America is 77% forested, with such native species as the White Ash, Basswood, Red Oak, White Pine, America Elm (along the streets of small towns), Balsam Fir, Black Willow, Norway Spruce, and the Horse Chestnut. If any particular wildflower says New England, it is the bluet that blossoms in May; in June, the higher altitudes are adorned with mountain laurel. Other commonly seen wildflowers include the Rose Mallow (July-October), Fireweed (July-September), Bayberry (along the coast, used by the colonists to add scent to their candles) False Lily-of-the-Valley (May and June), Rhododendrons, and other flowers native throughout the country.

Because so much of New England has reverted to woodland, it supports a comfortable animal population, the largest of which is the American moose of Maine, followed by the black bear; smaller creatures include the beaver, woodchuck, grey and flying squirrel, muskrat, porcupine, the white tail deer, raccoon mink, grey and red foxes and, on the coast, harbour seals. The summer bird population is also sizable, and in quiet corners of the region you may see such unusual visitors as the great horned owl, the coot, cormorant, great blue heron, Baltimore Oriole, belted kingfisher, bluebird, and several species of hawk.

**A Brief Survey of New England Letters**

In Adam's Fall
We sinned *All*

states the widely used New England Primer of 1683, at once introducing Puritan children to the first letter of the alphabet and the Calvinist belief of natural depravity. The Puritans' heavy handed God, who influenced every aspect of daily life, is naturally the subject of the earliest American literature; concepts such as predestination, the Biblical covenant between God and man, the precarious path from Original Sin, and the belief that God directed the Puritans to the New World to build 'the City on the Hill' are the main themes of 17th-century literature, much of it didactic and confirming God's approval of their successful enterprises and the Devil's hand in their misfortunes.

*Of Plymouth Plantation,* by Plymouth leader William Bradford, is not only our best historical record of the settlement, but it is surprisingly well written by a self-made man of the period. It set the tone for future essays and historical works, a style made ludicrous in *New English Canaan* by the jolly malcontent Thomas

Morton (1579-1647) who set up a maypole in present-day Quincy, Massachusetts, which he called Merry-Mount, and lived like Bacchus with a bevy of Indian concubines. Outraged to find a pagan in the suburbs of Boston, the Puritans clapped him in stocks and exiled him every time he returned to New England. Morton got his revenge in what was for a long time the only humorous American contribution to literature: 'Repent you cruell Schismaticks, repent!' he mocked his persecutors, whom he accused of inhumanity compared to the Indians. The first American poet to achieve any kind of distinction was Anne Bradstreet, ancestress of Oliver Wendell Holmes. Because the Congregational church educated girls as well as boys, New England's women early on held a place in the region's literature.

Staunch Puritans were always a minority of settlers in New England, and as the colonies became wealthy, the ministers began to lose their control over the people. Those not born into the religion were repelled by its extremes, particularly the witchcraft hysteria. Cotton Mather (1663-1728), minister of the Old North Church in Boston and at once one of the most educated and most ignorant men of his day, did his best to maintain the moral and political influence enjoyed by his father, Rev. Increase Mather, and his minister grandfathers. He personally contributed much to the overthrow of New England tyrant Sir Edmund Andros, led the crusade for smallpox inoculations in New England, and as a scientist belonged to the Royal Society for many years. His literary output could be measured by the pound instead of page; his masterwork, *Magnalia Christi Americana* (1702) is a ponderous hagiography of such New England 'saints' as William Bradford and Governor William Phips. He is better known for his 1693 *Wonders of the Invisible World,* his treatise on the Devil in the New World and defence of the Salem Witchcraft Trials, which he wholeheartedly supported. His belief that Satan had a personal claim on New England and was exerting great effort to corrupt God's children before the millennium by taking the form of innocent people is an instructive background to the large body of superstitions and oft-times gloomy folklore of the region.

Where Cotton Mather largely failed to maintain the Puritan theocracy, his counterpart in Northampton, Massachusetts, Jonathan Edwards (1703-1758) managed to terrify sinners with his sermons into returning to the bosom of the church. Sermons like the classic *Sinners in the Hands of an Angry God* (1741) where Edwards depicts humanity 'over the pit of hell, much as one holds a spider, or some loathesome insect over the fire' made his listeners moan in the aisles and gave birth to the Revivals of the

1730s and '40s in New England and in Britain itself.

The Enlightenment reached New England in the last half of the 18th century, but had less effect than in the more tolerant climes of Pennsylvania and Virginia, which produced deists like Thomas Jefferson and Benjamin Franklin, the latter born in Boston but forced to leave at a tender age because of his beliefs. Ethan Allen, leader of the Green Mountain Boys of Vermont, was perhaps New England's most notorious deist, whose book, *Reason, the Only Oracle of Man* (1784) caused a tremendous uproar. During the Revolution, the so-called Connecticut Wits produced a healthy body of satire and humour, perhaps most famously, *The Hasty Pudding* by Joel Barlow. Also during this period, Phyllis Wheatley (died 1784), a freed woman of Boston, wrote *Poems on Various Subjects, Religious and Moral,* considered the first book written by a black American.

After the Revolution, New England began to rapidly industrialize and forsake its spiritual mission; in reaction, Ralph Waldo Emerson developed the philosophy of Transcendentalism, a form of Idealism based on the intuitive knowledge of the unity of God, Man and Nature in the Universal Soul. In its exaltation of the individual, solitude and nature, it was similar to German Romanticism (as transmitted through Thomas Carlyle), but different in enough aspects to make it uniquely American. Concord, Massachusetts, was the centre of the Transcendental movement from 1830 to 1860, where Emerson held forth and the Transcendental Club (1836) held its meetings, with such illustrious members as William Ellery Channing (founder of the Unitarian Church, which introduced humanism into Calvinism), Margaret Fuller (early advocate of women's rights), Orestes A. Brownson (labour reformer), Amos Bronson Alcott (idealistic father of novelist Louisa May Alcott), and George Ripley (founder of the commune at Brook Farm), all of them ardent abolitionists. Emerson's essays have established a place for him in the world's literature, although more widely read today are two works of his disciple, Henry David Thoreau, whose masterful *Walden, or Life in the Woods* (1854) and *On Civil Disobedience,* describing his refusal to pay a poll tax to the government that began the ignoble Mexican War, are classics that, if anything, have become more significant with the passage of time.

Meanwhile, Nathaniel Hawthorne (1804-1864), born in Salem and resident of Concord, became the leading light in the American Renaissance. His greatest works, *The Scarlet Letter* (1850) and *The House of the Seven Gables* (1851) evoking a strong sense of New England past, ruminating on morbid psychological themes in a fine style of shadow and light, became instant classics on either side of the Atlantic. His classmate at Bowdoin College, Henry Wadsworth Longfellow (1807-1882) became the household poet of American Romanticism, and the first American to be honoured with a niche in the Poets' Corner of Westminster Abbey. Quaker and abolitionist editor John Greenleaf Whittier (1807-1892), his contemporary, particularly favoured New England themes; his masterpiece, *Snow-Bound, A Winter Idyl,* on the surface conjures up a typical New England scene, but its meaning is universal. Brahmin poet James Russell Lowell (1819-1891) also wrote on many regional subjects, and is best known for the hoary old line 'What is so rare as a day in June?' and *The Biglow Papers,* an example of the understated Yankee humour of the Downeast School. The major exponent of Downeast humour was Maine's Seba Smith (1792-1868) who created the stock, rustic and naively wise Yankee character in his Major Jack Downing, which Mark Twain, a longtime resident of Hartford, Connecticut, borrowed for his *A Connecticut Yankee in King Arthur's Court.* His neighbour in Hartford, Harriet Beecher Stowe, wrote *Uncle Tom's Cabin,* the sentimental banner of the abolitionist cause that led to the Civil War.

Later New Englanders, like poets Emily Dickinson, Edna St. Vincent Millay and Robert Frost, and novelists like Kenneth Roberts, Henry James and Willa Cather (whose *Ethan Frome,* the novel of the broken pickle dish, may be the most pessimistic view ever written of New England) have assured New England a place in America's, and the world's literature. For a more topical view of New England today, there are a number of magazines – *Yankee Magazine, Down East, Vermont Life,* etc. and the more scholarly *New England Quarterly,* not to mention the folksy *Old Farmer's Almanac,* which give fair sampling of the charms that await the visitor in New England.

## Getting Around New England

One might think it would be easy to get around New England using public transport – and so it is, compared to the rest of the United States, but that's not saying much. Getting from town to town by bus or by train isn't impossible, but you'll always have to schedule your time around the idiosyncrasies of the bus timetables and it's difficult to find public transportation to state parks and other natural areas.

**By Air.** Boston's Logan International Airport and Bradley International Airfield north of Hartford, Connecticut, are the main gateways to New England. It is also easy to get there from

Kennedy in New York City, by limousine service to Connecticut, or by taking the Carey Bus to the terminal in Manhattan and taking the train or bus to New England. The Carey Bus terminal is at 38th Street and First Avenue; the Port Authority Bus Terminal is at 40th Street and 8th Avenue; Grand Central Station is at 42nd and Vanderbilt Avenue; Penn Station is at 32nd Street and 7th Avenue, all on the East Side and not too far to walk unless you're really laden with baggage and skis. There are dozens of smaller airports throughout New England, served by New England Air, and a number of smaller airlines (see individual states).

**By Car.** The USA is a pathologically automobile-dependent culture. Almost everyone has a car, and because so many of the places in this book are inaccessible by public transport we have written as though the reader had one. Lately the cost of public transport has become so high that if you have a companion or two, it is literally cheaper to rent a car if you plan to travel a lot, even with big companies like Hertz or Avis, which have offices all over. To rent a car, you must have a major credit card to make the deposit (although foreigners can make the hefty deposit in cash). Americans must be 21 years old, and in some places (like New York City) 25, but foreigners who are 18 or older, have a valid International Driving Licence and a return ticket home will find a car to rent. Larger companies let you rent a car in one place and leave it in another. Recently homegrown companies like 'Rent a Junker' have sprung up, offering ten-year-old jalopies for rent at bargain-basement prices, though you really shouldn't count on finding one of these. But do shop around. The smaller the car, the more you'll save on gas. Most companies offer unlimited mileage and have lower prices the longer you keep the car.

Another option is to buy a used car and sell it when you're ready to go home. The best place to look for one is in the classified section of a small city newspaper; if possible, find a farmer or an older couple to buy the car from, because they take better care of them. A decent old car will cost between $200 and $350, and use the less expensive, leaded gas. Later models will cost more, but probably won't be worth it. Shiny bargains often turn out to be lemons (there has to be a reason why it seems cheap). After buying a car, you have to get a licence for it (temporary ones are available) and, in many states, insurance. When it's time to leave, sell the car through a newspaper or a used-car dealer.

If you are driving, the first thing to do is buy a good road map or pick one up from the state's tourist office. The Rand-McNally Road Atlas, covering the fifty states, plus Canada and Mexico, is sufficiently detailed. It is also a good idea to join an automobile club, such as the American Automobile Association (AAA) which has offices in practically every town in the country. They offer not only advice, maps and travel booklets, but also a discount on travellers' cheques, lists of campgrounds, a degree of insurance, bail bond, and cover the cost of a tow in an emergency. They can also help you get a licence if you buy a car, and provide a very useful booklet (free) for foreigners: *USA Travel Information* (write to AAA Headquarters, 811 Gatehouse Road, Falls Church, VA 22042). A year's membership in the AAA costs $28. Foreign visitors should also consider buying auto – and medical – insurance in their own countries to cover their trips in the United States; it will probably be cheaper.

A few words on driving in America: the national speed limit is 55 miles an hour on the highways, lower in populated areas. Exceed it at your own risk (most people do); a speeding fine averages $50. There are no international road signs; each state has a few of its own that may be hard to decipher. Although most Americans are good, cautious drivers, the ready availability of automobiles puts even the lunatic fringe in the driver's seat, so drive defensively and don't trust someone to stop until they actually do, especially in cities. Right turns on red are legal (except in New York City and where signs say otherwise) as long as you stop first and give pedestrians the right of way. Gasoline is priced by the American gallon (a fifth less than the Imperial gallon, or approximately 4½ litres). You generally save by going to a self-service station. When driving in New England, avoid the big highways and turnpikes unless you're in a real hurry. They are perfectly colourless, and nothing's very far anyway.

**Hitch-hiking.** Hitch-hiking is legal throughout New England, and the high density of students and former students here makes it relatively easy to find a ride. Some general suggestions: always go to the edge of a town or city before you start, travel lightly (if you're from abroad, sew a flag in a prominent position on your rucksack – Americans love foreigners), hold up a sign stating your destination, smile, and avoid doing it at night. A good way to find rides is to ask around at gas stations, truck shops or diners on the way. It is illegal to hitch-hike on expressways, but you may stand at an entrance ramp. It never hurts to be a little wary in accepting a ride; a woman thumbing alone is courting disaster, sad to say. On the positive side, there are many people who hitch-hike even when they own cars, just to meet the interesting kind of people who offer rides.

**By Bus.** The two interstate bus carriers, Greyhound and Trailways, each offer unlimited travel passes for a week, two weeks or a month, valid in Canada and the US. In New England a Trailways pass will probably take you to more places, and is worthwhile if you plan to hop about quite a bit. There are discounts for travellers over 65 and between 6 and 11 years old; children under five ride for free.

**By Train.** Amtrak, the national passenger train service, is due for some big cuts by the government, but the New England branches are well used and will probably be maintained. Massachusetts and Connecticut are covered quite well; there is one stop in Rhode Island but none at all in Maine, New Hampshire and Vermont.

**By Bicycle.** This is a lovely way to see New England in the summer and fall when it doesn't rain very much. Unfortunately, most of the way you'll have to compete with automobile traffic. A good book detailing routes in New England is *Northeast Bicycle Tours* by Eric Tobey and Richard Wolkenberg.

**By Foot.** The major trail in New England, the Appalachian Trail, begins at Mount Katahdin in Maine and passes through all the states except Rhode Island on its way down the east coast to Georgia. For information and a list of hiking clubs in New England, write to the Appalachian Trail Conference (Box 236, Harpers Ferry, West Virginia 25425).

**By Canoe.** Write to the Appalachian Mountain Club (Dept. 21, 5 Joy Street, Boston 02108) for copies of their *AMC River Guide I: Northeastern New England* and *AMC River Guide II: Central and Southern New England*. The first is $6, the second $7.95.

## Accommodation

**Hotels and motels.** Outside the downtown areas of large cities, hotels are scarce; motels are more common, but not always less expensive. We have listed after each state a small selection of the available commercial lodgings in each area that do not belong to chains. We are not merely being elitist – although chain motels do have a certain monotony, especially Howard Johnson's, very much in evidence in New England – we are simply saving space. If you prefer the security and national reservation networks of the chains, look for their toll-free numbers in the yellow pages of the phone book of any city, and their operators will be more than happy to tell you where to find their motels and make reservations for you. The least expensive New England chain is Chalet Suisse International (toll-free number: 800-258-1980).

Motel and hotel prices and quality vary greatly. What is inexpensive in Boston or a resort area in the summer season may seem astronomical in other places and at other times. The easiest room to find is the double with a double bed; a single will only be a few dollars less, an extra cot or bed only a few dollars more in most cases. Almost all hotel rooms and all motel rooms have at least a private shower and toilet, and it really is difficult to find one without a television. Generally, the best place to look for motels is on the periphery of cities and towns, along the highways and major routes, which is unfortunate for the visitor relying on buses. We have tried to list all the inexpensive and moderate-priced centrally located accommodation; usually the only pick is the local YMCA. When a hotel advertises 'American Plan' it serves three meals a day; 'Modified American Plan' means two meals. A place in this book listed as inexpensive will be between $18 and $25 a night for a double. Moderate runs from $25 to $40; expensive, from $40; very expensive, from $80 a night. (Rates are often substantially lower in the offseason.) If you stay more than a day at a place, leave at least one dollar per day for the maid when you leave.

**Inns and Guesthouses.** An 'Inn' in New England can mean inexpensive, but more often means the opposite. Most are picturesque old places, many surviving from the colonial era, with big fireplaces and elegant restaurants. A book called *Country New England Inns* (published by Burt Franklin & Co., 235 E. 44th Street, New York, NY 10017) will help you find them. Guesthouses, on the other hand, really are inexpensive, usually under $10 a night. Cape Cod is especially rich in guesthouses, which are actually rooms in private homes, sometimes with breakfast included. Corinne Madden Ross's *New England Guest House Book* may help locate these (East Woods Press, 820 East Boulevard, Charlotte, North Carolina 28203); another is *A Directory of Tourist Homes in the Eastern United States and Canada,* by Jon and Nancy Kugelman (McBride and Howe Books, 157 Sisson Avenue, Hartford, Conn. 06105).

**Youth Hostels.** The name is deceptive; these are for everybody regardless of age. Although primarily designed for travellers who arrive by bicycle or on foot, hostels may be found in some larger cities as well. Almost all require a youth hostel card, issued either abroad or, if you're an American, by the American Youth Hostel Federation (National Headquarters, Delaplane, Virginia 22025). A year's membership costs $14, but only $7 if you're under 18 or over 59 years old. When you join you receive the *AYH Guide and Handbook;* the far more detailed *Hosteling USA,* which describes a lot of the activities near each hostel, is also available from AYH headquarters, for $5.95. Staying in an American youth hostel is not the rigid experience it often is in Europe, although there are certain rules; no drinking, smoking or drugs, and you are expected to help out with the general chores. Check-out time each morning is 9.30. Reservations are recommended, and essential at some of the more popular hostels. Prices average $5 a night and often include meals. In the summer, many colleges and universities have dormitory rooms for rent at modest prices.

**Farm Vacations.** These have a strong appeal to city families in particular, and range from oldfashioned farmhouse accommodation, on working farms, to resort-style farms with a large number of recreational facilities. The best guide for these is *Country Vacations USA* (available from Adventure Guides, 36 East 57th Street, New York, NY 10022).

**Camping.** Camping means different things to different people. There are commercial campgrounds for the trailer and camper, and state park campgrounds on a first-come, first-served basis. Backpackers will find camping sports along the major trails. Each state can provide information on camping sites within its borders; other good sources are *Northeastern Campgrounds and Trailer Parks Guide,* published by Rand McNally and widely available, and the New England Campers Association (write to 211 High Road, Newbury, Mass. NY 01950).

**Handicapped Travellers.** As time passes, aeroplanes, airports, hotels, motels, restaurants, museums, etc., are taking care to make themselves more accessible to the handicapped. Specific information on facilities is provided in *The Wheelchair Traveler* by Douglas R. Annand (write to Ball Hill Road, Milford, New Hampshire 03055) and in *Where Turning Wheels Stop,* put out by the Paralyzed Veterans of America (3636 16th Street NW, Washington DC, 20010).

**Senior Citizens.** There are many discounts available for travellers over 65 years old. A good way to get in on them is to join the American Association of Retired Persons/National Retired

Teachers Association (write to them at 1909 K Street NW, Washington DC, 20006).

**Children.** Many chains take children free, others offer discounts. If they are young, bring along a sleeping bag. Cribs are available in many places; motels often have special playgrounds. Chains will usually supply lists of local babysitters, and in some cases, particularly at resorts, have their own babysitting service and special day programmes for children as well. If you need emergency help finding a place, or have any other questions, call or visit a *Travelers' Aid office;* there is one in most cities, listed in the phone book. Foreign visitors can also call a toll-free number for information: 800-255-3050; this is USA Desk, with multilingual operators on duty from 9am to 10pm Mondays to Fridays and 12am to 6pm on Saturdays and Sundays.

## Eating in America

Restaurants in this book (again we spurn the chains; they're harder to avoid than to find in most places) are rated by asterisks that reflect only price, not quality. One asterisk is inexpensive, around $5 for dinner; two means $5-$12; three denote $12 or more per person. Note that the tip is not included in these prices. In the world's largest democracy, people who work in restaurants receive sub-minimum wages and are expected to make it up in tips – 15% of the final tab before tax as a general rule. Only in chains, fast-food restaurants and cafeterias are you not expected to tip.

Foreign visitors are often impressed by the enormous portions most American restaurants dish out, usually more than the average person cares to eat, a child certainly. Many places offer children's portions at a lower price (occasionally adults may order these smaller dishes) or have 'kiddies' menus' with hamburgers, hot dogs, spaghetti and other foods that American children are addicted to. Another very popular feature in restaurants these days is the 'salad bar' where you serve yourself as often and as much as you wish. It takes many visits to many salad bars to shake the sensation of going to the pig trough, to tell the truth. A first-class restaurant will never have a salad bar, but many very expensive ones do.

Despite the economy, Americans eat out more today than they ever did in the past. New eateries open all the time; many of these are 'theme restaurants'. 'Theme parks' in the US are little spores of Disneyland with a central motif like the Wild West or Mother Goose; 'theme restaurants' are in castles, coalmines, train cars or anywhere else, although their façades usually help give them away as Disneylands of dining. A typical one will have the waiters and waitresses on roller skates or wearing Roman togas and fright wigs, menus with cutesy cocktails and entrées that sound so silly you're embarrassed to order them, and a décor that annuls the quality of the food, if it has any. Enter at your own risk.

If you are looking for an inexpensive meal but dislike the chains, and don't mind a bit of grease with your food, look for a diner. The classic American diner – streamlined in shiny chrome with little booths and a counter, a jukebox and twenty different kinds of pie reflected in a mirror – still exists in New England. The diners of the '30s and '40s may have been the highpoint in American restaurant aesthetics; the one in Salem, Massachusetts, is a classic. Diners are also good bets for fast, filling breakfasts, as are coffee houses.

If you're on a budget, check out the menu by the cash register before you sit down; eat a big lunch (when prices are lower) and go to the supermarket to find goodies for dinner. Buy your liquor at the state package store or at the supermarket, instead of ordering it at a restaurant where you'll pay twice as much. Even the cheapest motel has free ice.

American bars and taverns can be dark, gloomy holes where no one talks to anybody else and everyone stares at the television; or they can be lively and fun and good places to meet the natives. Some are pick-up bars, some are gay bars, some are sports bars, some are incredibly seedy, some are for businessmen. Ask around. The drinking age varies throughout the country from 18 to 21; if you look a little young, you will be asked to show identification before being served. Most bars close at 1 or 2 in the morning, and on Sunday.

## A Few Hints for Foreign Visitors

No matter what you think about the foreign policies of the United States, the average American is extremely friendly. Foreign visitors are still uncommon in most parts of the country, and people, especially outside the cities, will bend over backwards to be helpful to you. Americans have no hard feelings over the Revolution and War of 1812; indeed, the British are invariably the most popular of tourists. When you meet the natives, what they want to know most is your impression of the United States; Americans are very conscious of their image and seem to spend most of their time making or rejecting grandiose generalizations about themselves and their country. New

Englanders have a reputation for being less friendly, but it's a myth spread by Southerners. New Englanders may not be showy and say 'honey' all the time, but if you ask them for assistance, they'll gladly give it. Probably what they dislike most are pushy big mouths who think money talks, and people who try to be something they aren't.

**Dollars and Cents.** These are still common, despite American dependence on 'plastic money' – credit cards. The dollar (buck), with George Washington on one side and mystic symbols of the Great Seal on the other, is divided into the penny (1¢), nickle (5¢), quarter (25¢) and fifty-cent piece. The new dollar coins (the 'Suzie', portraying Susan B. Anthony) have been a dismal failure because they don't look like they're worth a dollar to Americans, despite lobbying efforts by the vending machine companies. Another rarity is the 'racetrack' two-dollar bill, another, but not as unpopular, Treasury boondoogle. The five, ten and twenty-dollar bills are the most common, the fifty and hundred fairly rare.

Everyone knows America has more than its share of crooks (although New England certainly has a lower crime rate than other parts of the country), so it's a good idea to buy travellers cheques in dollars before you come. Only large banks in urban areas have any kind of foreign exchange facilities. Unlike some countries in Europe, cashing travellers cheques in the US is a fairly painless process; just bring your passport and it usually takes less than a minute. Banking hours are generally from 9am to 3pm or 4pm, Monday to Friday, and some banks are open on Sunday mornings. They are closed for the following national holidays:

| | |
|---|---|
| New Year's Day | 1 January |
| Washington's Birthday | The closest Monday to 22 February |
| Memorial Day | The closest Monday to 30 May |
| Independence Day | 4 July |
| Labor Day | First Monday in September |
| Veterans' Day | This varies from state to state: 11 November to fourth Monday in October |
| Thanksgiving | Fourth Thursday in November |
| Christmas | 25 December |

**Post Office.** Every town, no matter how small, has a post office where you can buy stamps and aerograms, dispatch packages, and have your mail sent. (Have correspondents write to 'General Delivery' and 'Main Post Office' if it's a large city. They will hold your mail for thirty days, then send it back if it's not collected.) The cost of mailing a letter seems to go up every week. At writing it's 40¢ per half ounce for airmail overseas, and 20¢ per ounce for the US, Canada and Mexico (less for postcards and aerograms). Post offices are open Monday to Friday 8am-5pm, and Saturday 8am-12 noon).

**Telephone.** There are a number of telephone companies in New England, and the cost of a local call varies. Just put in your change, wait for the dial tone and dial (always 7 digits). For an out-of-town call, you may have to dial '1' first (if you misdial, a recording will tell you). If you are calling another state, you'll need to dial a three-digit area code first. Only Massachusetts (in New England) has two area codes, one for the eastern part of the state and one for the west. A map in every phone book will tell you what area code to use. Have a lot of change handy; the operator will tell you how much to put in. Whenever an area code is 800 the call is free (dial 1-800, then the number).

If you plan to call overseas on a pay phone, the easiest thing to do is call collect (reverse charges); barring that, buy a roll of quarters from any bank and ask the operator what to do (dial '0'; your money will return). A three-minute call to Great Britain costs three dollars. If you call from your hotel, expect the usual outrageous surcharges. Rates are lower after 5pm, lowest after 11pm and during the day on Sunday. Check the front pages of the phone book.

Most communities have an *emergency* number to dial if you need the police, ambulance or the fire company. It is usually 911, and you don't need to put in a coin to call. It will be printed on any pay phone, or in the phone book.

**Telegrams.** Telegrams in the US are sent by Western Union. Offices are only in large cities; most telegrams are sent by telephone. Sending a telegram overseas is an expensive proposition, because you have to pay for each word in the address. It is cheaper to call. Western Union does, however, telegraph money which you can send from or pick up at one of their offices.

**Medicines.** Even though Americans often get free medical care when they fall ill abroad, Uncle Sam does not return the favour for foreign visitors. Doctors, hospitals and medicine are all astronomically expensive here, and you really ought to consider some form of traveller's medical insurance before coming. If you need help quickly dial the emergency number on the telephone dial or else '0' for the operator. If it's serious, but not an emergency, most hospitals (especially city and county hospitals) have walk-in clinics. If you take any kind of medicine, be sure to bring it along with you.

**Crime.** If you are concerned about the kind of cops-and-robbers crime you've seen on exported American television shows, don't be, especially in New England; most of it happens only in the imagination of Hollywood writers. However, crime is a serious problem especially for poor people and minorities, who are by far the greatest victims. Car theft, mugging and rip-offs are the three crimes most likely to happen to travellers. Car theft is best prevented by not parking in secluded spots and driving an old heap. Always lock bags and packages in your trunk when you leave your car. Muggers – and rapists – go after lone people in secluded spots and particularly after dark, although this isn't much of a worry in small towns. Con games and rip-offs can be incredibly sophisticated or obvious, and are often connected with a sob story or with people pretending to give you something.

# Connecticut

Connecticut is the state of Yankee ingenuity. Outside a stretch of farmland along the Connecticut River Valley, dedicated to growing tobacco for cigar wrappers, 5,009 square miles are covered with thin rocky soil. It is the third smallest state in the Union, but its inhabitants enjoy the largest per capita income. Even in the earliest days of the Republic, Connecticut was synonymous with gadgets and new inventions sold by Connecticut 'Yankee Peddlers'; 19th century Americans told the time by Eli Terry and Seth Thomas clocks, wore hats made in Danbury, won the West with Winchester rifles and Colt revolvers, locked their trunks with Yale locks, rode on the vulcanized rubber tyres of Charles Goodyear, and dressed in clothes of cotton cleaned by Eli Whitney's cotton gin – all invented and manufactured in Connecticut. The 'Made in Connecticut' tradition continues whenever we punch an IBM computer card, use a coin-operated telephone or toss a frisbee.

In war time, Connecticut becomes America's arsenal. A Yalie named David Bushnell invented the submarine during the Revolutionary War, and later improvements led to Groton becoming the Submarine Capital of the World. Ships, guns, grenades, parachutes, helicopters, aircraft parts, machine guns and gas masks all poured out of the state during the Civil War and the two World Wars, nor has Connecticut fared too badly during the off-and-on Cold War.

Traditionally Connecticut is one the most conservative states. Its early days were entirely dominated by the Puritan ethic and Congregational Church; the anti-Catholic Know-Nothing Party flourished in the mid 19th century, and even today, despite the dominance of the Democratic Party, the state is fiscally a backwater, much in need of tax reform. Here the wealth of its own citizens works against the state's better interests. Nevertheless, Connecticuters can boast that their state contributed the basis of the American constitution in its 'Fundamental Orders' of 1639 (hence the nickname, ' Constitution State'), that it held the first public elections in America in 1670, and that it made the late Ella Grasso as the nation's first elected woman governor. Connecticut is also known for its contributions to education, due to the Puritan emphasis on Bible reading. Yale was the third institution of higher learning founded in the colonies, back in 1701; its raison d'être was the production of a Congregationalist clergy to maintain the Connecticut theocracy. Public education

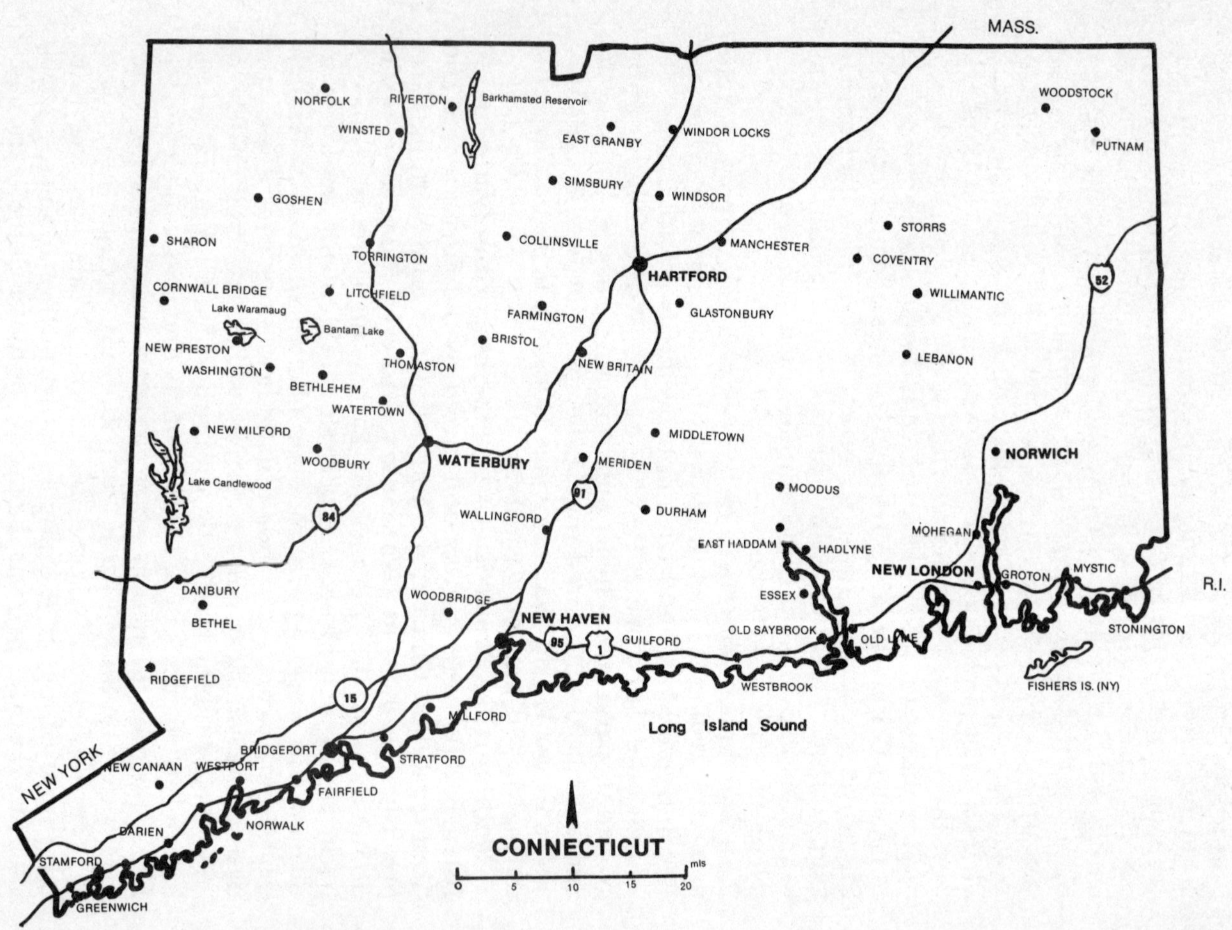
MASS.
R.I.
NEW YORK
NORFOLK
RIVERTON
Barkhamsted Reservoir
WINSTED
EAST GRANBY
WINDOR LOCKS
WOODSTOCK
PUTNAM
SIMSBURY
WINDSOR
GOSHEN
SHARON
COLLINSVILLE
MANCHESTER
STORRS
TORRINGTON
COVENTRY
HARTFORD
52
CORNWALL BRIDGE
LITCHFIELD
WILLIMANTIC
Lake Waramaug
FARMINGTON
GLASTONBURY
Bantam Lake
BRISTOL
NEW PRESTON
WASHINGTON
THOMASTON
NEW BRITAIN
LEBANON
BETHLEHEM
WATERTOWN
NEW MILFORD
MIDDLETOWN
WOODBURY
WATERBURY
NORWICH
MERIDEN
Lake Candlewood
91
MOODUS
DURHAM
84
WALLINGFORD
MOHEGAN
EAST HADDAM
HADLYNE
NEW LONDON
GROTON
MYSTIC
DANBURY
ESSEX
WOODBRIDGE
BETHEL
NEW HAVEN
OLD SAYBROOK
STONINGTON
95
1
GUILFORD
OLD LYME
RIDGEFIELD
WESTBROOK
FISHERS IS. (NY)
15
MILFORD
Long Island Sound
BRIDGEPORT
NEW CANAAN
WESTPORT
STRATFORD
FAIRFIELD
NORWALK
DARIEN
CONNECTICUT
STAMFORD
0 5 10 15 20 mls
GREENWICH

has existed since 1650, and the country's first school for the deaf was established in 1817.

None of this escaped the attention of Alexis de Tocqueville, who observed that Connecticut 'makes the clock peddler, the schoolmaster, and the senator. The first gives you the time; the second tells you what to do with it; the third makes your law and civilization.'

Today visitors to this citadel of Yankeeism come for the pleasant shoreline along Long Island Sound, for the pretty towns with their inevitable white-spired Congregationalist churches facing leafy town greens, for the famous repertory and summer theatres (many of which have contributed shows to Broadway), and to track down historic houses full of historic antiques. Old manufacturing centres like Bridgeport, Waterbury and Norwich are intriguing, while northern Connecticut, heavily wooded and studded with lakes, offers outdoor attractions and several ski resorts in the Berkshire foothills.

## Getting Around Connecticut

**By Air.** *Bradley International Airport*, north of Hartford, is the major airport in the state. There is a limousine service connecting the airport to the Sheraton Park Plaza Hotel in New Haven, the Holiday Inn in Meriden, and several hotels in Hartford. (In New Haven tel: 562-3165, in Hartford tel: 627-0213.) Connecticut Limousine service (tel: 865-5166) begins at the Sheraton in New Haven, with connections along the coast to Kennedy and La Guardia airports in New York. There are small commuter airports in Bridgeport and New London. At *Tweed Airport* in New Haven, Ocean Airways (tel: 468-6680) flies to Atlantic City and Asbury Park, N.J. and Washington; Pilgrim Airlines (tel: 787-5701) has shuttles to the New York airports and flights to Boston, Springfield, Long Island and Providence, R.I.; New Haven Airways (tel: 469-2364) has an air taxi service and scheduled flights to Islip, Long Island, Washington/Baltimore, Washington and Philadelphia.

**By Train.** *Conrail* commuter service (tel: 772-2093) has frequent trains between New Haven's Union Station and Grand Central in New York City, with stops in between. *Amtrak* (1-800-523-5720) serves Hartford and New Haven on the Boston-Washington line, with stops at Windsor Locks, Meriden, Wallingford, Bridgeport and Stamford; another route covers Mystic, New London, East Lyme, Old Saybrook and Madison.

**By Ferry.** Interstate Navigation Co. operates ferries from New London to Block Island, Rhode Island (tel: 442-7891). A ferry connects New London with Long Island and Fishers Island, N.Y. Another ferry operates from mid May to mid September, from Bridgeport to Port Jefferson on Long Island (tel: 367-3043 in Bridgeport).

**By Bus.** Interstate bus service to New York, Albany, Boston, New Hampshire, etc. is provided by Trailways (Union Place, Hartford, 527-2181, and 472 State Street, New Haven, 562-9991) and Greyhound (409 Church Street, Hartford, 547-1500, and 45 George Street, New Haven, 772-2470). Within the state, Connecticut Transit runs from Hartford (information booth at State & Main, tel: 525-9181) and New Haven (470 James Street, tel: 624-0151) to most other towns in the state.

## History

The native Indians of Connecticut gave us the state's clicking name; they called the land 'Quinnehtukqut' which means 'Beside the Long Tidal River'. Three main Algonkin tribes lived within the state's borders when the Dutch first traded along the coast in the early 17th century: the Matabesecs in the west; the Sequin 'River Indians' in the central valley; and the Pequot-Mohegan in the southeast. In 1633 Dutch and English Puritans set up posts along the Connecticut River. By 1636 they were in a life-and-death struggle with the Pequots, who murdered a group of traders and attacked the English fort at Saybrook, their old hunting grounds. In response, the Puritans attacked the Pequot stockade in Mystic during the night, set it afire, and shot any man, woman or child who attempted to escape the flames. 'It was a fearful sight to see them frying in the fire,' Cotton Mather wrote, 'but the victory seemed a sweet sacrifice, and they gave praise thereof to God.' The remaining Indian tribes, losing more and more of their land to the white invasion joined Philip of the Wampanoags (see *Rhode Island*) in the 1675 lost cause known as King Philip's War. Defeated in this last attempt to recover their heritage by force from Connecticut and Massachusetts, the Indians headed west.

Connecticut's 'Founding Father', a Congregationalist minister from England named Thomas Hooker, came to the valley in 1638 via Massachusetts Bay. Hooker was dismayed at the intransigent power of the Puritans in Boston, and the first thing he and Roger Ludlow did upon arriving in Connecticut was to establish the principles of the Fundamental Orders of 1639. The Orders advocated a separation of Church and State, and proclaimed that 'the foundation of authority is in the free consent of the people' – a radical concept at the time. But these admirable ideals were somewhat circumvented by requirements that, in order to vote, one should be white, male, a property-owner and approved by fellow voters (i.e. a member of the Congregational Church), ensuring an Orthodox Puritan government until 1912, when a state constitution replaced the Fundamental Orders.

The Puritan governor of the time somehow convinced Charles II to incorporate the Fundamental Orders into the Charter of 1662, which also gave Connecticut the Pacific Ocean as its western boundary. The charter, however, was too liberal for the Duke of York and he sent New England Governor Sir Edmund Andros to Hartford in 1687 to retrieve it. Sir Edmund and his armed escort met the town leaders one evening in a tavern and demanded the document. It was about to be handed over when suddenly someone blew out the candles, and in the confusion and darkness Joseph Wadsworth spirited the Charter away and hid in the trunk of a great oak a few blocks away. The oak became instantly famous as the Charter Oak, and Sir Edmund had to go home, leaving Connecticut independent.

Because Connecticut consisted of rural, zealously Puritan small towns, with little to trade, England was more or less content thereafter to leave the colony alone. Connecticut's conservative farmers also took care to do nothing that would attract British interest in their affairs, and taxes like the Stamp Act and Townshend Duties seemed like a great intrusion into their sovereignty. In 1766 they elected Jonathon Trumbull, a Son of Liberty from Eastern Connecticut, as governor, despite wealthy Tory sentiment in the west. Although past his sixty-fifth birthday when the Revolutionary War broke out, Trumbull was the leader of the cause in Connecticut and the only colonial governor to support the rebels. He answered Washington's requests for provisions so well that the General called Connecticut 'the provisions state'. Governor Trumbull's son, John Trumbull, later painted the most inspired and authentic images we have of the war. Connecticut also produced three of the Revolution's greatest leaders, General Israel Putman (Congress's second choice for commander, after Washington); Ethan Allen, later connected with the Green Mountain Boys of Vermont; and the brilliant and tragic Benedict Arnold.

After the war, a combination of population growth, lack of fertile soil, and conservative politics (Connecticut, for example, refused to support the war of 1812 and even held a convention on seceding) caused a great migration from the state westwards, many settling in the Western Reserve (northern Ohio), the strip of land Connecticut reserved for itself when giving up the rest of its westerly claims. So many people left Connecticut that, between 1789 and 1889, 34 Senators and 187 members of the House in the US Congress were born in Connecticut – but represented different states.

When economic necessity dictated that those remaining behind should turn to industry, there were not enough people left in the state to work in the factories. Connecticut manufacturers openly recruited workers from Europe, first from Ireland, later from Germany, Italy and Poland, as well as Canadians and also Jews from a number of other countries. By 1930 the native Yankee stock was only 35% of the state's population. The Industrial Revolution had totally changed the character of rural, Puritan Connecticut, but it took a while for the state's politics to catch up. Conservatives and, for a period, reactionary politicians (Connecticut elected a Know-Nothing governor from 1855 to 1857) dominated the scene until a Yale English Professor and Democrat named Wilbur L. Cross was elected in 1930.

There are two keys to Connecticut's rosy economic health these days. First, the inventiveness of the state's early manufacturers, in particular Eli Whitney who pioneered the concept of interchangeable parts in his Connecticut gun factory, replacing skilled craftsmen and enabling less skilled workers to work on only one piece of the final product. In the spirit of Whitney, Connecticut inventors have earned more patents per capita than any other state in the Union. The second factor is the megadollars of the insurance companies in the state; Hartford is the insurance capital of America. The first insurance companies were founded at the end of the 18th century, but only became prominent after the New York fire of 1835, when the president of the Hartford Fire Insurance Company rushed to the smouldering scene and swore to cover all claims – after other insurance companies had collapsed. The new business and trust in Hartford insurance companies was overwhelming. Accident insurance, automobile insurance, hailstone insurance and boiler insurance were first written in Hartford. Today the state has the headquarters of 47 insurance companies, with assets of over $40,000,000,000.

## What to See

**Southwestern Sector.** The southwestern corner of the state consists of New York City's more elite dormitory suburbs; the middle class live in New Jersey, the upper middle class and executives live along the Connecticut shore up to Westport, which is as far as anyone is willing to commute. **Greenwich**, on the New York line, is one of the wealthiest towns in America, with its opulent homes in a bucolic, woody setting. Because it originally belonged to the Dutch (until 1656) it never quite fitted Connecticut's Puritan mould. The *US Tobacco Museum* 100 W. Putman Avenue (open daily 1pm-5pm, closed Mondays and holidays), tells of colonial America's most lucrative crop, one that's grown in Connecticut as well, and contains an outstanding collection of pipes from around the world. To the east the residential neighbourhoods flow into **Stamford**, a modern city with the distinction of having the third largest number of corporate headquarters in the country (after New York and Chicago). It calls itself 'Research City' and has recently become famous for its *Fish Church* (First Presbyterian), designed in 1958 by Wallace K. Harrison, who worked on the United Nations building and is guilty of the Albany Mall. The church is located at 1101 Bedford Street (open daily 9am-5pm). Off Route 123 in **New Canaan** is the famous *Silvermine Guild of Artists*, where many New York artists summer, with constantly changing exhibitions.

Eastwards is **Norwalk**, founded in 1641 by Roger Ludlow, who wrote the 'Fundamental Orders'. The Connecticut state song and famous patriotic marching ditty, the derogatory 'Yankee Doodle' was inspired by Norwalk recruits and written by a West Albany surgeon who saw them march by his window during the French and Indian War. In 1864, a New York financier built a $2,000,000 Victorian palace in the town, the *Lockwood-Matthews Mansion* (295 West Avenue), now undergoing restoration but open for visitors Monday to Thursday, 9.30am-2.30pm; Sunday 1pm-4pm; admission free). Off the coast of Norwalk are several small uninhabited islands. From Cove Marina cruises pass these islands and tour Long Island Sound; the *Long Island Queen*, for example, sails to Northport on Long Island for lunch (tel: 838-9003 for schedules).

**Westport** fits many people's ideal of a perfect town, at once small yet sophisticated, the haven of TV executives. Its main claim to fame lies in the *Westport Country Playhouse*, founded in 1931 in a barn (Boston Post Road). Many of its productions go on to rave reviews on Broadway and plays are presented from June to Labor Day. During the same period, every evening at 8.00, there are free concerts of all kinds at the *Levitt Pavilion*, in a park on the banks of the Saugatuck River.

East along the coast is **Fairfield**, now a suburb of Bridgeport, a quiet town with several 18th-century homes, and the small

*Birdcraft Museum*, housing a display of 2,000 mounted Connecticut birds as well as carved decoys. Fairfield's famous *dogwood trees,* of which there are thousands, blossom in mid May, when the whole town seems to be covered in pink and white lace.

Blue-collar **Bridgeport** – once famous for its production of Warner's corsets and Remington arms, for the ill-fated quality car, the 'Locomobile', for the first American phonographs and sewing machines and a diverse number of other industries – has many surprises. P. T. Barnum, creator of 'The Greatest Show on Earth', found his two-foot-tall star attraction, Charles Stratton ('General Tom Thumb'), in Bridgeport and later adopted the city as his own. He served as mayor during 1875-76 and planted hundreds of trees in the city; he donated the land for pretty Seaside Park; he promoted Bridgeport and brought in many new concerns; Bridgeport was the winter quarters of his circus, and his elephants and their turbaned drivers ploughed the surrounding fields. In 1848, he built Iranistan, a Moorish-style fantasy house with innumerable onion domes. It burned down ten years later, but is recalled in Bridgeport's Iranistan Avenue and the fondness for onion domes in the city's older homes. Barnum may be famous for saying things like 'There's a sucker born every minute' and 'Everybody likes to be humbugged', but no one is held in higher esteem in Bridgeport. His portrait adorned the city's centennial coin and there is a Barnum festival every June in his honour.

People still wonder whether Walt Kelley created Pogo, or if Pogo created Mr Kelley. The latter, of course, was a son of Bridgeport, as was Pogo's Okeefenokee acquaintance, P. T. Bridgeport, who talked in circus poster script. Bridgeport's old city hall has recently been named in honour of another local hero, Jasper McLevy, the city's socialist mayor during 1933-57. Although the colourful Mr McLevy never built up much of a Socialist Party in Bridgeport, he was elected over and over again as an honest politician and a reformer.

Bridgeport may be no shining jewel of architecture or planning (although there are some fine Victorian houses) but it does have numerous fine parks, earning it the name 'Park City'. The most beautiful, *Beardsley Park* , on the banks of the Pequonnock, was laid out by Frederick Law Olmsted and contains the *Beardsley Park Zoo*, 'the biggest little zoo in New England', with some 600 animals (open daily 11am-4pm). The park also contains two small lakes and a Shakespeare Garden. In *Seaside Park* a statue of the seated Barnum commemorates his donation of the land to the city; there is a long sandy beach here ($10 a day per car).

The most famous attraction in Bridgeport, the *P. T. Barnum Museum*, is in the shadow of the Connecticut Turnpike, which the state saw fit to build right through the middle of town. Barnum himself designed the wonderful mosque-like building in 1890, surrounding it with elaborate carvings. Inside you can see such marvels as Tom Thumb's bed and wedding attire, an Egyptian mummy, a mechanical Swiss village, items from Jenny Lind's concert tour in America (promoted, of course, by Barnum, who paid the Swedish Nightingale a thousand dollars a day) and the *William R. Brinely Model Circus*, with half a million carved pieces and adding more every year. Located at 820 Main Street, it is open Tuesday to Saturday, 12pm-5pm, Sunday 2pm-5pm (admission). Another collection of Barnum and Tom Thumb memorabilia is at the *Museum of Art, Science, and Industry,* at 4450 Park Avenue (open Tuesday to Saturday, 2pm-5pm; closed holidays). The exhibits also include the Gear Gallery, the Transparent Woman and a large-scale model of the moon with the landings of the various Apollos carefully marked.

On Dewey Street the *Mountain Grove Cemetery* is the last resting place of Phineas Thomas Barnum (1810-91), Tom Thumb (marked by a marble shaft and a lifesize statue) and tiny Lavinia Bump Warren, who married Tom Thumb in New York in 1863. It was the media event of the year, thanks to Barnum, who found two other midgets to serve as best man and maid-of-honour for the ceremony. Lavinia outlived her husband by thirty years; her marker says succinctly: 'Wife'.

In **East Bridgeport** (where the frisbee evolved from flipping pie tins in the Frisbee Baking Company) a huge jai-alai court has recently been opened. Nearby **Stratford** is the home of the *American Shakespeare Theatre*, founded in 1951 and considered one of the top repertory theatres in America. The theatre itself, built on the banks of the Housatonic River, was modelled on the octagonal Globe Theatre in London and is surrounded by magnificent grounds. You can drive or boat there, and most theatre-goers eat a picnic lunch before the play. The Shakespeare Company performs throughout the summer; and as the theatre is also the *Connecticut Center for the Performing Arts,* other productions are scheduled throughout the year. (For programme information call 378-7321.)

Also on the Housatonic, *Boothe Memorial Park* was a gift to the city from the whimsical Boothe brothers, who added a personal touch to their lovely bequest, notably the *Technocratic Cathedral*, a monument to the Great Depression. Built of flat redwood boards, it symbolizes the state of the country in the '30s 'flat and in the red'. The cathedral contains a massive collection of Indian baskets; the Boothes' huge horseshoe collection may be seen in the *blacksmith shop*. The old wooden *Clock Tower* once belonged to a parish in Massachusetts – one of the brothers obtained it from the church members in exchange for a vacuum cleaner. Add to this a twelve-foot granite pulpit, an outdoor organ and basilica, and you have one of the oddest parks in the country. (The entrance is on Main-Putney Street, off Main Street.)

Nearby **Millford** has the lovely Silver Sands State Park (with a beach) and Charles Island, where you can walk at low tide. Captain Kidd is rumoured to have buried treasure here.

Leaving the coast, near the New York State border is **Ridgefield**, an extremely pretty little town founded in 1709. The *Aldrich Museum of Contemporary Art* at 258 Main Street is one of few small galleries devoted entirely to current works (same hours as Keeler Tavern). The sculpture garden is free to the public.

**Danbury**, once America's thriving 'Hat City', today has only one hat factory compared with fifty-one in the late '30s when every red-blooded American male wore a felt hat. In 1902 the hatters' union here organized a major strike against the Loewe company after it declared an open shop. The boycott called by the union was so successful that Loewe took the hatters to court under the Sherman Anti-trust Act. In 1915 the Supreme Court found the union guilty, in a case as infamous for labour as the Dred Scott Decision was for slavery. The union hatters had to sell their homes to pay $300,000 to compensate Loewe for lost business. In 1777, Danbury had an important cache of military supplies, and was consequently burned by the British. The houses that escaped the conflagration (all owned by Tories) today form part of the *Scott-Fanton Museum* at 43 Main Street (open Wednesday to Sunday 2pm-5pm; free admission). Included here is the 1790 Dodd Shop dedicated to the early hatting industry; the Rider House, with a working 18th-century kitchen; and the Charles Ives Birthplace. An insurance salesman, Ives (1874-1954) was New England's gift to modern music; his innovative, peculiarly American compositions are periodically popular on the concert circuit. North of Danbury, the man-made *Candlewood Lake* is the state's largest, with recreational facilities at *Squantz Pond State Park*.

**Waterbury** to the west owes its nickname of 'Brass City' to Alexander Hamilton's tariff on English brass and the Scoville Company, first in the US to make brass buttons. One of America's oldest corporations, Scoville has remained faithful to Waterbury when others would abandon it, today manufacturing Hamilton Beach blenders.

Two brutal highways have divided Waterbury into quarters.

From the interchange the *railroad station clock*, Waterbury's landmark, is clearly visible; 240 feet high, it recalls a glorious industrial past when the Waterbury Brass Clock Co. told the nation's time. Near the town green the *Mattatuck Museum* (open Tuesday to Saturday 12pm-5pm, Sunday 2pm-5pm) exhibits paintings by Connecticut artists, etchings by Whistler, and items of local historical interest. In Waterbury's neighbourhoods are numerous well-built 'triple decker' homes typical of New England.

**Restaurants in the Southwest.** *In Greenwich:* Café Bagatelle***, 18 W. Putnam; Boodles**, 21 Field Point Street; Manero's**, on the shore. *In Stamford*: Country Tavern***, Route 104; Pellicci's**. *In New Canaan:* Roger Sharman Inn***, 195 Oenoke Road. *In Norwalk:* Silvermine Tavern**, Perry & Silvermine Avenue; The Pier**, on the harbour. *In Westport:* Clambox*, Route 1; La Normandie***, 1300 Boston post Road; Café de la Plage*** (Peruvian cuisine), on the shore. *In Bridgeport:* Ocean Sea Grill**, 1328 Main Street. *In Ridgefield:* The Inn***; Stonehenge***. *In Danbury:* 1849 House***; Bella Italia**. *In Woodbury:* Curtis House**. *In Waterbury:* Red Bull Inn**.

## New Haven to Hartford

In 1638 a Reverend John Davenport and merchant Theophilus Eaton, both staunch Puritans, founded a settlement by the harbour which they called 'Quinnipiac' for the Indians who sold them the land; in 1640 they renamed it **New Haven**. Disturbed by the Anne Hutchinson controversy in Boston, New Haven's original colonists sought to create a more perfect 'Zion in the Wilderness' in their new territory. They adopted a constitution obedient to 'The Word of God' (no mention of the King) that called for the election of 'Seven Pillars' to lead the Church and State. The new colony was soon known as the strictest and most fanatical in New England.

When Charles II included New Haven in the liberal Connecticut Charter of 1662, New Haven was ready to take up arms to maintain its independence until an even more unsavoury attempt by the Duke of York on its sovereignty convinced the colonists to join the Hartford Colony. In 1716 a Congregationist college was transferred to New Haven from Saybrook. Two years later it was named Yale, after Elihu Yale, the governor of Madras, who donated £562 to the school. Today Yale is one of the America's top universities, almost synonymous with New Haven itself. New Haven also claims its share of Yankee know-how, being the first place to manufacture sulphur matches, the Colt revolver (developed at Eli Whitney's interchangeable-parts gun factory), the stone-crusher for highway construction, the corkscrew and the lollipop.

New Haven is enjoying a new prosperity of late, as a result of its efforts to recruit new businesses. Its harbour is now the third busiest in New England. Both Yale and the city have significant works by major new architects, and can claim to be the cultural centre of the state, with the University's museums, two famous theatres, the New Haven Symphony and the Connecticut Ballet.

Any tour of New Haven must start at the *Green*, the centre of the town since its foundation. Lovely and shaded, it served the colonists as a cow pasture, burial ground, arena of public punishment, and site of several public buildings, all since demolished. Three churches remain. *Trinity Episcopal Church*, an early attempt at Gothic Revival, was built in 1814 by local architect Ithiel Town. *Center Church* was also built in 1814 by Town (for the Congregationalists); it's the New England version of St Martin's-in-the-Fields, with an ancient crypt, a stained-glass window of Rev. Davenport delivering the first sermon in New Haven, and a seven-branched candlestick symbolizing the 'Seven Pillars'. The *United Church* (Old North Church), built in the same period by David Hoadley, is more representative of the local style of the period, and witnessed Henry Ward Beecher's famous sermon to a group of abolitionists about to join John Brown in Kansas in 1855. The offering that day was used to buy the men Bibles and rifles. The one tombstone remaining on the Green, the *Dixwell Monument*, marks the grave of regicide John Dixwell. After signing the death warrant of Charles I, Dixwell, Edward Whalley and Willian Goffe fled to New Haven in 1661 to escape the wrath of Charles II (see West Rock Park).

Facing the Green, at 169 Church Street is *City Hall*, the older part of which was designed in 1871 by Henry Austin. Fortunately the city decided to save this unique Venetian-Gothic pile when city government expanded; a new sandstone building stands behind the old façade. Also on Church Street is the *New Haven Visitor's Center* with maps and information.

Several events take place annually on the Green. *Powderhouse Day* in the spring commemorates Benedict Arnold's demand of the keys to the powder house after the conflict at Lexington and Concord. A vote had just been taken to remain neutral, but Arnold threatened to break down the door. The selectmen handed over the key, Arnold armed his troops and began his ill-fated role in the Revolution.

The *Yale Campus* begins west of the Green, through the *Phelps*

*Gateway* on College Street where the University's *Information Booth* is located. Highlights of a campus tour (where you will see at least one example of every major architectural trend in America) include *Connecticut Hall*, built in 1752 and the oldest building on campus; Nathan Hale, the patriot martyr, roomed here while a student, and a statue of him stands in front. On High Street, *Harkness Tower*, Yale's landmark crown tower (221 feet) was inspired by the Tour de Beurre of Rouen Cathedral. At the base of the tower you can enter *Branford Quadrangle*, the loveliest of the seven on campus.

On the corner of High and Chapel is the *Yale University Art Gallery* (open Tuesday to Saturday 10am-5pm, Sunday 2pm-5pm), founded in 1832, the first university art museum in the New World. Among its treasures are John Trumbull's paintings of the Revolution, the Elihu Yale tapestries, the Dura-Europos frescoes, a collection of Italian Renaissance paintings and art from almost every society and period in history. More specialized is the collection in the brand new *Yale Center for British Art* right across the street, the last work of architect Louis I. Kahn (his first commission was the new addition of the Art Gallery across the street). The paintings belonged to the collection of Paul Mellon, and include works by major British artists from the 15th to the 19th centuries (open same hours as Art Gallery). Nearby, at 1114 Chapel, is the *Yale Repertory Theatre,* founded in 1966 and located in an old Baptist Church. This professional theatre grew out of the widely acclaimed Yale School of Drama, and performs from September to May (tel: 436-8491 for information). Also here is the *School of Art and Architecture* of Paul Rudolph, not a very good example for the students who attend it.

Back on High Street between Elm and Wall is the enormous *Sterling Library* (1889); neo-Gothic and ecclesiastical with its stained glass, its nave-like entrance, stone carvings of ancient civilizations, high-vaulted ceiling and cloisters, it contains the sixth largest collection of books anywhere. Nearby stands Gordon Bunshaft's *Beinecke Rare Book Library* (1963), not much from the outside but awe-inspiring inside with its soft golden light. A copy of the Gutenberg Bible and Audubon's *Birds of America* are on display, as well as selections from the library's 400,000 rare works and manuscripts. At Grove and High Streets is the *Grove Street Cemetery*, with the fabulous *Egyptian gate* by Ithiel Town's apprentice, Henry Austin. Eli Whitney, Noah Webster and Charles Goodyear are among the famous buried here.

The *Payne Whitney Gymnasium* (York & Tower Parkway) is a

marvellous Gothic Revival stronghold built in 1932; across the street are the 1962 *Morse and Stiles residential colleges* by Eero Saarinen. Take Grove to *Hillhouse Avenue*, considered one of America's most beautiful streets in the 19th century; at no.15 the *Yale Collection of Musical Instruments* (open Tuesday to Friday 2pm-4pm, Sunday 2pm-5pm) displays instruments from 1550 to 1850. Hillhouse leads to Sachem Street where at the corner of Whitney is the famous *Peabody Museum of Natural History* (open Monday to Saturday 9am-5pm, Sunday 1pm-5pm; free admission on Mondays, Wednesdays and Fridays). This amazing collection contains such wonders as a 67ft brontosaurus, a mastodon, a prehistoric sea turtle 10 ft long, Mexican Indian artifacts, dioramas, and Rudolph F. Zallinger's famous murals of the Age of Reptiles. At 411 Whitney the *New Haven Colony Historical Society* (open 10am-5pm, 2pm-5pm Saturday and Sunday has a collection tracing New Haven's history, including Eli Whitney's original cotton gin, which revived slavery in the south.

Architectural novelties off-campus include the 1969 *Headquarters of the Knights of Columbus* by Kevin Roche at Church and Frontage Streets, Paul Rudolph's wonderful *Municipal Parking Garage*, and the *Armstrong Rubber Building* (1969) at 500 Sargent Drive. Near this is the *Long Wharf Theatre* (222 Sargent) located in an old food terminal warehouse near the harbour. It performs from October to mid June, and its many awards (including two Pulitzer prizes) and venturesome productions make it Connecticut's top repertory theatre. (For information call 787-4282.) From *Long Wharf Dock* you can cruise round New Haven Harbor and Long Island Sound on the *Liberty Bell*, from Memorial Day to Labor Day. (For times and information, call 562-4163.)

On either side of New Haven are two high points. Whalley Avenue leads to *West Rock Park,* a striking rock formation with a fine view of New Haven. In *Judge's Cave*, the regicides Whalley and Goffe took shelter from the British agents seeking their deportation in 1661. Their brief stay is recalled on a tablet: 'Resistance to Tyrants is Obedience to God.' South of here is the fine, rolling *Edgewood Park*, and south of that, the *Yale Bowl* (Derby Avenue and Yale), built in 1914; the *Walter Camp Memorial Arch,* added in 1928, honours the innovative coach who changed American football.

North of New Haven is **Meriden,** prettily situated between the Hanging Hills and Mount Beseck; this is one of Connecticut's traditional silver-making cities. At *International Silver* (500 Broad Street), 18th-century New England is re-created in the *Heritage House* (open Monday to Saturday, 10.30am-3pm). West of town you can hike to *Castle Craig*, a stone tower high up in the Hanging

Hills, for the views of Long Island (paths from Meriden in *Hubbard Park)*.

**New Britain** manufacturers much of the hardware that makes Connecticut America's leading producer; the Stanley Works are the largest, and it is Ukranians who seem to dominate the many ethnic groups who came to work in the factories. New Britain lies in the shadow of its 97-foot War Memorial shaft in *Walnut Hill Park*. The *New Britain Museum of American Art,* at 56 Lexington Street, contains a survey of American paintings from 1740 and fine murals by Thomas Hart Benton on the theme 'Arts in Life in America' (open Tuesday to Sunday 1pm-5pm, free admission).

**Restaurants.** *In New Haven:* Delmonaco's***, 232 Wooster; Basel's (Greek)***, 993 State Street; Sherman's Tavern***, 1032 Chapel; Casa Marra***, 321 East Street; Leon's**, 321 Washington; Old Heidelberg*, 1151 Chapel; Louis' Lunch*, 263 Crown Street (claims to have served world's first hamburger). *In Hamden:* Pippin's**, 1995 Whitney; Mac Andrew's**, 1125 Dixwell. *In Wallingford:* Wallingford House**, 30 Quinnipiac Street; Yankee Silversmith Inn**.

## Hartford

The capital of Connecticut and insurance capital of America, Hartford has recently undergone a 'renaissance' like New Haven, with not entirely happy results. A new highway, I-84, was built through the centre of the city and literally in the backyard of the Capitol. The roof of the city's new arena came crashing down several years ago, and the Phoenix Mutual skyscraper, the new building Hartford is proudest of, is an essay in gimmicky mannerism: 'the only two-sided building in the world'. The other new structures sin mainly by being dull, except for the Civic Centre Mall, one of the most attractive urban malls in the country.

Originally called 'Suckiag', Hartford was a Dutch trading post before the Puritan colonists, under Thomas Hooker, took over. Angrily the Dutch called the English *jankes* or thieves, a term which soon came to be spelled 'Yankees'. Hartford's first prosperity derived from agriculture, and even today Hartford handles the business end of the Connecticut tobacco industry; several manufacturing firms got their start in Hartford, most importantly Pratt and Whitney, developers of the modern aircraft engine. The insurance business began in 1794; today insurance company campuses are a definite feature of the cityscape, in a large, dull way. The city has sizable Italian, black and Slavic populations, and – interestingly – proportionately the greatest Jewish population of any city in the US outside New York.

The *State Capitol*, built on the highest point in *Bushnell Park,* is a massive miasma of architectural styles of the past, designed by Richard Upjohn and finished in 1879, six years after a referendum was passed to make Hartford the sole capital of Connecticut (until then legislative sessions were held alternately in Hartford and New Haven). Inside you'll find the usual battle flags, a statue of Nathan Hale, a plaster cast of the Genius of Connecticut (it once stood on top of the dome) and, in the Senate chamber, the Lieutenant Governor's chair, carved from the Charter Oak (which fell in a storm).

Across the street from the Capitol is the Italian Renaissance-style *State Library and Supreme Court*, housing such treasures as a duplicate of the famous 1662 Charter (according to the story, a lady cut her bonnet lining out of the document hid in the Charter Oak) and the table where Lincoln signed the Emancipation Proclamation. In Bushnell Park, a round shelter protects an antique but still whirling *Carousel*.

The older part of Hartford's downtown area is northeast of Bushnell Park, some of it torn down for the *Hartford Civic Center*, 70,000 square feet of well designed shopping mall, exhibition space, and the repaired *Veterans Memorial Colosseum*. Two interesting buildings near the centre deserve a look: the ornate *Society for Savings Bank*, on the Pratt Street Mall, and the *Goodwin Building* on Asylum Street, built in 1881. J. P. Morgan Senior, born in Hartford, lodged here whenever he visited his home town.

*Main Street* to the east has been the main thoroughfare of the city since its inception. Near the corner of Main and Pratt Streets stands *Christ Church Cathedral*, built in 1829 and one of the earliest Gothic-style churches built in America. The beautiful Romanesque *Cheney Building* on the other side of Main Street was designed by H. H. Richardson in 1877 and built of Connecticut brownstone. South of Main Street is the *Old State House*, built by Charles Bullfinch in 1792 – the first of his many public commissions (including the rebuilding of Washington DC). Considered one of the first federal-style buildings still standing, the State House served as Connecticut's co-Capitol from 1796 until 1878. Inside there is an elegant curved staircase and a Gilbert Stuart portrait of Washington, an interesting collection of political memorabilia and the *Hartford Visitors Information Centre* (open Monday to Saturday 10am-5pm, Sunday 12pm-5pm). Behind the State House on State Street is urban renewal's contribution to Hartford: *Constitution Plaza*, with the aforementioned headquarters of the Phoenix Mutual Life Insurance Company.

Back on Main Street, the *Ancient Burying Ground* lies adjacent to the white-spired *Center Church*, built in 1807 on the site of Thomas Hooker's First Church. The church is reflected in the golden glass of I. M. Pei's *Bushnell Tower* next door, but also note its own fine Tiffany stained-glass windows.

Across the street, the tower of the *Travelers Insurance Company Buildings*, the dominant feature of Hartford's skyline, used to be the tallest structure in New England until the Prudential Building in Boston topped it. On one wall a plaque mentions that this was the site of the Zachary Sanford Tavern, where the famous Charter Oak incident took place (see Section on History). Below the top of its 527-ft tower an *Observation Deck* (open from June to August, Monday to Friday 8.30am-3.30pm, free admission) affords fine views across the city.

Near the Travelers Building on Main Street, the *Wadsworth Atheneum* was the first public art museum in America, founded in 1842; it houses a famous collection of guns, Meissen porcelain, silver, 19th-century French Baroque paintings, and archaeological finds from the Orient (open Tuesday/Wednesday/Friday 11am-3pm, Thursday 11am-8pm, Saturday/Sunday 11am-5pm; admission).

*Burr Mall*, home of Alexander Calder's 'Stegosaurus', separates the museum from the ornate *Municipal Building* constructed in 1914 and one of the jewels of Hartford architecture. Next door the *Hartford Public Library* (1957) straddles a highway.

West of downtown, on the other side of I-84 there are several things worth seeing, including *Elizabeth Park* with its enormous rose garden. Nearby, at 1 Elizabeth Street, the *Connecticut Historical Society Museum* exhibits furniture, paintings, crafts, and an unusual collection of tavern signs (open daily 9am-5pm except Sundays, holidays and Saturday afternoons in the summer).

In Old Nook Farm, at the corner of Farmington and Forest Streets, are the *Mark Twain and Harriet Beecher Stowe Houses* (both open June to August daily 10am-4.30pm; and September to May Tuesday to Saturday 9.30am-4pm; Sunday 1pm-4pm). Mark Twain wrote many of his best works while living in this riverboat-shaped house from 1874 to 1891. He moved to Hartford because his publisher lived here, but he also liked the rural atmosphere of Nook Farm, so close to the city. Highlights of the house include the billiards room, the small conservatory where his children performed plays, and Mark Twain's Venetian bed in which the humorist claims to have slept backwards, to look at the carvings on the headboard that cost him so much money. His neighbour Harriet Beecher Stowe came to Hartford after writing

*Uncle Tom's Cabin*, and after the Civil War that Lincoln jokingly said the novel had provoked. Her white 'cottage' was built in 1871 and contains many of her possessions. *Trinity College*, on the south side of Hartford, has a neo-Gothic campus and a beautiful *chapel*, built in 1932. The carvings inside are a result of a competition between the workmen, who used their children and relatives as models.

Outside Hartford, Route 160 leads to **Rocky Hill** and the *Glastonbury-Rock Hill Ferry*, in operation (daily, 9am-5pm), since 1655. It crosses the Connecticut from April to October, 7am-8pm. Also here, in *Dinosaur State Park* dinosaur footprints may be seen in the sandstone, dating back 200 million years. **Newington**, another southerly suburb of Hartford, is the home of the *American Radio Relay League* (225 Main Street) where all manner of electronic communications equipment is exhibited and demonstrated (weekdays 9am-4pm; free admission).

Residential **West Hartford** was the birthplace of lexicographer Noah Webster; the *Noah Webster House*, at 227 S. Main Street, a fine example of a saltbox farm house, contains memorabilia relating to the author of *The Blue Backed Speller* and America's first dictionary (open Sunday, Tuesday 1pm-4pm, Thursday 10am-4pm; admission). Just to the west, in **Farmington**, one of Connecticut's prettiest towns, is the *Farmington Museum*, located at 37 High Street in a beautiful 17th-century New England style house with period furnishings (open Wednesday/Saturday 10am-12pm, Tuesday to Sunday 2pm-5pm; admission).

**Restaurants.** *In Hartford:* Rising Sun*** (Japanese), Civic Centre; Carbone's***, 588 Franklin Avenue; Honiss' Oyster House**, 44 State; Brownstone**, 124 Asylum Street; Bombay Cuisine*, 481 Wethersfield. *In Wethersfield*: The Clam Box**. *In Glastonbury:* Blacksmith's Tavern***, 2300 Main Street. *In West Hartford:* Brock's***, 1245 New Britain Avenue; Fiorello's**.

## The Northwest

Numerous lakes and the Berkshire foothills make this corner of Connecticut the most scenic, especially in the fall and also in the spring, when the mountain laurel blooms. North of Hartford begin the tobacco plantations, covered with white cheesecloth tents in the summer; the shade maintains the even temperature needed for the best Connecticut broadleaf used for cigar wrappers. At **Windsor Locks**, to the north, the airport's *Bradley Air Museum* has a fascinating display of over fifty aircraft, from a 1909 Bleriot to a supersonic jet (open daily 10am-6pm, admission). Route 20 from here leads to **East Granby** and the infamous *Old Newgate Prison and Copper Mine*. Newgate began as a copper mine in 1707; during the Revolution, cabins built in the shafts incarcerated British prisoners and Tory sympathizers. This ghastly dungeon continued in use until 1827 (open daily 10am-4.30pm from Memorial Day to October; admission).

To the west, near **Simsbury** the 165 ft *Heublein Tower* in *Talcott Mountain State Park* may be reached in an hour's climb; the view is magnificent. North of *Peoples State Forest,* the *Hitchcock Chair Factory* in **Riverton** has been making chairs since 1818. Visitors may observe craftsmen woodworking, rushing and stencilling the chairs, still made from the old patterns. Nearby, in an old church, the *John Tarrant Kenney Hitchcock Museum* displays antique furniture (open Tuesday to Saturday 10am-5pm from June to October, Saturdays only from November to May; free admission).

*Indian Lookout*, on Mountain Road near Torrington, provides the best spot to see Connecticut's mountain laurel blooming in June. Little **Litchfield** (Route 202) played an important role supplying the troops during the Revolutionary War. In 1784 Tapping Reeve (1744-1823) founded the first law school in America here, graduating two vice-presidents (including Aaron Burr, Reeve's brother-in-law) and 130 members of Congress. *The Tapping Reeve House and Law School* may still be seen on South Street (open mid May to mid October 11am-5pm, closed Sunday and Monday; admission). In 1810 Rev. Lyman Beecher came to Litchfield, and his two famous abolitionist children, Henry Ward and Harriet, were born here (in North Street, see plaque); Ethan Allen, patron saint of Vermont, was born in High Street. The *Litchfield Historical Society* on the Green contains exhibits relating to the town's history and some very early American paintings (open 15 May to 15 October: Tuesday to Saturday 11am-5pm, Sundays 2pm-5pm; 16 October to 14 May: Tuesday to Saturday 2pm-4pm, free). The *Litchfield Nature Center*, towards Bantam, has a lovely wild flower garden; there is a public beach at *Bantam Lake*.

Litchfield and **Goshen** to the north are Connecticut's dairy centres; Goshen's Lewis Norton invented the hard 'pineapple cheese' that made the village famous when it was sold commercially. West of here, on the other side of Mohawk Mountain and its ski lifts lies some remote and wild countryside, the Appalachian Trail, and several picturesque old towns like **Cornwall.** Cornwall was the site of a Foreign Mission School founded in 1817, designed to instruct Indians and Hawaiians and make them missionaries to their own peoples. The experiment lasted only until 1826, when two Indians married local girls, which caused an uproar. The *Cornwall Historical Society*, at Routes 7 and 45, contains items related to the mission and old Cornwall (open weekends 1 May to 15 September, 1pm-5pm free admission).

On Route 7, a 200-ft waterfall is the star attraction in *Kent Falls State Park*. **Kent** itself has a famous prep school and the *Sloane-Stanley Museum and Kent Furnace* (Route 7). The ruined Kent Furnace smelted iron in the 19th century; the museum of old American tools was founded by artist Eric Sloane with help from the Stanley Tool Co. (open May to October, Wednesday to Sunday 10am-4.30pm).

**New Preston**, on Lake Waramaug, is a popular summer resort area; and in pretty little **Washington** to the east, the *American Indian Archeological Institute and Museum* on Curtis Road displays an important collection of Indian artifacts from Connecticut and elsewhere (open Tuesday to Saturday 10am-4.30pm, Sunday 1pm-4.30pm; admission).

The Connecticut clockmaking industry originated in three towns north of Waterbury. **Thomastown** was named for Seth Thomas, who made his first clocks here in 1812, after learning the trade from Eli Terry of nearby **Terryville**. In the gable of the Congregational Church here, one of Terry's clocks with wooden works still tells the time. Terry's grandson James founded the Eagle Lock Company in town, and in the *Lock Museum of America* at 114 Main Street you can see some of his products among the 18,000 locks on display (open May to November: Tuesday to Sunday 1.30pm-4.30pm). Largest of the three towns is **Bristol**, for many years a giant clockmaking centre and today home of the *American Clock and Watch Museum*. Located at 100 Maple Street in an 1801 mansion, the museum displays over a thousand clocks made by various American manufacturers (open April to October 1pm-5pm; admission). Today Bristol is famous for its chrysanthemums and for *Lake Compounce*, one of the oldest amusement parks in America, just south of town. It began in 1846 and hosts annual sheep barbecues.

**Restaurants in the Northwest.** *In Windsor:* Windsor House**, 219 Broad Street. *In Simsbury:*Chart House***, 4 Hartford Road. *In Morris (near Litchfield)*: Deer Island Inn (German)**. *In Kent:* Bull's Bridge Inn**, Route 7. *In New Preston:* The Birches Inn**; Le Bon Coin**. *In Washington:* Mayflower Inn**, Route 47.

## Southeast Coast

Safe from New York's tentacles, the southeast coast of Connecticut retains many vestiges of its seafaring past. The oldest house in Connecticut still stands in **Guilford:** now the *Henry Whitfield State Historical Museum* (Old Whitfield Street) this stone house was built in 1639 and has a medieval appearance; a well tended herb garden grows next to it (open Wednesday to Sunday 10am-5pm, closed 15 December to 15 January). The *Green* has many fine old houses and a pretty *Congregational Church* in the Greek Revival style.

A railway built by Civil War veterans still operates from charming **Essex** (north of Old Saybrook) to Deep River. The *Valley Railroad Co. Steam Excursion Train,* equipped with two steam locomotives built in 1910, chugs along a scenic ten-mile track; one can combine this with a riverboat and cruise on the Connecticut River. (The train runs daily from 18 June to 5 September and at weekends from 7 May to 13 June and 10 September to 23 October; for schedules tel: 767-0103.) Essex has many lovely old homes and the *E. E. Dickinson plant,* which produces that obscure elixir, witch-hazel.

Across the Connecticut is **Old Lyme,** the calendar-picture New England town and an old art colony. In the *Florence Griswold House* at 96 Lyme Street are the headquarters of the historical society, with paintings by the Old Lyme Art Colony members and a historical collection (open Tuesday to Saturday 10am-5pm, Sundays 1pm-5pm; in winter Wednesday to Friday and Sunday 1pm-5pm). The *Congregational Church* on the Green – built in 1816, burned in 1907 and faithfully reproduced in 1910 – is considered the epitome of its type in New England, and is the subject of numerous paintings. At 2 Ferry Road, is the *Nut Museum* devoted to nuts around the world (open from April to November: Wednesday/Saturday/Sunday; admission $1.00 – and a nut).

The *Eugene O'Neill Memorial Theater* in **Waterford** (Route 213) has become a leading experimental theatre, built in honour of the playwright who lived in New London for many years. It's the home of the National Theater for the Deaf, the National Theater Institute and the National Drama Critics' Institute. New plays are presented in the summer (for information, tel: 443-5378). To the south is *Harkness Memorial State Park,* the former summer estate of philanthropist Edward Harkness; his Italian-style mansion contains the entire collection of Rex Basher's lifesize bird paintings, donated to the state by the artist (open from Memorial Day to Labor Day, 10am-5pm). The park itself, open all year, has formal flower gardens, picnic grounds and a beach, but no swimming. Bathing is permitted, however, in nearby *Ocean Beach Park,* on the other side of the Eugene O'Neill

Theater.

In 1658, a small town named Pequot on the Monhegin River, with a vision of future mercantile glory, renamed itself **New London** and its river, the Thames (pronounced 'Thames' not 'Tems'). It became New England's major privateering port during the Revolution, capturing so many valuable British cargoes that the British sent a force under Benedict Arnold to attack it in 1781. Fort Trumbull, guarding the town, was taken by a ruse, and New London was burned.

Shortly after the war, New London's whaling industry began. Along with Nantucket and New Bedford, Massachusetts, New London had an enormous fleet of vessels that sailed from the Arctic to the Antarctic in search of whales, their precious smokeless oil, and tremendous profits. Before the discovery of petroleum in Pennsylvania ended the market for whale oil, it almost seemed as if the town on the Thames would live up to its name.

The north waterfront of New London is the home of the *US Coast Guard Academy* (Mohegan and Park Avenues). Of particular interest here is the beautiful sailing ship, the *Eagle* – formerly the German *Horst Wessel,* captured during the war, refurbished and now used to train cadets. Across the street from the Academy on Mohegan Avenue, the *Lyman Allyn Museum* is a memorial to a whaling captain, with a diverse collection of early American furniture, dolls houses and Roman artifacts, as well as fine art (open 10am-5pm, Sunday 2pm-5pm, closed Mondays). It is next to the campus of *Connecticut College*, where the *Arboretum* contains a stand of virgin hemlocks over 400 years old.

The *Tale of the Whale Museum* at 115 Huntington Street, located in a Greek Revival House near City Hall, contains numerous exhibits on whales and their hunters.

Across the Thames from New London is **Groton**, 'Submarine Capital of the World' thanks to the presence of the Electric Boat Company, which builds the Navy's submarines, and the US Naval Submarine Base, headquarters of the Atlantic Fleet. One of the bloodiest massacres of the Revolution took place here; after Benedict Arnold burned New London, he sent Colonel Eyre across the river to take Fort Griswold with over 800 troops. Fort Griswold's defenders were few, but under Colonel William Ledyard they managed to hold the British back for some time and inflicted heavy losses. When finally forced to surrender, Ledyard handed his sword to an officer who ran him through with it, setting off a British rampage in which 85 Americans, many wounded in the battle, were killed. Today, at the corner of Park and Monument Avenues, you can visit *Fort Griswold State*

*Park* with its 134-ft granite monument and splendid views of the area. The Monument House nearby contains battle memorabilia. In the river off Thames Street is the *USS Croaker Submarine Museum* (open daily 9am-5pm; admission). Built by Electric Boat, the *Croaker* served in World War II and the museum traces the history of the submarine. The curious may also visit the *US Submarine Base*, where there is another submarine museum. In the summer the *'See the Submarine by Boat' cruise* takes visitors up the Thames past the base and Coast Guard Academy (87 Fairview Avenue; tel: 445-7401 for information).

Partly in Groton and partly in Stonington, **Mystic** has a long seafaring and shipbuilding tradition. During the California Gold Rush, it produced a number of swift clipper ships, including the famous *Andrew Jackson*, which in 1860 rounded the Horn to San Francisco in a record 89 days and 4 hours, beating the *Flying Cloud* by 9 hours. West Mystic claims to have built the first ironclad ship in America, the *Galena*, which predated the more famous *Monitor* by several months.

The *Mystic Seaport Museum* recreates the spirit of maritime New England in the 19th century. Here you can board the last of the wooden whaling ships, the *Charles W. Morgan* of New Bedford; visit the shipyard dedicated to preserving the museum's sailing ships; watch seafaring and craft demonstrations; tour the re-created village (the houses were brought in from various locales); and look at all manner of sea memorabilia. In the summer there are cruises on a refurbished steam boat. (Open March to November 9am-5pm, to 8pm from May to September, to 4pm from December to March. Admission for adults is $5.00, $2.50 for children over 6.) On Route 27 the *Mystic Marinelife Aquarium* houses 2,000 specimens including performing whales, dolphins and seals to give the underwater point-of-view (open daily 9am-6pm, admission $4.50 adults, $1.75 children aged 5-14).

In **Stonington**, near the Rhode Island border, the colonial mansion *Whitehall* (Route 27) has authentic furnishings and three-foot shingles (open daily 2pm-4pm, closed Saturdays; admission). On the Point, Connecticut's oldest lighthouse is now the *Old Lighthouse Museum* with locally made artifacts and Indian items (open July to Labor Day, 11am-4.30pm; closed Monday).

**Restaurants.** *In Branford:* Beefsteak Tavern**, 377 E. Main Street. *In Guilford:* Sachem Country House**, Goose Lane; Little Stone House**, town dock. *In Essex:* Griswold Inn***. *In Old Lyme:* Bee & Thistle Inn**, Old Lyme Inn***, both in Main Street. *In Waterford:* Poor Richard's***. *In New London:* Anthony's Steam Carriage*** in Union Station; The Gondolier**, Whale Oil

Row; Pier One*, Harbour. *In Groton:* Yankee Fisherman***, Long Point. *In Mystic:* Seamen's Inne***, Mystic Seaport; Yesterday's Manner***, Route 184; Chuck's Steakhouse**, downtown; Sailor Ed's**. *In Stonington:* Harbour View***.

## Northeast Connecticut

This is one of the most sparsely inhabited areas of the Northeast Corridor, much of it under forest cover. Between Essex and Hartford there are several state parks along the Connecticut River; in the *Gillette Castle State Park* near **Hadlyme** stands one of America's feudal castles, built in 1914 by the famous Sherlock Holmes actor, William Gillette. Overlooking the river, it is a curious palace designed and decorated by Gillette himself (open Memorial Day to Columbus Day, 11am-5pm).

North along the river, the lovely restored *Goodspeed Opera House* in **East Haddam** once again presents new and revived musicals from June to Labor Day. (For information, call 873-8664.)

**Moodus**, to the north, has become a small resort centre; in the past it was known for the mysterious 'Moodus Noises' on Mount Tom. Early settlers believed the weird subterranean rumblings were caused by local witches quarrelling. In 1765 a certain Dr Steele from Great Britain removed two pearls from the mountain's cave, which he claimed had caused the blasting. The mountain was quiet until 1791 – when it made explosive noises and caused a tremendous earthquake.

North along the Connecticut is **Middletown**, home of the *Wesleyan University* and once the largest and most prosperous city in Connecticut. Its wide streets downtown remind one of the Mid-West. The main centre of attraction in the university, the *Olin Library*, designed by Henry Bacon, houses the original manuscript of the *Theory of Relativity* by Albert Einstein and other rare works. The 1828 Russell House, now the *Honors College*, is a Roman Temple in a Brownstone medium. Other fine houses dating from Middletown's glory days of West Indian trade may be seen along High Street.

Eastwards, **Coventry** has an attraction called *Nathan Hale's Homestead* (South Street), although it was built by Nathan's father and finished after his son was hanged in 1776. It is a fine house, containing many of its original furnishings (open 15 May to 15 October, 1pm-5pm). On Silver Street the *Caprilands Herb Gardens* will interest the gardener for their variety and beautiful arrangements (open April to December).

On the main campus of the *University of Connecticut* at nearby

**Storrs** are the *William Benton Museum of Art* in a Gothic revival building (open Monday to Saturday 10am-4.30pm, Sunday 1pm-5pm) and the *Nutmeg Summer Playhouse*, with performances from mid June to mid August (tel: 429-2812 for information).

Little **Lebanon**, south of Willimantic, was the home of Revolutionary War Governor Jonathon Trumbull, without whose assistance, Washington once said, 'the war could not have been carried to a successful termination'. *Trumbull's House and War Office* on the Common are now museums and contain many Revolutionary memorabilia, as well as Governor Trumbull's secret office and a self-portrait by John Trumbull, the Governor's son (open 15 May to 15 October, Tuesday to Saturday 1pm-5pm).

Hilly **Norwich** on the Thames, industrial yet charming, is known as 'the Rose of New England' for its beauty and many rose gardens, especially in *Mohegan Park*. Norwich was given by Uncas, chief of the Mohegans, to Thomas Leffingwell, who had helped him battle the Narragansetts in King Philip's War (the Mohegans fought for the English). Benedict Arnold was born in Norwich, as were the ancestors of several presidents.

Like Pittsburgh, Norwich is located on the banks of three rivers; the Yantic, the Shetucket and the Thames. **Norwichtown**, on the Yantic, is the town's historic district, with numerous 18th-century homes. Here, the *Leffingwell Inn*, built in 1675, has been turned into a museum (open summer, Tuesday to Saturday 10am-12pm and 2pm-4pm, Sunday 2pm-4pm; winter weekends only). South along Washington Street is the site of Benedict Arnold's birthplace (corner of Arnold Place) and further down, at 108 Crescent, is the *Slater Memorial*, containing several interesting collections of Japanese, Indian and American art (open September to May, Monday to Friday 9am-4pm, weekends 1pm-4pm; June to August, Tuesday to Sunday 1pm-4pm). A nearby monument honours Captain Samuel Reid, a hero of the War of 1812 and designer of the modern American flag, with a star added for every state.

At the corner of Washington and Sachem Streets is the *Uncas Monument* erected by order of President Andrew Jackson, where several Mohegan Sachems are buried. Nearby is the narrow gorge called *Indian Leap*, over the edge of which, according to legend, the Mohegans drove their enemy the Narragansetts in a battle. Just south of here the *Yantic Falls* bring the river down to the Thames.

When Norwich became a steamship terminus to New York, (the company was the beginning of the Vanderbilt fortune) a new downtown was built on the Thames; the *City Hall* building and ornate Victorian homes on Broadway recall the old prosperity. Up the Shetucket, in **Taftville** the château-like *Ponemah Mills*, originally used to weave fine cloth, are still used for manufacturing today.

On *Uncas Hill* in **Mohegan** are the ruins of Uncas' cabin. His direct descendants run the *Tantaquidgeon Indian Museum* (Route 32), with reproductions of New England Indian dwellings and crafts made by the Mohegan Indians (open daily 10am-6pm).

**Restaurants.** *In East Haddam:* Gelston House**, Goodspeed's Landing. *In Middletown:* Town Farm Inn***, Silver Street; La Boca (Mexican)*, 526 Street. *In Manchester:* Cavey's***, 45 E. Center Street. *In Warehouse Point:* Coachlight Dinner Theater***. *In Willimantic (near Lebanon):* The Clark's**. *In Norwich:* Gentleman Jim's**, Norwich Motel.

## Annual Events in Connecticut

**First Saturday in May:** Powderhouse Day, *New Haven.* Festive celebration of Benedict Arnold's demanding of the powderhouse keys.
**Second weekend in May:** Dogwood Festival, *Fairfield.* Typical New England church fair amid blossoms. Also in Fairfield, the Bird Carver's Show exhibit and sale of prize bird carvings. Also: Shad Derby and Festival, in *Windsor.*
**End of May:** New England Fiddle Contest, Bushnell Park, *Hartford.*
**End of May/June:** *Old Lyme* Spring Exhibit, Lyme Art Association Gallery. Also: New England Exhibition of Painting, Drawing and Sculpture, Silvermine Galleries, in *New Canaan.*
**Last weekend in May:** Yale Harvard weekend, in *New London,* with Regatta.
**Mid June to 4 July:** Barnum Festival, *Bridgeport.*
**Last half of June:** Rose Festival, *Norwich.*
**Late June:** Mountain Laurel Festival, in *Winsted* and *West Torrington.*
**4 July:** Enormous parade in *Bridgeport.*
**Second Saturday in July:** International Festival, *New London.*
**July weekends:** Deep River Muster, *Deep River.* Fife and Drum shows.
**Mid July:** *North Stonington* Agricultural Fair. Also, in *Hebron,* Bluegrass Festival.
**Late July:** Village Fair Days, *New Milford.*
**Second weekend in August:** *Mystic* Outdoor Art Festival, largest in state.
**Mid August to Mid October:** Bluefish Tournaments, *East Lyme.*

**First weekend in September:** Antiques Weekend, in *Farmington.*
**Mid September:** Oyster Festival, in *Norwalk.* Also: Four Town Fair, *Somers.* Oldest agricultural fair in the state. Also: Chrysanthemum Festival, in *Bristol*, through mid-October.
**First weekend in October:** Connecticut Antiques Show, Armory, *Hartford.*
**First week in October:** *Danbury* State Fair, state's largest. Also: Apple Harvest Festival, in *Southington.*
**Mid November to December:** Silvermine Christmas Exhibition, *New Canaan.*
**Mid December:** Christmas Torchlight parade, in *Old Saybrook,* with carols and muster.

## **Accommodation in Connecticut** (area code: 203)

**Southwest**
Showboat Inn, Steamboat Rd, tel: 661-9800, *Greenwich.* Expensive modern, with pool and baby-sitting.
Homestead Inn, 420 Field Point Rd, tel: 869-7500, *Greenwich.* Cosy inn near Long Island Sound, not too expensive.
Shippan Point Inn, 1404 Shippan Ave, tel: 323-1910, *Stamford.* Moderately expensive, with waterbeds and fireplaces.
Silvermine Tavern, Perry Ave, tel: 847-4558, *Norwalk.* Average-priced old country inn.
Norwalk Motor Inn, 99 East Ave, tel: 838-5531, *Norwalk.* Modern motel near beach and State Park.
Inn at Longshore, 260 Compo Rd, tel: 226-3316, *Westport.* Expensive; docking available.
Bridgeport Motor Inn, 100 Kings Hwy, tel: 367-4404, *Fairfield.* Moderately priced, near Connecticut turnpike.
West Lane Inn, 22 West Lane, tel: 438-7323, *Ridgefield.* Expensive, in Ridgefield's historic district.
Ridgefield Motor Inn, Rt. 7, tel. 438-3781, *Ridgefield.* Moderate, with pool.
Stonehedge Inn, Stonehedge Rd, tel: 438-6511, *Ridgefield.* Charming small inn, good restaurant, expensive.
Ethan Allen Inn, I-84, tel: 744-1776 *Danbury.* Colonial-style motel near fairgrounds and Candlewood Lake; expensive.
Stratford Motor Inn, Main St, tel: 378-7351, *Stratford.* Moderately priced, with good restaurant, on river.
Plaza Motel, 345 Old Gate Lane, tel: 878-0685 *Milford.* Inexpensive, near jai-alai.
YMCA, 909 Washington Blvd, tel: 375-7000, *Stamford.* Modern, inexpensive, men & women over 18.

**New Haven to Hartford**

*In New Haven:*

The Colony Inn, 1157 Chapel St, tel: 776-1234. Moderately expensive, near downtown and Yale.

Duncan Hotel, 1151 Chapel St, tel: 787-1273. Inexpensive, near Yale.

New Haven Motor Inn, 100 Lily Pond Ave, tel: 387-6651. Moderately priced, with pool.

Three Judges Motor Lodge, 1560 Whaley Ave, tel: 389-2161. Inexpensive, but a ways from downtown.

YMCA, 52 Howe St, tel: 865-3161. Men & women, inexpensive.

International Center Residence Halls, 406 Prospect, tel: 787-3531. Open summer only (closed last two weeks of August), $5 a night.

Sleeping Giant Motel, 3400 Whitney Ave, tel: 288-2505, *Hamden.* Inexpensive.

Yale Motor Inn, Rt 5, tel: 269-1491, *Wallingford.* Moderate, with pool.

YMCA, 110 W. Main St, tel: 235-6386, *Meriden.* Men & women, cheap.

Burritt Hotel, 67 W. Main St, tel: 223-2703, *New Britain.* Inexpensive, with restaurant.

**Hartford area**

*In Hartford:*

Governor's House Hotel, 440 Asylum, tel: 246-6591. Next to Civic Center, moderately expensive.

Hotel Sonesta, 5 Constitution Plaza, tel: 278-2000. Expensive, downtown.

Hartford Hilton, Ford & Pearl Sts, tel: 249-5611. Downtown, with restaurant; expensive.

Swiss Chalet Inn, 185 Brainard Rd, tel: 525-9306. Inexpensive, but two miles out of town.

YMCA, 135 Broad, tel: 525-1163. Women only, reservations necessary. New building with kitchens.

YMCA, 160 Jewell St, tel: 522-4183. Fancy Y, men and women, air-conditioning, but inexpensive.

West Hartford Motor Inn, 900 Farmington Ave, tel: 236-3221, *West Hartford.* Moderately expensive, five miles from Hartford.

Grantmoor Motor Lodge, 3000 Berlin Tpke, tel: 666-5481, *Newington.* Moderate.

Madison Motor Inn, 393 Main St, tel: 568-3560, *East Hartford.* Inexpensive.

**Northwest Connecticut**

Windsor Towne House, 19 Maple Ave, tel: 688-6261, *Windsor.* Moderately expensive.

Bradely International Inn, 34 Old Country Inn, tel: 623-2533, *Windsor Locks.* Moderately expensive, near airport.

Executive Inn, 969 Hopmeadow, tel: 658-2216, *Simsbury.* Moderate to expensive.

Hillside Motel, Rt 44, tel: 693-4951, *Canton.* Inexpensive, near museum.

Yankee Peddlar Inn, 93 Main St, tel: 489-9226, *Torrington.* Moderate, with restaurant.

Club Getaway, S. Kent Rd, tel: 927-3664, *Kent.*Expensive resort-style.

Inn on Lake Waramaug, Rt 202, tel: 868-2168, *New Preston.* expensive resort in charming inn.

Boulders Inn, Rt 45, tel: 868-7918, *New Preston.* Expensive resort, furnished with antiques.

Hopkins Inn, Hopkins Rd, *New Preston.* Charming lakeside inn, moderate.

Bantam Lake Youth Hostel, East Shore Rd, tel: 567-9258, *Lakeside.* near Bethlehem. Beautifully located, open year round. Card required.

Red Bull Motor Inn, Scott Rd, tel: 756-8123, *Waterbury.* Expensive, with restaurant and entertainment.

Waterbury Motor Inn, 91 Scott Rd, tel: 756-7925, *Waterbury.* Moderate, with restaurant.

YMCA, 136 Main, tel: 754-2181, *Waterbury.* Cheap, but men only.

**Southeast Coast**

Branford Motor Inn, Exit 55 Conn. Turnpike, tel: 488-8314, *Branford.* Moderate, with pool.

Coastway Motel, 327 Boston Post Rd, tel: 669-2275, *Clinton.* Inexpensive.

Old Saybrook Motor Hotel, US 1, tel: 388-3463, *Saybrook.* Moderate, beach.

Admiral House Motel, Exit 66 off I-95, tel: 399-6273, *Saybrook.* Expensive, near beach and charter fishing.

Griswold Inn, 48 Main, tel: 767-0991, *Essex.* Moderate, restaurant.

Old Lyme Inn, 85 Lyme St, tel: 434-2600, *Old Lyme.* Moderately expensive with good restaurant.

Lighthouse Inn, 242 Lower Blvd, tel: 443-8411, *New London.* Expensive, overlooking Long Island Sound.

Oakdell Motel, 983 Hartford Tpke, tel. 442-9446, *New London.* Moderate

YMCA, 19 Meridian St, tel: 443-5368, *New London.* Inexpensive.

Mitchell College Youth Hostel, 355 Pequot, tel. 447-3787, *New London.* Open all year, card required.

On The Thames Motel-Boatel, Thames St, tel: 445-8111, *Groton.* Moderate, by the docks, beach privileges.

Windsor Motel, Rt 184, tel: 445-7474, *Groton.* Inexpensive; efficiencies.

Mystic Motor Inn, Rt 1, tel: 536-9604, *Mystic.* Moderate to expensive.

Taber Motel, Rt 1, tel: 536-4904, *Mystic.* Moderate to expensive.

Seaport Motor Inn, Rt 27, tel: 536-2621, *Mystic.* Moderate, with restaurant.

**Northeast Connecticut**

Banner Lodge, Banner Rd, tel: 873-8652, *Moodus.* Golf included in rates, restaurant, pool, summer only; deluxe resort.

Riverdale Motel, E. Hampton Rd, tel: 342-3498, *Portland.* Inexpensive.

Crestline Motel, Rt 66, tel: 347-6955, *Middletown.* Inexpensive.

Middletown Motor Lodge, Washington St, tel: 346-9251, *Middletown.* Inexpensive.

Essex Motor Inn, 100 E. Center, tel: 646-2300, *Manchester,* Moderate X-rated motel.

King's Inn, Rt 52, tel: 928-7961, *Putnam.* Moderate, with restaurant.

Berris Motor Inn, Rt 6 & 52, tel: 774-9644, *Danielson.* Moderate, with restaurant and sports facilities.

Norwich Motel, 181 West Town St, tel: 889-2671, *Norwich.* Moderate, pool and restaurant.

**For more information and a list of campsites,** write to the Department of Economic Development, 210 Washington Street, Hartford, Conn. 06106.

**Detailed information on parks and recreation** may be had from the State Department of Environmental Protection, State Office Building, Hartford, Conn. 06115.

# Rhode Island

Rhode Island, tucked between Connecticut and Massachusetts, may be the smallest state in the Union, but as one of its governors has said, it should be measured 'not by the foot, but by the head'. Roger Williams, the state's founding father, set the pace when he insisted on freedom of religion and civil rights for Indians in 1636; Newport, Rhode Island's largest colonial city, attracted a yeasty mix of Quakers, Jews, Baptists and Anglicans, and was the cultural centre of New England until the Revolution. Of all the states, Rhode Island was the first to declare independence from Britain, it was the last to sign the Constitution, it had five capitals until the mid 19th century and at one time had two governors. It also has the longest official name of the states: Rhode Island and Providence Plantations, but the shortest motto – *Hope*.

With nearly one million inhabitants, Rhode Island is the most densely populated state after New Jersey. The Industrial Revolution in America began in Pawtucket, and today the state is highly industrialized, producing such diverse products as costume jewellery, electronics, lace, machinery, metals and yachts. Outside the northeast corner of the state, however, Rhode Island is rural with a fetching charm.

The greatest geographical feature of the state is Narragansett Bay, a miniature version of Chesapeake Bay, where lobsters, hard clams (quahaugs), flounder, scup, cod and whiting compose the main commercial catch, while sportsmen come to challenge the giant bluefin tuna. The state feast, were there such a thing, would be the clambake: clams, lobsters, sausage, corn and sweet potatoes are put in a steaming pit lined with seaweed, with flavoursome results. Early settlers learned the clambake technique from the Indians, and the tradition has been handed down in certain families of bakemasters, who keep their secret to themselves. The other Rhode Island speciality you can find at certain festivals is the cornmeal Johnnycake, a corruption of 'Journey Cake', first made in Usquepaug.

Not only does Narragansett Bay supply seafood, but it creates sheltered harbours at Providence and Newport. In past centuries great sailing ships set sail from these ports to the West Indies, Africa, China and California, making fortunes for a number of now entrenched aristocratic families. Newport's mild climate attracted others in the summer, first from the steamy south and then from New York, until it became one of the most fashionable resorts in the world, setting off a building spree of opulent

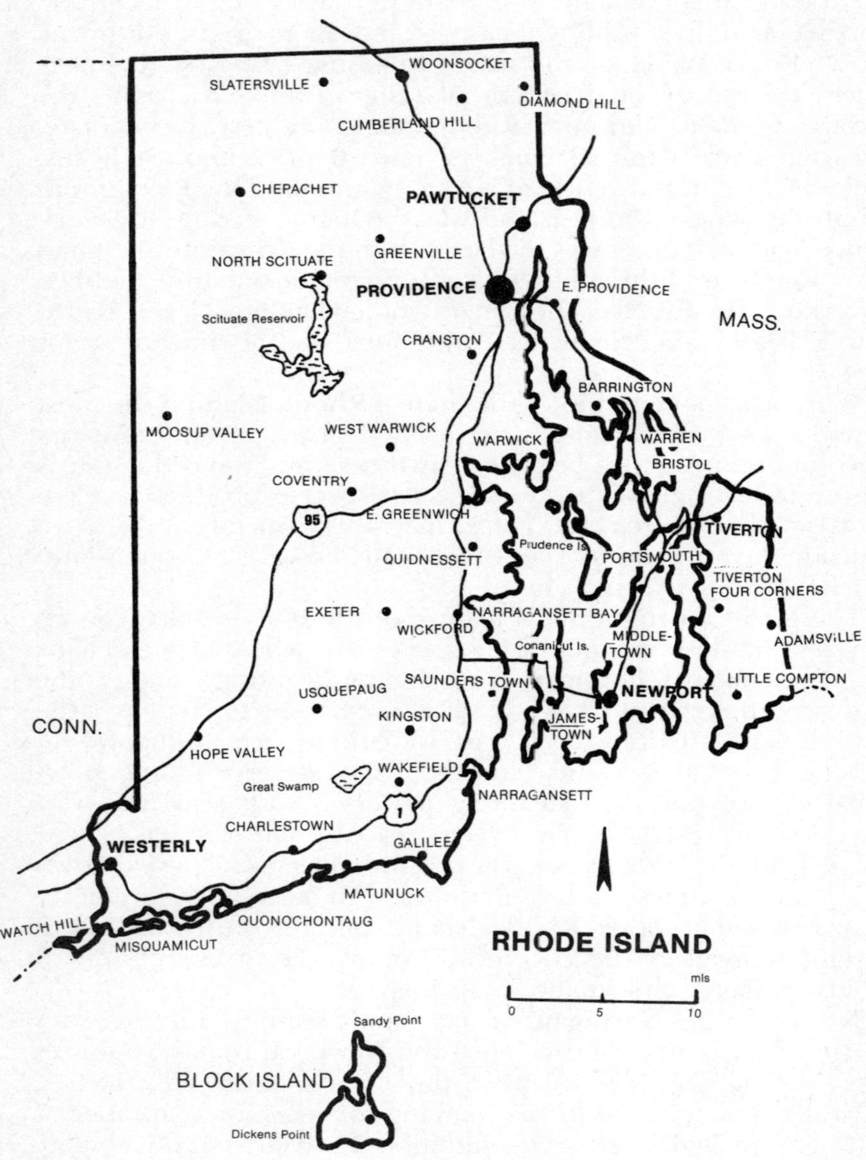
WOONSOCKET
SLATERSVILLE
DIAMOND HILL
CUMBERLAND HILL
CHEPACHET
PAWTUCKET
GREENVILLE
NORTH SCITUATE
PROVIDENCE
E. PROVIDENCE
MASS.
Scituate Reservoir
CRANSTON
BARRINGTON
MOOSUP VALLEY
WEST WARWICK
WARWICK
WARREN
BRISTOL
COVENTRY
95
E. GREENWICH
TIVERTON
Prudence Is.
QUIDNESSETT
PORTSMOUTH
TIVERTON
FOUR CORNERS
EXETER
NARRAGANSETT BAY
WICKFORD
MIDDLE-
TOWN
Conanicut Is.
ADAMSVILLE
SAUNDERS TOWN
LITTLE COMPTON
USQUEPAUG
NEWPORT
KINGSTON
JAMES-
TOWN
CONN.
HOPE VALLEY
WAKEFIELD
Great Swamp
NARRAGANSETT
1
CHARLESTOWN
WESTERLY
GALILEE
MATUNUCK
WATCH HILL
QUONOCHONTAUG
MISQUAMICUT
RHODE ISLAND
mls
0
5
10
Sandy Point
BLOCK ISLAND
Dickens Point

mansions that will never be equalled. Today sleek yachts instead of China Clippers ply the waters of the bay; with its many islands and quaint coastal villages it makes splendid sailing. For landlubbers the 'Ocean State' offers a series of lovely beaches along its southwestern shore and on charming Block Island, ten miles to the south.

## Getting Around Rhode Island

One of the major advantages to a Rhode Island holiday is that you are never much more than an hour away from any other point in the state; it is America's first city state, where you can get by decently without a car.

**By Air.** The largest airport in Rhode Island is *T. F. Green State Airport* at Warwick, served by major carriers and the smaller New England lines like Pilgrim and Air New England. There is a daily Newport shuttle service to the airport from 1 America's Cup Avenue (tel: 846-2500). There is a commuter air service between *Westerly State Airport* and Block Island as well (tel: 596-2460).

**By Train.** Amtrak (tel: 1-800-523-5720) has service to Providence Railroad Terrace on its Boston—New York—Washington route, with less frequent stops in Westerly, Kingston, Shannock, Wickford and East Greenwich.

**By Ferry.** To take your car on a Block Island ferry, you must reserve a place in advance, in writing, to Interstate Navigation Co., P O Box 482, New London, tel: Conn. 06320. Cars are taken only on ferries from Galilee and Providence. Year-round service to *Block Island* sails from Galilee; summer service from Newport, Providence and New London, Connecticut. For schedules in Galilee, tel: 783-4613; in Providence tel: 421-4050; in New London, tel: (203) 442-7891. From Church Street Wharf, Bristol, there is a service to Prudence and Hog Islands every day (tel: 245-7411). A cruise boat will take passengers from Block Island to Montauk, Long Island (New York) in summer only.

**By Bus.** Interstate bus lines operating out of Providence to surrounding cities and towns in New England and New York are Bonanza Bus Lines (27 Sabin Street, Providence; tel: 751-2868) and Greyhound (1 Sabin Street, Providence; tel: 751-8800). Because Rhode Island is so small, it has its own in-state bus lines to all points in its borders: *Rhode Island Transit Authority* (headquarters at 256 Melrose Street, Providence; tel: 781-9400).

## History

In October 1635 the Puritans of Massachusetts Bay banished Roger Williams, a Salem elder, for he 'hath broached and divulged new and dangerous opinions against the authority of magistrates'. His sin was that he had suggested that the land they lived on really belonged to the Indians, and that Indian religions might be superior to Christianity in the eyes of God. For such heresy Williams and his followers had to leave. They sailed south in the wilderness to the Mohassuck and Woonasquatucket (Providence) Rivers, where they purchased land from the Narragansett Indians and founded a new colony, which Williams named Providence. Religious freedom, the basis for the new colony, soon attracted others discontented with the Puritan theocracy – mainly Quakers, Williams' fellow Baptists, and, by 1650, Jews from Europe.

In 1639 Roger Williams helped buy Aquidneck Island from the Indians, and here Anne Hutchinson, also banned from Boston, founded Portsmouth. Other dissenters founded Newport, and a fourth settlement was founded on the mainland: Warwick. These four towns became a political entity under the Charter of 1643 and under the famous Charter of 1663, in which Charles II bade Rhode Island 'to hold forth a lively experiment that a most flourishing civil state may stand and best be maintained with full liberty in religious concernments'.

Because of Roger Williams' respect for their rights, Rhode Island's relations with its Indians were quite good. These Indians, the Narragansetts, were one of the most powerful tribes in New England at that time and they played an important role in King Philip's War (1675-6), the most severe threat New England ever faced. Its cause may be traced, as may be expected, to the Puritans. King Philip, whose Indian name was Metacom, was the young chief of the Wampanoags, a small tribe in the Plymouth Colony – his father, Massasoit, did much to assist the early settlers there. When Massasoit died, the Plymouth colonists immediately forgot all the help they had received and turned on Philip, ordering him to pay them tribute in an attempt to totally subjugate the Wampanoag tribe. Philip then realized that unless the Indians united against the white settlers, they would lose all their ancestral lands to the usurpers. A number of smaller tribes rallied to his cause, which the Puritans shrugged off, until their own stupidity caused them to lose their great allies, the Narragansetts.

The Narragansett chief, Canonchot, became Philip's field general. Together they caused a reign of terror, burning settlements throughout the Connecticut Valley, their strategies and desperate courage taking the Puritans by surprise. At the end of 1675 New England's whites honestly feared they would be wiped out – until their great victory in December. Canonchot and the Narragansetts had built a fort in Rhode Island's Great Swamp, near South Kingstown, believing themselves safe; the swamp, however, froze that year, and the English attacked, overwhelming the surprised Indians. The Narragansetts never recovered from this blow, and without his most powerful ally, King Philip was fighting a losing battle. He was murdered in August 1676, ending the war that had cost New England over 600 men. Fifty-two of New England's ninety towns had been damaged or destroyed and it took years for the colonies to recover. (The Indians, however, never recovered, and those who survived the war went west.)

First to prosper was Newport, which survived King Philip's War without a scratch. Located on a magnificent harbour, it did not take the first settlers long to realize the commercial possibilities it offered. Jewish merchants began producing spermaceti (whale oil) candles, making Newport the leader in their manufacture. Ships were built and were used to smuggle molasses in from the West Indies to make rum. In the early 18th century this developed into the notorious 'triangular trade' in which Rhode Island led the other colonies: rum was sold in Africa for slaves, who were sold in the West Indies in exchange for molasses to make the rum in New England. Many slaves were processed through Newport as well and these various enterprises made Newport one of the wealthiest and busiest ports in the colonies. The taint of slavery did not, however, prevent Newport from becoming the pre-Revolution intellectual and artistic centre of New England, where Baptists, Jews and Quakers lived and disputed in heady freedom.

Rhode Island shed the first blood in the Revolution. For several years prior to the war, Newport's merchants, squeezed by British enforcement of anti-smuggling laws, set fire to customs vessels in protest; in 1772, *HMS Gaspee* was attacked in Providence, its crew captured, its captain wounded and the ship burned to the waterline. In May 1776, Rhode Island declared its independence, antedating the other colonies by two months (Rhode Island was also the last state to ratify the Constitution, and so functioned as an independent Republic for fourteen years).

Brilliant colonial Newport suffered a devastating blow when the British occupied it in 1776, ending its trade. Providence, until that time half the size of Newport, rose to take its place; at the back of the bay it was far less vulnerable. It became 'the backdoor to Boston', bringing in much needed supplies through trade and extensive privateering. After the war, Providence's merchants turned to the China trade to maintain their wartime prosperity; Newport remained a staid backwater until the mid 19th century, when the affluent began to summer there once more, as their forefathers had during the glory days of the slave trade.

In 1798, according to legend, Samuel Slater arrived in Pawtucket from a journey in England, where he had memorized the closely guarded secret of the Arkwright power spinning frame. He built his own version of the mill on the Blackstone River, and in effect started the Industrial Revolution in America. Canadians, Irish, French and Italian immigrants flocked to the state seeking jobs, in the process making Rhode Island the second most densely populated state in the union.

## What to See

Unlike other New England towns, Providence, Rhode Island's capital, was not founded around a Common or Green with a church centrepiece – a result of Roger Williams' insistence on a separation of Church and State. The earliest settlement spread along the eastern bank of the Providence River, but when manufacturing became the city's livelihood after the War of 1812 and Jefferson's trade blockade, the heart of Providence moved westward, where downtown Providence is today.

Dominating Providence on all sides is the *State Capitol,* an inordinately large building for such a small state, topped with an unsupported marble dome, second largest after St Peters in the Vatican. On top of this stands a bronze figure in a lionskin – not the apotheosis of Roger Williams but of *The Independent Man,* symbolic of Rhode Island's historical prerogative of going its own way. The Beaux Arts Capitol itself, made of white Georgia marble, was designed by the great architectural firm of McKim, Mead and White in 1892. The exterior of this fine building is everything (especially at night, when illuminated), although there is a Gilbert Stuart portrait of Washington in the Governor's Reception Room inside, and the Gettysburg Cannon (loaded until 1962) near the rear entrance.

Just east of the Capitol, in Providence's lovely *East Side,* is the site of Roger Williams' original settlement in 1636, now the *Roger Williams National Memorial and Spring* (N. Main and Spring Streets). Nothing remains of 1636 Providence, but an educational exhibit has been set up near the natural spring that supplied the first settlers.

Up the hill and parallel to Main Street runs *Benefit Street* (built for the 'benefit' of the inhabitants). At 150 Benefit Street the *Old State House* (1762) served as one of Rhode Island's five capitols until 1900. Overlooking this on *Prospect Terrace* is the *Roger Williams Monument,* where the founder's remains were interred in 1939. The panoramic view from the terrace of downtown Providence is the best in town. Near here, at 62 Prospect Street, the Rhode Island School of Design has a gallery in the *Woods-Gerry House* (open Monday to Friday 8.30am-4.30pm, weekends 1pm-4pm), an enormous Victorian mansion built in 1860 on the highest point in the city.

Take Prospect South to College Street for *Brown University,* the seventh oldest university in America. Originally affiliated with the Baptist Church, it was named in 1804 after a descendant of the Brown brothers – 'Nick, Joe, John and Mo' – who lived in the late 18th century and left an indelible mark on Providence. Extraordinarily wealthy, the family made its initial fortune in sea trade, spermaceti candles and rum; it played a major role in Rhode Island politics – in particular John Brown, who led the conspiracy to burn the British schooner *Gaspee.* Moses Brown, a Quaker, was a leading abolitionist; Joseph Brown, a first-class architect, built Providence's finest homes and the First Baptist Meeting House; Nicholas, an industrialist, owned a great foundry.

The oldest building on campus, *University Hall,* lies just inside the grand *Van Wickle Gates.* This four-storey brick Georgian building, built in 1770 by Robert Smith, served as a barracks for American and French troops during the Revolution, and today houses the Administration offices. Here you can begin a student tour of the campus (Monday to Friday on the hour; autumn Saturdays; not available in January or May). At Brown and George Streets, on the College Green is the great stone *John Carter Brown Library,* housing a collection of early Americana considered the most extensive in the world. Across Prospect from University Hall are two other libraries: *John Hay Library,* with special collections from Lincolniana to the papers of H. P. Lovecraft, and the new *John D. Rockefeller Library* with the University's main collections.

Take College Street back to Benefit Street; here, at number 251 is the Greek Revival *Providence Athenaeum,* built in 1838, although the library company itself dates back to 1753. Here Edgar Allen Poe courted poetess Sarah Whitman, thought to be the model for his Annabel Lee. The books on the shelves, many from the

18th century, and the atmosphere of the place have changed little since then. At the corner of Benefit and Power stands Providence's loveliest mansion, the *John Brown House* (open Tuesday to Friday 11am-4pm, weekends 2pm-4pm, admission). Designed by Joseph Brown in 1784 for his wealthy, slave-trading patriotic brother, this was the first house built on the hill over the wharves and one of the finest early American mansions. The house was given to the Rhode Island Historical Society by John Nicholas Brown, and has been restored to mint 18th-century condition, with some of the furniture made in Newport for the Browns, porcelain brought back in the China trade (John Brown sent the first Rhode Island ship to the East) antique dolls, and John Brown's 'chariot', reputedly the oldest American-made vehicle.

Take Main Street north to 75 North Main and the lovely *First Baptist Meeting House,* also by Joseph Brown and finished in 1775 (open Monday to Friday 10am-3.30pm, Saturday 9pm-12 noon, Sunday at 12 noon). This church, built by the 118 members of the Baptist congregation founded by Roger Williams, seats 1,200 – it was specifically designed not only for Sunday service but also for Brown's commencement ceremonies, which still take place there after a long procession down the hill from the university. The interior is maintained in the colonial style, with the original chandelier. Interestingly, although Roger Williams founded the Baptist Church in America and was its first minister, he withdrew from it only a few months later, believing Christiandom was irreparably corrupt.

The *Rhode Island School of Design* on North Main is one of America's leading art schools, and appropriately enough it has one of the best little art museums: the *R. I. School of Design Museum of Art,* at 224 Benefit (open Tuesday to Saturdays 11am-5pm, Sundays and holidays 2pm-5pm, free on Saturdays; closed August). The museum houses Greek and Roman collections, a large amount of Orientalia, French Impressionists, American art, British watercolours, and an addition devoted to Charles Pendleton's collection of 18th-century American furnishings.

Down the hill, at the corner of College and South Water and facing Providence River is the *Market House,* built in 1773 and the centre of colonial mercantile life. Designed by Joseph Brown and Governor Stephen Hopkins (in those days, remember, architectural design was not a profession, but a hobby of colonial gentlemen who learned from books and pictures), the Market was originally only two storeys; a third was added by the Masons. Rochambeau's troops lived here during the Revolution, and it served as Providence's City Hall until 1880.

## Downtown Providence (the Weybosset, or West Side)

In the early 19th century, the heart of Providence's commercial life moved west to *Kennedy Plaza.* Here stands the palatial *City Hall,* designed by Samuel J. F. Thayer in 1878 and inspired by the palace of the Tuileries. In City Hall Park an equestrian statue honours General Ambrose Burnside (father of the sideburn), who served as Rhode Island Governor and Senator after the Civil War.

One of Providence's newest-oldest attractions is its *Arcade,* southeast of City Hall at the beginning of Weybosset Street. Built in 1828, this Greek Revival skylit structure was America's first indoor shopping mall. It has recently been restored and reopened in the style of Boston's Quincy Market, containing eateries and boutiques. South of Weybosset, at Abbott Park Place is *Johnson and Wales College,* where master chefs are trained; in the spring and summer the college sponsors weekends of gourmet instruction and feasting. At the corner of Weybosset and Empire rises the golden dome of the *Beneficent Congregational Church,* or 'Round Top Church', built in 1810, the oldest church on the west side, with a 5,700-piece crystal chandelier. Empire Street continues to Washington Street and the Lederer Theater (formerly the Majestic movie palace), now the home of the *Trinity Square Repertory Company* (for performance information, tel: 351-4242).

Above all this, at the top of Westminster Street is the Gothic Revival *Cathedral of St Peter and St Paul,* facing onto I. M. Pei's excellent *Cathedral Square*, a pleasant multi-level brick plaza with trees and an unusual fountain. To the south on Elmwood Street are the rolling hills of *Roger Williams Park,* with a Temple of Music, an Oriental Garden, a *Museum of Natural History and Planetarium* (open Monday to Friday 8.30am-4.15pm, Saturday 10am-4.15pm), and a zoo (open daily 10am-4pm; free admission).

**Restaurants.** L'Apogee***, on top of the Biltmore Plaza Hotel, with views; Capriccio***, 2 Pine Street; Camille's Roman Gardens***, 71 Bradford; S.S. *Victoria***, 515 South Water Street (dine on a New York City steamship); David's Potbelly**, 100 North Main; Rue de l'Espoir**, 99 Hope Street; Coffee's Café and Restaurant*, 357 Dyer Avenue (Italian); Luke's*, 59 Eddy Street (Chinese).

## Eastern Rhode Island: Pawtucket to Newport

Just north of Providence is **Pawtucket**, 'the place by the waterfall'. In 1793, English immigrant Samuel Slater brought the Arkwright spinning frame to Pawtucket, founding Slater Mill on the Blackstone River and manufacturing the first cotton cloth spun by water power in America. The new textile technology quickly spread across New England: Slater's organization of the factory and its production are the basis of American industry.

Today the *Slater Mill Historic Site,* on Roosevelt Avenue, has been restored and is unique in the respect that the machines actually work, with all the whirring and oily smells of the Industrial Revolution; you can imagine the little children darting in and out of the heavy machinery, tying the broken threads. In the *Wilkinson Mill,* an eight-ton waterwheel will soon be hooked up to power the 19th-century machine tools; in the *Slater Mill* itself, bales of cotton are turned into yarn. A house on the property, the *Sylvanus Brown* house, built in 1758, was converted to workers' dwellings and is still furnished in that manner. Slater Mill is easily reached off I-95, Exit 28, or by 98 or 99 bus from Kennedy Plaza in Providence (open June to 5 September, Tuesday to Saturday 10am-5pm, Sunday 1pm-5pm; other weekends 1pm-5pm, closed Christmas to February; admission). Note the *Pawtucket Public Library*, built in 1902 as a copy of the Erechtheum in Athens, with marble panels depicting various civilizations. In eastern Pawtucket, near the Massachusetts border, is *Slater Memorial Park* (Route 1A) with a zoo and a carousel.

**Warren,** to the southeast, is an old seafaring town on a deep harbour; whaling, shipbuilding and dredging oysters were the main activities. There are many early 19th-century homes and churches near the waterfront, numerous antique shops, and a museum: the *Charles R. Carr Collection* in the library on Main Street, with artifacts from North American, Pre-Columbian and Peruvian Indians (open Monday to Friday 12pm-8pm, Saturday 1pm-3pm; closed Saturdays in the summer).

The first battle of King Philip's War occurred in **Bristol,** another seafaring town to the south; the last battle took place here as well, when Philip, hiding on Mount Hope, was murdered by another Indian in August 1676. In the early 19th century Bristol prospered, building ships for the China Trade. Today Bristol shipbuilders build yachts, and the town is known for its many museums and historic homes. The most elegant of these, *Linden Place* (Hope and Wardwell), was built by Russell Warren for the prominent De Wolf family, who earned their fortune in the slave and China trades; the mansion is lacy, gracious and highly detailed and remains in the family today. The ballroom built for the house on Wardwell Street is now the *Bristol Art Museum,* where exhibitions are changed every two weeks (open 1pm-5pm, Friday evenings 7pm-9pm, June to October). The Romanesque Revival *Burnside Memorial Building,* on Hope and Court Streets, was built in 1883 to honour the Civil War General and inventor of the breech-loading carbine rifle, which he manufactured in Bristol. On the eastern side of town, on Tower Street is Brown University's *Haffenreffer Museum of Anthropology* with permanent and changing exhibits from around the world (open 1pm-5pm, Tuesday to Sunday, June to August and 1pm-5pm at weekends during April/May and from September to November).

To the south, on Ferry Road, are the beautiful *Blithewold Gardens and Arboretum.* Blithewold itself was the summer estate of Augustus Van Winkle, a Pennsylvanian coal magnate, but his house is largely ignored in favour of the grounds, still very much as they were when landscaped in the 19th century, with various flower gardens and a variety of exotic trees including the largest Giant Sequoia east of the Rocky Mountains (open 10am-4pm daily except Mondays; admission). From the Church Street Dock you can take a ferry to *Prudence Island* and *Hog Island,* both known for excellent fishing off their coasts (tel: 245-7411 for the schedule).

East of Bristol and Aquidneck Island are the *Sakonnet Lands,* today a quiet corner of the state, but during the Revolution a centre of patriotic activity, opposing the British occupation of Newport. *Fort Barton* was constructed at **Tiverton,** where it was suspected the British would cross if they made an attempt on Boston. It was the base for the Battle of Rhode Island in August 1778. From here Lafayette, Nathaniel Greene and General John Sullivan launched a major attack on the British in Newport; unfortunately the French fleet suffered in a storm and was unable to provide the planned sea support, and the Americans were forced to retreat from Middletown after an unsuccessful siege. Today you can visit the Fort Barton Redoubt, the nature walk, and climb the observation tower erected near the fort for a view of the whole of Aquidneck Island.

**Tiverton Four Corners** is a pretty village to the south of Tiverton and the birthplace of Captain Robert Gray, discoverer of the Columbia River and claimant of the Northwest Territory on behalf of the United States. **Adamsville** to the east was the birthplace of the Rhode Island Red, America's first meaty chicken; in its honour, the *Rhode Island Red Commemorative Monument,* the only one anywhere to a chicken, stands near Crandall Road. **Little Compton,** to the south, was founded by Congregationalists when the Sekonnet Lands were claimed by Massachusetts. Thus, unlike the majority of towns in Rhode Island, it has a *Common,* a beautiful public square where the first church town hall building was constructed, now replaced by the United Congregational Church. The burial ground next to it contains the graves of Elizabeth Pabodie, first white woman born in the English colonies, and Benjamin Church, who fought in King Philip's War and ordered Philip's body beheaded and quartered. For years he kept Philip's hand around his house as a souvenir.

Connected by bridge both from Bristol and Tiverton, **Aquidneck** (or Rhode) **Island** was discovered by Verrazano in 1524; he was so taken by its charms and abundant wild roses that he named it Rhode Island (the isle of Rhodes in Greece was also named for its roses) and spent a kind of two-week holiday in its waters. All three of its towns – Portsmouth, Middletown and, most famously, Newport – have something to offer the visitor.

**Portsmouth,** originally Pocasset, was the second settlement founded in Rhode Island (1638). During the Battle of Rhode Island, *Butts Hill Fort* (Sprague Street) was occupied by American troops, many of whom were black – Rhode Island, unable to recruit its quota of freemen for the cause, offered slaves in the state their freedom if they fought. At the junction of Routes 114 and 24 there is a *Memorial to Negroes*, honouring their role in the First Rhode Island Regiment. Near here, off Route 114 on Cory's Lane are the *Green Animals Topiary Gardens,* today operated by the Preservation Society of Newport County (see Newport). Besides some eighty whimsically sculpted scrubs, Green Animals has flowerbeds, rose arbours, fruit trees, and the New Rhode Island Children's Toy Museum in the house of Mr Thomas Brayton, who developed the gardens (open May to September, and October weekends, 10am-5pm; admission).

**Middletown**, between Portsmouth and Newport, retains its agricultural livelihood to this day. One of its earliest residents was George Berkeley, then Dean of Derry and later Bishop of Cloyne, who came to Newport in 1728 en route for Bermuda where he intended to found a divinity school. He never made it, spending three years in Middletown (then part of Newport), waiting for money from England to proceed on his mission. Those three years were not wasted; Berkeley wrote *Alciphron* here, helped found the Newport Philosophical Club, preached in the church and discovered 'Tar Water' – a brew introduced to him by the Indians, believed to be a potent cure for a variety of ailments. Tar water became an obsession in Berkeley's life, which he brought back with him and popularized in England. Berkeley was a formulator of the Idealist philosophy, which states that what is perceived is not what exists – which may explain why one of the front double doors of his Middletown home, *Whitehall* (311 Berkeley Avenue), is false. The original fireplace and some 18th-century furnishings remain (open from July to Labor Day, 10am-5pm daily, and June and September 2pm-5pm, admission).

Just west of here are the *Hanging Rocks,* where a fifty-foot overhanging rock extends for a mile, very near another natural wonder, *Purgatory Chasm,* a giant cleft in the rock.

**Restaurants.** *In Warren:* Wharf Tavern***, Water Street; Fore 'n' Aft***. *In Pawtucket*: Donald Anthony's Hose Co. 6*, 636 Central Avenue. *In East Providence*: Arboretum***, 63 Warren Avenue. *In Bristol:* The Lobster Pot**, 119 Hope Street; Balzano's Café*, 189 Mount Hope Avenue. *In Tiverton:* Sunderland's**, 2753 Main Road. *In Little Compton:* Abraham Manchester Tavern**, Main Road. *In Portsmouth:* Pocasset Country Club**, Bristol Ferry Road.

## Newport

America's most aristocratic resort, **Newport** had a thriving summer colony even before the Revolution; Southern planters would bring their families here to escape the summer heat of the Carolinas and West Indies. The climate was excellent, and at that time Newport was a bustling seaport equal to New York or Boston, a cosmopolitan cultural centre attracting masterbuilders and craftsmen who built some of the finest colonial structures and furniture in the New World. But the colonial planters who vacationed in Newport came to do business as well – to buy slaves. Slaving, smuggling and privateering, and a monopoly in the manufacture of spermaceti candles made colonial Newport wealthy and rebellious, until the British sent 6,000 troops to occupy it from December 1776 to October 1779. Their presence struck a blow to Newport's trading activities from which it never recovered.

During the Civil War, when sentiments in Annapolis were decidedly Southern, the US Naval Academy was transferred to Newport for the duration. It brought a sparkle that was to continue after the war, when the nouveau riche rediscovered Newport and its refreshing summer climate. As fortunes in banking, railroads and commerce grew, so did the size of the 'summer cottages' south of town, which eventually matured into the most opulent palaces of the 19th century, inhabited only seven weeks of the year. Yachting, polo, tennis and golf became the rage of Society's Four Hundred; the women thought nothing of spending $100,000 for a party. The Gilded Age lasted from 1880 until the advent of World War I, when it and so many other American dreams became badly tarnished. Thanks to the Preservation Society of Newport, however, we can still marvel at the French châteaux and Italian palazzi that big money built for itself before strong unions, improved anti-trust and tax laws, child labour and minimum wage laws, and a loss of innocence put an end to such outrageous pretensions. The wealthy still come to Newport in the summer, but less obtrusively today.

Because Newport never developed much industry, and because the summer colony left the old town to rot while they built their cottages on the outskirts, colonial Newport with its colourful, tidy frame houses and narrow streets has remained intact and lived in all year round. Part of it, the waterfront area around Washington Street, was a merchants' and craftmen's quarter. During the Revolution, British bombardment from Goat Island caused heavy damage; today it is a lovely neighbourhood of restored homes, some brought here from other locations in Newport and New England. Near the Goat Island Bridge (take it to the island for the view of Newport), *Hunter House,* at 54 Washington Street, is the most elegant of the pre-Revolution mansions erected by Newport's colonial elite. A carved pineapple tops its doorway; the fruit has been the symbol of Newport hospitality ever since an impaled pineapple in front of the house meant that a ship from the South had come in and that refreshments were available inside. Hunter House contains furniture made by Newport's master craftsmen, Goddard and Townsend, and five of the rooms still have their original panelling (open April weekends and daily from 1 May to 1 November, 10am-5pm; admission; discount combination tickets for any two or more of the Preservation Society's seven mansions and the Green Animals Topiary Gardens are available here and at the Society's other properties).

At nearby 31 Walnut Street, Matthew Calbraithe Perry was born, the younger brother of Oliver Hazard. Matthew fought in the Battle of Lake Erie with his brother, then later, a naval commander in his own right, he was the first Westerner to sign a trade treaty with Japan (1854). At the end of Walnut Street, on Farewell Street, the *Common Burial Ground,* laid out in the 18th century, contains some excellent examples of colonial stone-carving. In the adjacent *Island Cemetery* stands a monument dedicated to the Perry brothers.

*Thames Street,* the main commercial thoroughfare of old Newport, begins at the Old Burial Ground. *The Brick Market* on Thames at *Washington Square,* the heart of colonial Newport, was built by Peter Harrison in 1760. Its Palladian windows and Ionic pilasters make it very much a temple of commerce, reflecting the prosperity of 18th-century Newport. Today a shop in the Market run by the Preservation Society sells Newport crafts. Facing the Market on Washington Square, the *Old Colony House* was built in 1739 in a more typically colonial mould by Richard Munday. It served as the seat of colonial and state government in alternate years until 1900, when Providence became the sole capital of Rhode Island. The British used it as a barracks and the French as a hospital; Washington met Rochambeau here. It is one of the few colonial brick structures in Newport – the bricks were imported from England.

There are numerous things to see in the Washington Square area, none more than a few blocks apart. Among them is the *Wanton-Lyman-Hazard House* at 17 Broadway, built in 1690, the oldest house in Newport. Remodelled in the 18th century and after, it gives visitors an interesting view of how tastes have changed during the last two hundred years. It has a colonial garden, and offers demonstrations of 18th-century cooking (open from June to Labor Day, Monday to Saturday 10.30am-5pm, admission). At 26 Marlborough Street, the *White Horse Tavern* claims to be the oldest tavern in America, in continuous operation from 1687 to the present (it is a restaurant today). The *Friends Meeting House* at Marlborough and Farewell Streets was built in 1699, but later enlargements have obscured much of the original structure. The wealthy Quakers who came to Newport contributed much to its economy and intellectual life; their meeting house here is the oldest in America (open from June to Labor Day, Monday to Saturday 10am-5pm).

*Touro Synagogue,* at 72 Touro Street, was the masterwork of Peter Harrison; built in 1759, it is the oldest surviving synagogue in the country. Named for Isaac de Touro, the spiritual leader of Newport's Jeshuat Israel congregation, the synagogue combines Georgian architecture with Sephardic ritualistic specifications; its diagonal position on the lot allows worshippers to face Jerusalem when praying at the Holy Ark. Although serenely simple on the outside, the synagogue is ornate and elegant inside, adorned with five brass candelabra and a Scroll of Laws from 1658. When Newport's Jewish population moved en masse to New York after the Revolution, Touro Synagogue was closed for many years, but kept alive by bequests of Isaac de Touro's sons. It reopened permanently for services in 1883 (open to visitors

10am-5pm Monday to Friday; 10am-6pm on Sunday; Saturdays only for services).

The *Newport Historical Society* at nearby 82 Touro Street (open Tuesday to Friday 9.30am-4.30pm, Saturday 9.30am-12 noon) contains a large collection of Newport memorabilia, furniture and a maritime collection; adjacent is the *Sabbatarian Meeting House,* the first Seventh-Day Adventist Church in the United States, built in Newport in 1729 (the congregation was founded in 1671) and recently moved to this site. It has an impressive pulpit.

Just south of Washington Square, at 23 Clarke Street is *Newport Artillery Company Armoury,* built in 1835. The Newport Artillery Company itself was founded in 1639 to protect the settlement from the Indians, making it the oldest military organization in America. Today its museum contains an unsurpassed collection of military items and uniforms from the seven wars that the company has served in (open May to September, Tuesday to Sunday 9.30am-4pm).

South of Clarke, on Spring and Church Streets rises the famous steeple of *Trinity Church,* a colonial gem built in 1724. Rhode Island's first Anglican parish was founded in 1698, when Puritan excesses brought many back to the fold. Trinity Church, designed by Richard Munday and inspired by Boston's Old North Church, is the best preserved wooden church of the early 18th century; its clock tower and steeple are original (unlike the tower of Old North Church) and topped with a bishop's mitre weathervane. The three-tiered wineglass pulpit inside is the only one in the country. Many have worshipped here, including Washington and Queen Elizabeth II; Dean Berkeley preached here often during his three-year stay in Newport. He sent the organ to the church from England (after Handel tested and approved it). The church is open daily in the summer, 10am-4pm. **St Mary's,** a few blocks south on Spring Street, is Rhode Island's oldest Catholic church. In September 1953 an American legend was created here when Senator John F. Kennedy married Jacqueline Bouvier.

Return south to Thames Street via Pelman to *Bowen's Wharf,* the restored cobblestone quay with several 18th- and 19th-century buildings. Among the pleasure craft docked here is the reconstructed *Frigate Rose,* the British vessel that attempted to stop Newport's smugglers by blockading the port from 1774 to 4 May 1776. As the *Rose* sailed away, Rhode Islanders declared their independence from the Crown.

Lavish *Bellevue Avenue,* Newport's most esteemed address from the Gilded Age to the present, begins at the eastern end of Touro

Street. At the corner here is the *Jewish Cemetery,* where headstones in Spanish and Portuguese recall the Sephardic ancestry of the first Jewish settlers. In *Touro Park,* just to the south of Bellevue, is an odd stone tower seemingly placed there for the sole purpose of mystification. Known as the *Old Stone Mill,* many believed it to have been built by the Vikings, although recent scholarship has proven its mortar to be identical to the mortar in Governor Benedict Arnold's house (Benedict Arnold the traitor's great-grandfather). The land itself originally belonged to Arnold, and the tower was a base for his mill.

Across Bellevue is the famous *Redwood Library*, built in 1748 and the oldest library still in use in the United States. Designed as a wooden Roman temple (painted to look like stone) with Palladian windows by Peter Harrison, the library was built by the Newport Philosophical Club, founded by Dean Berkeley, Abraham Rivera and Quaker Henry Collins. Inside there is an excellent collection of early American paintings by such masters as Gilbert Stuart and Rembrandt Peale (open Monday to Saturday 10am-6pm). Next to it, at 76 Bellevue, is the *Art Association of Newport,* in one of the earliest houses designed (in 1863) by Richard Morris Hunt, the favourite architect of the Gilded Age. It is interesting to compare this charming Victorian mansion with Hunt's later 'summer cottages' further south on Bellevue. Also his is the *Travers Block,* the medieval-style commercial building at Bellevue and Memorial Boulevard.

This corner, however, belongs to Stanford White's *Newport Casino,* now the *International Tennis Hall of Fame and Museum,* an outstanding example of the Shingle style (Tudor revival, half timbering, the use of different textures and materials in a building). The first national tennis championship was played at the Casino in 1881; in early June the Miller Hall of Fame Championships take place here. The Museum (open May to November 10am-5pm; November to May 11am-4pm, admission) contains the expected tennis memorabilia, the most fascinating concerning the legendary Pierre Etchbaster, world indoor court tennis champion from May 1928-54, when at the age of sixty he decided to retire. In the Casino's theatre there are performances by a local company; behind it, on Casino Terrace, the *Newport Automobile Museum* has a large collection of antique and classic cars (open daily 10am-7pm, winter 10am-5pm, admission). Across the street, the Bellevue Shopping Center stands on the site of Stone Villa, owned by *New York Herald* publisher James Gordon Bennett Jr, who financed Stanley's quest for Livingston and introduced the sport of polo to the United States.

Next to the shopping centre on Bellevue and Bowery is **Kingscote,** thought to be the first house in the country built exclusively for summer use – in 1839. Bulky, assymetrical and Victorian, it was designed by Richard Upjohn for George Noble Jones of Georgia and bought by William Henry King in 1864, from whence its name. The dark Gothic interior is lightened by Tiffany windows, Mr King's collection of chinoiserie, and the dining room, added in 1881, that Stanford White lined with cork – a 'first' (open April weekends and daily from 1 May to 1 November, 10am-5pm, admission).

Back on Bellevue, *The Elms* (same hours as Kingscote) was designed by Horace Trumbauer on the model of the Château d'Asnieres near Paris, which many say Trumbauer improved on. It was built in 1901 – one of the last of the 'cottages' – for Edward J. Berwind of Philadelphia, who made his money in coal. He did not, however, like the thought of coal wagons delivering fuel to his home across his lawn, so he had an elaborate underground railway built from beyond his property to his furnace! The Berwinds were great art collectors, as the furnishings attest; a number of paintings in the house are on loan from the Metropolitan Museum of New York. The formal gardens behind the house are the most beautiful in Newport.

Across Bellevue near Shepherd Street is the opulent Victorian *Château-sur-Mer* (same hours as Kingscote). This granite pile was built in 1852 by Seth Bradford, and enlarged in 1870 by Richard Morris Hunt for William S. Wetmore, who earned his wad in the China trade. Hunt's ballroom is thought to be the first in Newport; he also designed some of the furniture. Other features are an Eastlake oaken stair, stained glass by John La Farge, a Chinese Moongate and a Victorian toy collection. On nearby Shepherd Street the *Watts-Sherman House* is a beautiful example of the Shingle style, despite the additions built when it served as a school.

Shepherd Street leads to Ochre Point and the grandest of the grand, *The Breakers,* built for Cornelius Vanderbilt by Richard Morris Hunt in 1895 (open daily from April to 1 November; also Wednesdays and Sundays until 8pm; admission). The moment you walk through the seven-ton iron gates, you know you're in for some pretty fancy architectural cheesecake. Vanderbilt himself spent only a few months here before his death; the house was last owned by Countess Lazlo Szechenyi, who offered it as an air raid shelter during World War II (the mansion is fireproofed with iron plates, according to Vanderbilt's specifications). Spectacularly located beside the sea in park-like grounds designed by Olmsted and Vaux, suffice to say that this is the most grandiose and lavishly decorated tourist attraction in America. Outlying amenities include the *Children's Playhouse* (a small Victorian mansion); the *Breakers Stable* (Coggeshall Avenue: separate admission), containing the Vanderbilts' private battalion of coaches and carriages; and the famous *Cliff Walk*, at the end of Ruggles Avenue. For three miles, past numerous mansions, this path skirts the rocky and often precipitous Atlantic coast; it is beautiful, but don't send young children on it by themselves.

Back on Bellevue, at the corner of Marine Avenue is the terracotta *Rosecliff,* designed in 1902 by Stanford White for Mrs Hermann Oelrichs, a social leader of the day (open April to 1 November 10am-5pm, Monday until 8pm). This French château, styled after the Grand Trianon at Versailles, is subtle (at least after the Breakers) and gained much of its current fame when used as the setting for the 1974 film version of *The Great Gatsby,* where Robert Redford languishes amidst billowing white draperies. Stanford White designed Rosecliff's most famous feature, the heart-shaped stair, and Augustus Saint-Gaudens added the Court of Love, à la Marie Antoinette.

The last of the Preservation Society's estates on Bellevue is *Marble House* (open from April to 1 November, daily 10am-5pm, winter weekends 10am-4pm), built in 1892 by Richard Morris Hunt for the William K. Vanderbilts. As conspicuously lavish as the Breakers, it is somewhat smaller but no less monumental with its great Corinthian columned façade. The ballroom here is almost overwhelming; the Gothic Room and the dining room are impressive. In the grounds near the cliffs is a pagoda-shaped Chinese Tea House awaiting restoration funds.

Between Rosecliff and Marble House is *Beechwood,* built in 1856, formerly the home of Mr and Mrs William Blackhouse Astor. Today it is operated by the Beechwood Foundation, which attempts to give the visitor a 'feel' of the Gilded Age with costumed maids and butlers, and an audio-visual presentation on American Society with a capital S in the library (open all year round, 9.30am-7pm; cost $4.50, under 12's free). *Belcourt Castle* on the other side of Marble House is another work of Richard Morris Hunt, built in 1892 for Oliver H. P. Belmont (a descendant of Com. Matthew Perry) and his wife, the former Mrs W. K. Vanderbilt. Today it is owned by the Tinney family, who grace it with their fabulous collection of antiques from all over the world. The castle itself, one of Hunt's later works, was inspired by a Louis XIII hunting lodge, and is an example of medievalism run amuck; stained glass and carved wood fill every crack and crevice. The Royal Arts Foundation has a display here of French furniture and a Golden Coronation Coach (open from April to

November 10am-5pm; admission).

*Ocean Drive* begins at the southern end of Bellevue Avenue and follows the southern tip of Aquidneck Island, offering marvellous scenery along the way; at *Price's Neck* you can pull off the road and have a picnic. If you come during the America's Cup race, this is the best vantage point to view the yachts. On Harrison Avenue, a branch of Ocean Drive, is *Hammersmith Farm,* the last working farm in Newport. Built in 1887, the Shingle-style house has been in the Auchincloss family ever since, and it hosted the wedding reception for John Kennedy and his bride, the daughter of Mrs Hugh Auchincloss; the Kennedys often returned here in the summer. The gardens are the work of Frederick Law Olmsted (open from April to October and weekends in March and November 10am-5pm; from Memorial Day to Labor Day, hours are 10am-8pm; admission). Adjacent to Hammersmith Farm is *Fort Adams State Park.* The granite fort, one of the largest in America, was begun after the departure of the British and dedicated on 4 July 1799. Named for President John Adams, its purpose was to defend Narragansett Bay. The government continued work on the fort until 1857, although during the Civil War it was already obsolete. Never attacked, it served as a coastal command post through World War II.

**Restaurants in Newport.** Whitehorse Tavern***, Marlborough and Farewell; The Pier***, W. Howard Street; Christie's***, Christie's Landing; Salas**, 343 Thames Street; Clare Cokke House**, Bowen's Wharf.

## Conanicut Island and Block Island

In 1969 a bridge was built from Newport to **Conanicut Island,** named for Narragansett Indian Sachem Canonicus. **Jamestown**, the only town on the island, was founded in 1656; its most famous landmark is the *Old Watermill* on North Road, built in 1787 and recently restored to operating condition. Near here, the *Sydney L. Wright Museum* features Indian and colonial artifacts from the area (in the Jamestown Philomenian Library; open Monday/Wednesday/Friday 10am-5pm and 7pm-9pm; Tuesday/Thursday 7pm-9pm). *Fort Wetherall State Park* faces Fort Adams in Newport and affords fine views over the cliffs. At the southernmost end of Conanicut Island the *Beavertail Lighthouse* dates from 1856 and has lovely sea views.

There are several pleasant ferries that go to **Block Island,** nine miles south of western Rhode Island. The only year-round service is from Galilee (tel: 783-4613); other summer ferries depart from India Pier in Providence (via Newport) and from New London, Connecticut (tel: (203) 442-7891). If you want to take a car (really not necessary) you have to make reservations in advance. There are also cruises to and from Montauk on Long Island.

Named after the Dutch explorer Adrian Block who passed here in 1614, the first white settlers came in 1662, and for many years their descendants eked out a rugged living by fishing the rich coastal waters. In the 19th century a breakwater was constructed at the Old Harbor, allowing large ships to dock here; the holidaymakers began arriving shortly thereafter, and by the late 19th century Block Island was a fashionable resort, with its lovely Victorian cottages, hotels and beaches.

After a long lapse Block Island is becoming popular again for its beaches (the public beach is at *Block Island State Beach*), fishing (tuna, marlin, swordfish) and 19th-century ambience. Add some spectacular scenery, particularly the *Mohegan Bluffs,* where clay cliffs rise 200 feet straight out of the sea, some in the form of rugged Indian profiles (easily seen by rented bicycle from the Old Harbor). The lighthouse here and the northernmost one at *Sandy Point* are crucial; some thousand ships have been wrecked off the coast of Block Island, which is often shrouded with fog. The most famous wreck took place off *Dickens Point* in the south-east, inspiring Whittier to write 'The Palatine Light'. You can still see the Palatine Graves and *Settler's Rock,* where the first settlers on the island landed. At Town Road and Ocean Avenue the *Block Island Historical Society* has a number of exhibits on Island history (open 11am-4pm weekdays, 17 June to 30 September; admission).

**Restaurants on Block Island.** Ballard's Inn***, Old Harbor; 1661 Inn***, Spring Street; Narragansett Inn***, New Harbor; Dead Eye Dick's**, New Harbor; Baroni's**.

## Western Rhode Island

In the northeast corner of the state, **Diamond Hill State Park** derived its name from a great vein of shining quartz in the rock. During the winter the park is one of the state's main ski areas. The northwestern corner of Rhode Island is rural farmlands, lakes and forests, with many woodland trails and recreational facilities centred in **Pulaski State Park** near the Connecticut border. One of the main towns in the area, **Chepachet**, on the Chepachet River, is famous in Rhode Island history as the headquarters of lawyer Thomas Wilson Dorr, instigator of

Dorr's Rebellion, which called for universal white male suffrage in 1842 (until then Rhode Island had been operating under its Colonial Charter of 1663, which made property a qualification for voting). Dorr was elected People's Governor by his supporters, and so for a time Rhode Island had two governors. After a brief military confrontation, Dorr surrendered; however, the Rhode Island legislature had written a new constitution including his reforms by the end of 1842. Today Chepachet is a charming village with many of its original houses, churches and buildings intact, including the *Stagecoach Tavern* (Route 44), built in 1800 and military headquarters of the Dorrites in 1842, and a restaurant today. To the south lies **Scituate,** beside the Scituate Reservoir, in the centre of one of the most scenic regions of the state.

**Warwick**, south of Providence, one of Rhode Island's four original towns included in the 1643 charter, was founded in 1641 by Samuel Gorton. Banned not only from Boston but from Providence by Roger Williams after he instigated a street riot, Gorton was one of America's first anarchists, disputing both religious and civil authority. However, when his own claim in Warwick was disputed by Massachusetts Bay Colony, Gorton bustled off to England and had the Earl of Warwick help him secure a title to the land, hence the settlement's name. In the 19th and 20th centuries, Warwick grew to become Rhode Island's second largest city with its industry and commercial activity, although it was only incorporated in 1931. At *Gaspee Point* (Warwick Avenue) the British schooner *Gaspee* ran aground while patrolling Narragansett Bay for illegal shipping. When news of the *Gaspee's* troubles reached John Brown in Providence, he organized the party that captured the British crew and burned the vessel on 9 June 1772. Despite a large reward offered by the king and an inquiry in Newport, the conspirators were never named or caught. The event, one of most important preceding Lexington and Concord, is celebrated in Warwick with an annual festival and clambake. The *Warwick Museum* at 334 Knight Street contains displays relating to Warwick's long history (open Tuesday to Saturday 11am-4pm, Sunday 1pm-5pm; admission).

In nearby **Coventry,** at 50 Taft Street, the *General Nathaniel Greene Homestead* was built by Greene for his new wife in 1774, although lived in only until the Revolution. In the war Greene, originally a Quaker, was second in rank to George Washington; after the war he and his wife moved to a Georgia plantation. His simple fourteen-room farmhouse is partly restored (open March to November, Wednesday/Saturday/Sunday 2pm-5pm; admission).

South on the bay is **East Greenwich,** a centre of Rhode Island's effort in the Revolutionary war; the Kentish Guards Militia was founded here in 1774, giving the American cause two brigadier generals, Nathaniel Greene and James Mitchell Varnum. Still standing are the Greek Revival *Armoury of the Kentish Guards*, 90 Pierce Street, and the *General James M. Varnum House,* an elegant hilltop mansion at 57 Pierce Street, built by Varnum in 1773. It survives almost unchanged and contains 18th-century furniture, marine displays and a colonial garden (open June to September, closed Monday and Thursday 1pm-4pm; admission).

South towards Wickford is **Quonset Point,** where the former Naval Air Station gave birth to the 'Seabees' and the Quonset Hut. **Smith Castle** (1677), near Cocumscussoc Park just north of Wickford, is considered to be the only building left in Rhode Island where Roger Williams visited, to preach to the Indians. The original house, built in 1640, was burned by the Indians in King Philip's War; in the grounds is a cemetery of settlers killed in the action. The house tour includes a fine 18th-century garden (open Monday to Saturday 10am-5pm, Sunday 2pm-5pm, closed Thursdays and 15 December to 15 March; admission).

The village of **Wickford**, part of North Kingstown, is a jewel of a place, set on a pretty harbour whence the crops of Rhode Island's southern plantations were shipped to Providence and Newport. The most important structure in Wickford, the *Old Narragansett Church* on Main Street, was built in 1707, one of Rhode Island's original four colonial parishes and one of America's oldest Episcopalian churches. The church, a simple white-frame building styled after New England meeting houses, contains old box pews and a wine-glass pulpit. In **Exeter**, just to the west, the *Tomaquag Indian Memorial Museum* features not only artifacts but also an Indian restaurant and trading post and cultural centre (open April to November 11am-5pm).

To the south on Gilbert Stuart Road is the *Gilbert Stuart Birthplace and Snuff Mill,* where America's most famous portraitist of the 18th century was born in 1755. His father, a Scottish immigrant, began the first snuff mill in the country – a replica of the mill runs by water power on the first floor. The house itself is simple but beautifully situated (open daily except Fridays 11am-5pm, winter 11am-3pm, admission).

To the south, **Narragansett** was once a resort to rival Newport, until the great fire of 1900 destroyed the Casino and great Victorian hotels. All that remains are the *Towers* of the Casino over Route 1A in the middle of *Narragansett Pier;* the original Casino, like the one in Newport, was designed by McKim, Mead and White. Today thousands of people still come to Narragansett for its glorious beaches, including *Scarborough State Beach* on the east side of the peninsula, and *Sand Hill Cove* and *East Matunck State Beach* to the west, the latter two near the villages of Galilee and Jersalem (Galilee is a year-round terminus for Block Island).

The village of **Kingston** just to the north is a pretty 18th-century settlement. Among the many old houses in Kingston is the simple *George Fayerweather House,* built in 1830 by a blacksmith whose father had been a slave in the area. It is now the headquarters of the Fayerweather Craft Guild, which demonstrates and sells its work from May to December, Thursday to Sunday, 11am-4pm.

From Route 2 in West Kingston a path leads to an obelisk marking the *Great Swamp Fight* on 19 December 1675, where the Massachusetts and Connecticut militia decimated the Narragansett warriors during King Philip's War. In retaliation the Indians destroyed many of the towns in Rhode Island, particularly in the west. The swamp itself, some 2,600 acres in size, was formed by a glacier thousands of years ago, and is home to a number of unusual creatures.

Along the south coast of the state are more beaches, most famously *Moonstone Beach* with its moonlike rocks. **Charlestown,** named after Charles II, was the site of the Narragansett Indian reservation from 1709-1880, now the *Historic Village of the Narragansett Indians.* Here you can see the Protestant church that the converted members of the tribe built in 1859 on Narrow Lane, still used by the Narragansetts on Sundays and during their festival in August.

The beaches continue west along the coast: *Charleston Beach, Quonochontaug* and *Misquamicut State Beach*, south of Westerly. **Westerly** itself, subject to a border dispute with Connecticut until the mid 18th century, is a pretty town surrounding one of the loveliest small urban parks in America, *Wilcox Park,* designed by Olmsted and Vaux in 1898.

**Watch Hill** to the south is a beautiful old resort town overlooking the sea. A *statue of Ninigret,* chief of the Niantic tribe, and the *Flying Horse Carousel* on Bay Street, one of the oldest in America and still operating, delight visiting children.

**Restaurants.** *In Woonsocket:* El Dorado**, 401 Clinton. *In North Providence:* Jimmy Burchfield's Classic Restaurant***, 1058 Charles Street. *In Cranston:* Twin Oaks***, 100 Sabra Street. *In West Warwick:* West Valley Inn**, 4 Blossom Street. *In Warwick:* Bank Café***, 40 Post Road; Rocky Point Park*, Rocky Point. *In North Kingstown:* Custy's***, 7759 Post Road. *In Charlestown:* Old Wilcox Tavern***, US-1; Windswept Farm**, US-1. *In*

*Wakefield:* Larchwood Inn***, 176 Main Street. *In Westerly:* Swiss Chalet***, Post Road; Shelter Harbor Inn**, Post Road.

## Annual Events in Rhode Island

**May Day Breakfasts:** All over the state Rhode Islanders get up early to celebrate 1 May with a special breakfast of Johnnycakes, sausages, baked beans and pie; the oldest annual breakfast is at the Oaklawn Community Baptist Church. It is the official opening of *Rhode Island Heritage Month,* celebrating the state's declaration of independence in May 1776. The third Sunday in May is Forefather's Sunday, celebrated at the First Baptist Church in *Providence;* house tours take place on College Hill, *Providence* (1-2 May), *Wickford* and *North Kingston,* which also hosts a Johnnycake festival and village festival; in *Cranston* there is an Azalea and Rhododendon Show at 44 Marden Street.
**Last weekend in May/first weekend in June:** Gaspee Day, *Warwick.*
**Mid June:** La Fete Saint-Jean-Baptiste, *Warwick;* also Strawberry Festival in Dovecrest Indian cultural centre, *Exeter.*
**4 July:** Ancient and Horribles Parade, *Chepachet;* cannon salute at noon in *Newport;* festivities in Roger Williams Park, *Providence.*
**Mid July:** Blessing of the Fleet Festival in *Galilee;* Green Bean Thanksgiving and Clam Bake, at Dovecrest in *Exeter.*
**End of July:** Newport Outdoor Art Festival, *Touro Park.*
**July/August:** Newport Jazz Festival, for two days – then it moves to New York City.
**Beginning of August:** American Indian Federation Pow-Wow, at Indian Hall, *North Kingstown* (Lafayette); second week the Narragansett Tribe August Meeting in *Charlestown* with Pow-wow and festivities. Also: Fair at the Elms in *Newport,* and Old Stone Church Clambake in *Adamsville.*
**Mid August:** Warwick Rotary International Air Fair, at Quonset State Airport, *North Kingstown;* Yachting Race Week in *Newport* (yachting activities throughout July and August); Glocester Heritage Days, *Chepachet;* Reenactment of the 1778 Siege of *Middletown;* Sandcastle-building contest at town beach, *Narragansett.*
**Early September:** Annual Moosup Valley Grange Clambake, *Foster;* Florentine Faire, Renaissance-style festival at Roger Williams Park, *Providence.*
**Labor Day weekend:** Rhode Island Tuna Tournament, *Galilee.*
**Mid September:** Polish Picnic, St Joseph's Church, *Central Falls;* Apple Festival, at Smith-Appleby House, *Smithfield;* Our Lady of the Rosary and Santo Cristo Festival, *Providence;* Harvest Fair, at Coggeshall Farm, *Bristol;* America's Cup, every three years,

*Newport.*
**1-4 October:** International Jumping Derby, Grand Prix horse event, *Portsmouth;* also, Cranberry Festival and Indian Summer Ceremony at Dovecrest, *Exeter;* Narragansett Indian Fall Festival, *Charlestown;* Aquidneck Island Harvest Festival, *Middletown.*
**Last weekend in October:** Usquepaug Johnnycake Festival, *Richmond* (South Kingstown).
**Thanksgiving:** Harvest Thanksgiving Dinner, at Dovecrest in *Exeter;* Thanksgiving Procession and Pilgrim Service in *Peace Dale* and *Pawtucket.*
**Christmas season:** Christmas in *Newport,* Christmas on a Plantation in Yankeeland, at Smith's Castle, *North Kingstown;* Luminaria, tours of historic homes in *East Greenwich;* the Hanging of the Greens, First Baptist Church, *Providence.*

## **Accommodation in Rhode Island** (area code: 401)

**Providence**
Biltmore Plaza, Kennedy Plaza, tel: 421-0700. Deluxe centrally located hotel.
Wayland Manor, 500 Angell St, tel: 751-7700. Moderately priced, with dining room.
Providence Mariott, Charles & Orms St, tel: 272-2400. Expensive, in town resort style hotel.
YMCA, 160 Broad St, tel: 456-0100. Men only, cheap.

**Pawtucket to Newport**
Howard Johnson's, 2 George St, tel: 723-6700, *Pawtucket.* Moderately priced, indoor pool.
New Yorker Motor Lodge, 400 Newport Ave, *East Providence,* tel: 434-8000. Moderate.
Almeida Court, Bay View Ave and Bristol Motor Lodge, 400 Metacom Ave in *Bristol,* connected to Roger Williams College (tel: 255-1000). Open 8 June to 16 August.
Harriet Bradford Inn, 423 Hope St, tel: 253-6400, *Bristol.* Moderate.
Founders Brook Motel, 310 Boyds Land, tel: 683-1244, *Portsmouth.* Moderate.
Twin Spruce Tourist, 515 Turpike Ave, tel: 683-0673, *Portsmouth.* Inexpensive.
Prudence Island Inn, Sandy Point Landing, *Prudence Island,* tel: 683-4142. Moderate.
Gateway Motel, West Main Road, tel: 847-2735, *Middletown.* Inexpensive.
Paradise Motel, Aquidneck Ave, tel; 847-1500, *Middletown.*

Inexpensive.
Floradale Motor Court, 985 East Main Road, tel: 847-9726, *Middletown.* Inexpensive cabins.
Easton's Inn on the Beach, 30 Wave Ave, tel: 846-0310, *Middletown.* Moderately expensive, dining room.
Stone Bridge Inn, 1 Lawton Ave, tel: 624-6601, *Tiverton.* Small, moderate, with restaurant.

**Newport**
The Inn at Castle Hill, Ocean Drive, tel: 849-3800. Deluxe, tennis, restaurant, entertainment, beach cottages available.
Shamrock Cliff, Ocean Drive, tel: 847-7777. In mansion built like Irish castle, deluxe.
Sheraton Islander Inn, Goat Island, tel: 849-2600. Resort style hotel, deluxe.
Hotel Viking, 1 Bellevue Ave, tel: 847-3300. Expensive, near mansions.
Harbor Base Motel, Coddington Hway, tel: 847-2600. Moderate, view of harbour.
Bella Vista Guest Manor, 1 Seaview Ave, tel: 846-4262. Moderate.
Yankee Peddler Inn, 113 Touro St, tel: 846-1323. Moderately expensive.
Armed Services YMCA Multi-Center, 50 Washington Sq, tel: 849-7746. Youth hostel card required, very inexpensive.

**Conanicut and Block Islands**
Bay Voyage Inn, Conanicus Ave, tel: 423-0540, *Jamestown.* Expensive, beach, entertainment.
Ferry Boat, Ferry Wharf, tel: 423-0101, *Jamestown.* Moderate-priced rooms on old New York ferry boat, with restaurant.
Jamestown Shores Motel, Eldred Ave, tel: 423-0023, *Jamestown.* Moderate, summer only.
There are many hotels and inns on **Block Island,** most open only June-September. Among them:
Narragansett Inn, Ocean Ave, tel: 466-2626. Expensive, restaurant, entertainment.
1661 House, Old Harbor, tel: 466-2421. Expensive, good restaurant, year-round.
Neptune House, Connecticut Ave, tel: 466-2100. Expensive, tennis, year-round.
Surf Hotel, Dodge St, tel: 466-2241. Moderate, family hotel.
Blue Dory Inn, Dodge St, tel: 466-2254. Moderate.
Holiday Haven Guest House, Center Rd, tel: 466-2676. Moderate.

**Western Rhode Island**

Woonsocket Motor Inn, 333 Clinton St, tel: 762-1224, *Woonsocket.* Moderate, with water beds.

YMCA, 43 Federal St, tel: 769-0791, *Woonsocket.* Men only, inexpensive.

Lakeside Motel, US 55, tel: 949-0371, *Chepachet.* Moderate.

White Rock Motel, US 44, tel: 568-4219, *Chepachet.* Moderate.

Stone House Motel, US 6, tel: 647-5850, *Foster.* Inexpensive.

Hillside Motor Lodge, 101 New London Ave, *Cranston.* Inexpensive.

Rhode Island Inn, 2081 Post Rd, tel: 739-0600, *Warwick.* Fairly expensive, owned by Johnson & Wales College and features school's continental cuisine.

Open Gate Motel, 840 Quaker Lane, tel: 884-4490, *Warwick.* Inexpensive.

Leprechaun Motel, 325 Quaker Lane, tel: 828-1509, *West Warwick.* Inexpensive.

Greenwich Hotel, 162 Main St, tel: 884-4200, *E. Greenwich.* Moderate.

Dutch Inn by the Sea, Great Island Rd, tel: 789-9341, *Narragansett.* Expensive, tennis, pool beach, entertainment.

Sweet Meadows Inn, Point Judith Rd, tel: 783-7315, *Narragansett.* Expensive.

Neptune Inn Motel, 113 Ocean Rd, tel: 783-4704, *Narragansett.* Moderately expensive, on the sea.

Driftwood Motel, 1084 Boston Neck Rd, tel: 783-2847, *Narragansett.* Moderate.

Gray's Motel, 7835 Post Rd, tel: 294-9551, *N. Kingstown.* Expensive, small resort type motel.

Bob Bean Motel, 600 Boston Neck Rd, tel: 294-2411, *N. Kingstown.* Inexpensive, near beaches.

Kingstown Motel, 6530 Post Rd, tel: 884-1160, *N. Kingstown.* Moderate, near Wickford.

Larchwood Inn, 176 Maine St, tel: 783-5454, *Wakefield.* Expensive; old country mansion with restaurant and entertainment.

Tower House Motor Inn, US 1 and Rt 138W, tel: 783-2516, *South Kingstown.* Expensive, near University.

Wonder View Tourist Home, 38 Seaview Ave, tel: 789-8147, *Wakefield.* Moderate.

University of Rhode Island Youth Hostel, Memorial Union, Rt 138, tel: 789-3929, *Kingstown.* In old farmhouse, one mile from URI. Very inexpensive.

Charlestown Willows, US 1, tel: 364-7727, *Charlestown.* Resort motel, but not very expensive, open April to November.

Sea View Motor Court, Post Rd, tel: 364-7727, *Charlestown.* Moderate, family motel.

The Summer House, Schoolhouse and Charlestown Beach Rds, tel: 364-6926, *Charlestown.* Moderate-priced rooms and efficiencies.

Breezeway Motel, Winnapaug Rd, tel: 348-8953, *Misquamicut.* Moderately expensive, beach privileges, pool.

Pleasant View House Motor Inn, 65 Atlantic Ave, tel: 348-8200, *Misquamicut.* Expensive, private beach, pool, restaurant.

Ocean House, Bluff Ave, tel: 348-8161, *Watch Hill.* Deluxe, private beach, good restaurant, lovely views.

Weekapaug Inn, Weekapaug Rd, tel: 322-0301, *Westerly.* Expensive resort, private beach.

Narragansett Inn, Bay St, tel: 348-8912, *Watch Hill.* Moderately expensive, views of Watch Hill Harbor.

S & S Motor Lodge, 171 Post Rd, tel: 322-0304, *Westerly.* Moderate, conveniently located.

Pony Barn Motel, Shore Rd, tel: 348-8216, *Westerly.* Moderate family motel.

Traveltel Motel, Post Rd, tel: 596-7475, *Westerly.* Inexpensive budget motel.

# Massachusetts

Feisty little Massachusetts has long been America's most fertile breeding ground for new ideas, the seeds planted by its Puritan founders. We may rightfully think today that the Puritans were stiff-necked prudes who hated nothing as much as the idea that somewhere someone was having fun, who at their most extreme executed dissenters from their self-righteous philosophy; but they were also literate, argumentative, and in general more interested in the word than in the deed. From the blood-curdling sermons of Jonathan Edwards, the enthusiastic Revolutionary propaganda of Samuel Adams, the Abolitionist rallies of Wendell Phillips and the campaign for women's suffrage of Susan B. Anthony to the philosophies of Ralph Waldo Emerson, Henry David Thoreau, Henry James and George Santayana, to the 1972 election when it was the only state to choose McGovern over Nixon, Massachusetts has been in the vanguard of American public opinion and thought, embracing causes long before they are popular anywhere else.

When you look at a map of Massachusetts you see a trapezoid that blossoms out towards the Atlantic, the long finger of Cape Cod beckoning the east. From its earliest days the 'Bay State' has derived its livelihood from the sea, from trade with the West Indies and later with China, from the great whaling fleets of Nantucket and New Bedford, from the fish and lobster caught by the intrepid fishermen of Gloucester and New Bedford.

In the 19th century, Massachusetts, like the rest of New England, turned to manufacturing. The textile mills at Lowell became the model for benevolent paternalism; the nearby mills at Lawrence became, in the famous 1912 strike, notorious for their working conditions. Lynn was synonymous with shoes, Springfield with rifles, Northbridge with machines. Today the state has cleverly attracted a large number of electronics firms, due to its pool of skilled workers.

Massachusetts has three well defined and popular tourist destinations: Boston and its numerous historic and cultural attractions, the preppy-trendy capital of America; Cape Cod and the islands, with sandy shores, quaint villages, cranberry bogs and an atmosphere as thick as clam chowder; and the Berkshire Hills, ski land in the winter and resort land in the summer, home of the famed Tanglewood concerts. In between there are enough things to see to take up your whole holiday, so beware. Massachusetts may be small (45th in the Union) but it spreads a rich feast.

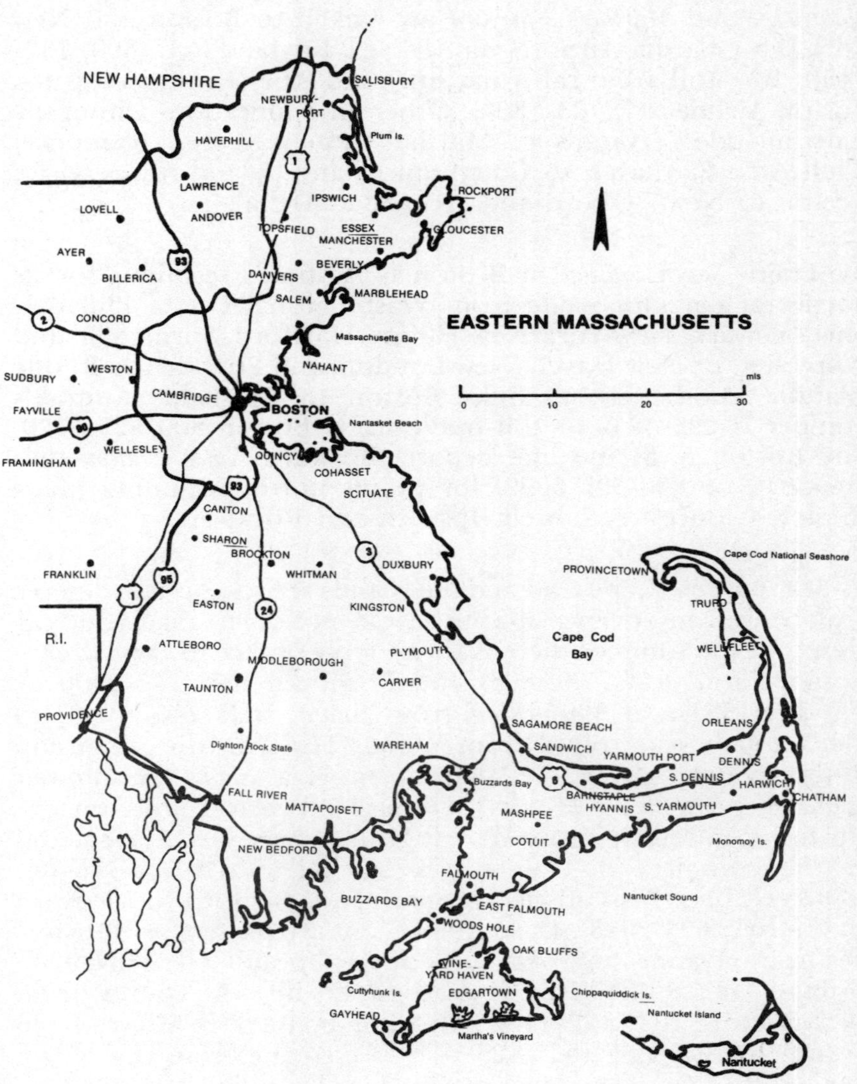
EASTERN MASSACHUSETTS
NEW HAMPSHIRE
SALISBURY
NEWBURY-PORT
Plum Is.
HAVERHILL
LAWRENCE
ANDOVER
LOVELL
IPSWICH
ROCKPORT
GLOUCESTER
TOPSFIELD
ESSEX
MANCHESTER
AYER
BILLERICA
BEVERLY
DANVERS
SALEM
MARBLEHEAD
CONCORD
Massachusetts Bay
NAHANT
SUDBURY
WESTON
CAMBRIDGE
BOSTON
FAYVILLE
Nantasket Beach
WELLESLEY
FRAMINGHAM
QUINCY
COHASSET
SCITUATE
CANTON
SHARON
BROCKTON
WHITMAN
DUXBURY
FRANKLIN
EASTON
KINGSTON
R.I.
ATTLEBORO
MIDDLEBOROUGH
PLYMOUTH
CARVER
TAUNTON
PROVIDENCE
Dighton Rock State
WAREHAM
FALL RIVER
MATTAPOISETT
NEW BEDFORD
BUZZARDS BAY
Buzzards Bay
MASHPEE
COTUIT
FALMOUTH
EAST FALMOUTH
WOODS HOLE
OAK BLUFFS
VINE-YARD HAVEN
EDGARTOWN
Cuttyhunk Is.
GAYHEAD
Martha's Vineyard
Chippaquiddick Is.
Nantucket Island
Nantucket
Nantucket Sound
Monomoy Is.
CHATHAM
HARWICH
DENNIS
S. DENNIS
S. YARMOUTH
HYANNIS
BARNSTAPLE
YARMOUTH PORT
SANDWICH
SAGAMORE BEACH
ORLEANS
WELLFLEET
TRURO
PROVINCETOWN
Cape Cod National Seashore
Cape Cod Bay
mls
0
10
20
30

## Getting Around Massachusetts

**By Air.** *Logan International Airport* in Boston Harbor is the major airport in the state and northern New England; western Massachusetts is also served by *Bradley International Airport* in Windsor Locks, Connecticut. Small airports in *Provincetown, Hyannis, Nantucket* and *Martha's Vineyard* are linked to Boston and New York (La Guardia Airport) via Air New England (tel: (800) 732-3450 for toll-free information) and the Provincetown—Boston Airline (tel: 723-7800). Other air connections within the state include: Hyannis to Martha's Vineyard and Nantucket (Gull Air); Fairhaven to Cuttyhunk Island (Island Air Service); Boston to New Bedford and Worcester (Delta).

**By Train.** *South Station* in Boston is Amtrak's terminus for its northwest corridor route from Washington DC (via Philadelphia, Newark, New York/New Haven, Hartford, Springfield and Worcester, or New Haven, New London, and Providence, Rhode Island). Another route links Boston to Pittsfield. Amtrak's number is 292-5252 or toll-free outside Boston 800-523-5720. The Boston & Maine line departs Boston's *North Station* (tel: 227-5070 or 800-392-6099) for points north, including Manchester, Gloucester, Lowell, Ipswich and Rockport.

**By Sea.** Because Cape Cod and the islands are so popular, reserve a place well in advance if you have a notion to take your car along. In the summer there is direct ferry service to *Provincetown* from Boston (tel: 723-7800) and Plymouth (tel: 747-2400 or 800-242-1304); to *Marblehead* from Salem (tel: 745-6070); to *Nantucket* all year round from Woods Hole on the Steamship Authority (tel: 800-352-7104) and from Hyannis in the summer (will take cars). To *Martha's Vineyard* all year round on the Steamship Authority from Woods Hole to Vineyard Haven, and in the summer to Oak Bluffs as well (carries cars; tel: 800-352-7104). Also all year around, New Bedford to Vineyard Haven (tel: 693-2088). In summer there are passenger-only ferries from Hyannis (tel: 693-1555) and Falmouth (tel: 548-8000), both to Oak Bluffs. To *Cuttyhunk Island,* all year round, from New Bedford (tel: 992-1432). In summer there is a ferry from Boston to *Gloucester* (tel: 426-8419) departing from the North Avenue Bridge.

**By Bus.** Main hubs are Boston, Worcester, Hyannis and Pittsfield. *Greyhound* with its own terminal in Boston (tel:

423-5810) and *Trailways* at South Station (tel: 482-6620) are the main intrastate bus lines. Cape Cod is served by *Plymouth & Brockton St. Railway Co.* buses from the Greyhound Terminal in Boston (tel: 423-5810) as well as by *Bonanza Buses* (Greyhound Station, Boston, tel: 548-7588; and New York City (tel: (212) 564-8484) from the Port Authority Terminal. *Peter Pan Buses* from Springfield to Cape Cod, Boston and New York City. Peter Pan, Greyhound and Bonanza pretty much cover the other routes in the state, and there are several services (the *Cape Ann RTA,* the *Berkshire RTA, Southeastern RTA* and *Worcester Bus Co.* and *Cape Cod Bus Lines*) that cover limited areas. The Boston Metropolitan Area is served by the 'T', the light rail and buses of the efficient if often penniless *MBTA* which has a line direct to Logan Airport.

## History

The principal Indian tribes of Massachusetts were the Mohegan, Poktumtuk, Wampanoag and Massachuset, all of the Algonkin family; the latter gave their name to the Bay, the Colony and the Commonwealth (like Pennsylvania, Massachusetts is not a state but a Commonwealth). Indian assistance was invaluable to the first colonists, especially the Pilgrims. Massasoit, sachem of the Wampanoags, signed a friendly peace treaty with them, and the famous Squanto, orphan of the disease-decimated Patuxet tribe, taught them how to grow and fertilize hardy Indian vegetables like squash and corn when the seeds brought from England failed to sprout.

The 128 Pilgrims who founded Plymouth in 1620 are America's sentimental favourite first settlers. Neither the first Spanish (St Augustine, Florida, was the first on American soil) nor the first English settlement (Jamestown, Virginia, has that honour), Plymouth nevertheless set the tone of subsequent colonizations; the Pilgrims were representatives of Europe's new middle class, seeking the religious and political representation they lacked in the Old World. On board the puny ship *Mayflower* they crossed the Atlantic, anchored in Plymouth Bay, and drafted the 'Mayflower Compact' giving the majority 'the Civil Body Politick', the right to make laws.

Half the Pilgrims died during the first winter. The survivors built a small hamlet and invited Massasoit and his tribe to a Thanksgiving feast when the first crops were harvested in the autumn. This, a sort of American Passover feast, re-enacted every November throughout the country (in between televised football games), was the high point in Indian—white relations in Massachusetts. After this, the English stole the Indians' land and treated them with such abuse that Massasoit's own son and successor Metacom, or Philip, led a violent multi-tribal war against the whites to force them back to Europe – and almost won (see 'Rhode Island').

Eight years after the founding of Plymouth Colony, Massachusetts Bay Colony was founded. Far more organized and populous than the Mayflower expedition, more commercially oriented and more determined to create a religiously homogenous society, Massachusetts Bay immediately surpassed Plymouth in size and influence. Very rapidly the colony dispersed, some members seeking better farmlands, others dissenting with the harsh Puritan codes of John Winthrop, governor of the colony from 1627. When Salem minister Roger Williams in 1635, and Anne Hutchinson and John Wheelwright the following year, dared to question his ideals, Winthrop's General Court banished them. Roger Williams left to found Rhode Island, Wheelwright founded New Hampshire, and Thomas Hooker, a decent Puritan minister who disagreed with Winthrop's harsh methods, founded Connecticut. Less fortunate were Quaker Mary Dyer, hanged in 1660 after returning from her banishment, and the twenty Salem 'witches' executed by Governor Phips's court in 1692 – all of the victims, not accidentally, considered enemies by Reverend Samuel Parris of the Salem parish.

Governor Phips, by the way, was the first Royal Governor of Massachusetts under a new charter that united Plymouth and Massachusetts Bay in 1691. The original charter, revoked in 1682, had been replaced by the Dominion of New England under Sir Edmund Andros in 1686. It lasted as long as King James II; in 1689, the good people of Boston tossed Andros and his cronies into the calaboose as soon as news of the 'Glorious Revolution' reached the Colony.

By 1700 Massachusetts counted 80,000 inhabitants. Shipbuilding and the 'triangle trade' of African slaves and West Indies molasses, and later smuggling, when the Acts of Trade and Navigation were passed by Parliament, permitting the colonies to trade only with England, were the basis of many a Brahmin fortune. After several events in Boston – the Boston Massacre, the Tea Party and the Blockade of Boston Harbour – revolution was inevitable. The 'shot heard around the world' was fired on 19 April 1775 in Concord, Massachusetts, beginning the American Revolution.

After the war Massachusetts became a bulwark of Federalism and elected one of its own, John Adams, to the presidency in 1800. It was an era of great commercial ventures, not only for

Boston but for Salem, New Bedford, and the other ports, most profitably in the China trade and trade with Britain, now in the throes of the Industrial Revolution. As in Connecticut and Rhode Island, James Madison's War of 1812 put an abrupt halt to international trade, encouraging merchants to invest their money in new American industries, and to manufacture goods formerly purchased from Britain. Textile mills and machine works sprouted up along the major rivers of the three states. Massachusetts became the largest textile state in the Union for almost one hundred years, until the companies headed South for the cheaper, non-unionized labour.

After the Civil War, Massachusetts confronted a new problem in the massive influx of immigrants, mainly Irish, into the state. When foreign workers took over the factory jobs for lower wages than the Yankees were willing to accept, industrialists were quick to take advantage of them, until conditions were so bad that the workers went on strike: the Lynn shoemakers in 1860 (the largest strike in American history up to that time) and the Lawrence Mill Workers in 1912. The radical International Workers of the World rallied around the latter cause, only to be defeated when the mills were closed down for good in retaliation. The Irish in Boston, mostly poor victims of the potato famine, were treated like second- or even third-class citizens until by their sheer numbers they gained political and economic status. After the Irish broke the Yankee stranglehold over state politics, other Massachusetts ethnics followed their example. Brahmin pride suffered again when one of their own, a Peabody, lost the race for the US Senate in 1966 to Edward Brooke, the first black to win a seat in the Senate since the post-Civil War period. Brooke in turn lost his seat in 1978 to a son of Greek immigrants, Paul Tsongas.

Today, with a Catholic majority, Massachusetts is much more of an Irish, Italian, French Canadian, Portuguese and Polish state than a Puritan Yankee state. Young, well educated professionals are the newest immigrants, making a heady and argumentative mix, particularly in Boston. The old fishing port of Gloucester has become a Moonie stronghold – it remains to be seen what comes of that, as Massachusetts plunges headfirst into the 21st century with its computers, its diversity, its liberalism, its headaches and its reputation as the brains trust of America.

## Boston

. . . two ladies on the train from the suburbs, and one

says to the other: 'I go into Boston every week to get scrod.' And the other one says: 'So do I but I didn't know it had a past tense . . .'

Boston joke.

A city that is set on a hill cannot be hid.

Matthew 5:11

Boston is the only American city where virtue is an issue, or at least an occasional concern; it's a very self-conscious town, and it usually has good reason to be. From the days of the genuinely noxious Puritan Fathers to the Revolution to the pre-Civil War New England Renaissance, through the spectacular career of the Boston Irish to the present day, when the city sends more steadfast liberals to Congress than most states do, Boston has communed with its conscience and consulted with its reason towards effecting the millennium. While the rest of the nation has been off making real-estate deals, Boston has loyally been carrying on our moral and intellectual battles, at times (like the election of 1972) singlehandedly.

The Puritans who stayed home in England were eventually able to work out their complexes by taking over the country and chopping down all the may-poles; those transplanted to New England had to settle for spying on their neighbours, and, left to their own devices, the first Bostonians turned their aspiration of a 'city on a hill' into a bad dream. The aspiration lived on, through Unitarianism, Transcendentalism, Brook Farm, abolitionism, Christian Science, and the New Deal coalition, and although the red hot cussedness of the Puritan clergyman was replaced by the likes of Reverend Phillips Brooks of Trinity Church (who wrote 'O Little Town of Bethlehem'), the millenarian tendency has persisted in increasingly healthier guises. From the beginning, there has been a great contradiction. Colonial traders wrote home from Boston that they had never seen so many whores in one place. In our own century, the busy little beavers of the Watch and Ward Society made 'banned in Boston' the greatest honour – and eventually the most profitable one – that any publisher could hope for, while over at Scollay Square things were going on that would have drawn a raid in New York. And also in this century, tolerant, progressive Boston contributed one of the greatest travesties of justice in American history when it sent the immigrant anarchists Sacco and Vanzetti to the chair. What is most fascinating about all this is that Boston has come through its long and tortuous history with such a delicious sense of humour.

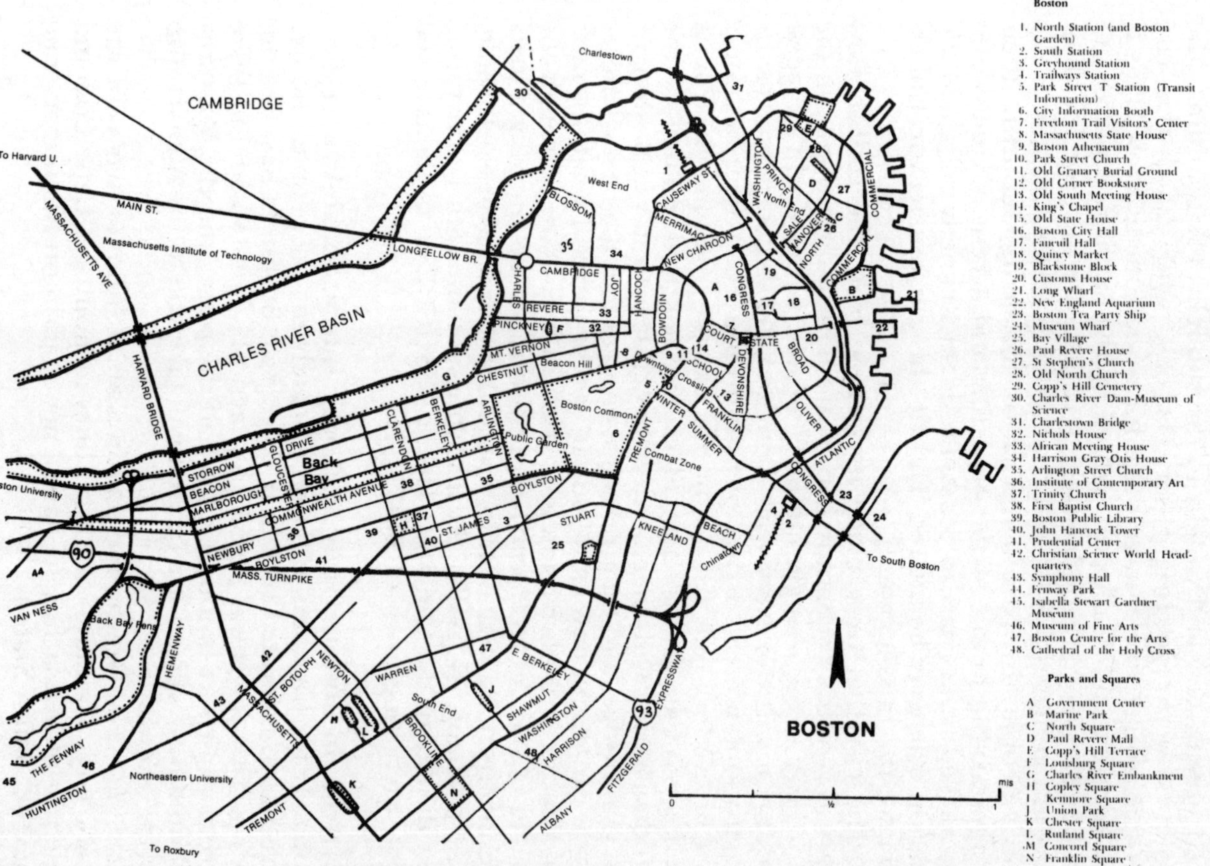


**Boston**

1. North Station (and Boston Garden)
2. South Station
3. Greyhound Station
4. Trailways Station
5. Park Street T Station (Transit Information)
6. City Information Booth
7. Freedom Trail Visitors' Center
8. Massachusetts State House
9. Boston Athenaeum
10. Park Street Church
11. Old Granary Burial Ground
12. Old Corner Bookstore
13. Old South Meeting House
14. King's Chapel
15. Old State House
16. Boston City Hall
17. Faneuil Hall
18. Quincy Market
19. Blackstone Block
20. Customs House
21. Long Wharf
22. New England Aquarium
23. Boston Tea Party Ship
24. Museum Wharf
25. Bay Village
26. Paul Revere House
27. St Stephen's Church
28. Old North Church
29. Copp's Hill Cemetery
30. Charles River Dam-Museum of Science
31. Charlestown Bridge
32. Nichols House
33. African Meeting House
34. Harrison Gray Otis House
35. Arlington Street Church
36. Institute of Contemporary Art
37. Trinity Church
38. First Baptist Church
39. Boston Public Library
40. John Hancock Tower
41. Prudential Center
42. Christian Science World Headquarters
43. Symphony Hall
44. Fenway Park
45. Isabella Stewart Gardner Museum
46. Museum of Fine Arts
47. Boston Centre for the Arts
48. Cathedral of the Holy Cross

**Parks and Squares**

A Government Center
B Marine Park
C North Square
D Paul Revere Mall
E Copp's Hill Terrace
F Louisburg Square
G Charles River Embankment
H Copley Square
I Kenmore Square
J Union Park
K Chester Square
L Rutland Square
M Concord Square
N Franklin Square

Boston, with its medieval streets and resistance to diffusion, is one of the few real cities in New England (with Portland, Maine, Providence, Newport and New Haven). It is built of red brick and green trees, and caught in the sunlight it is beautiful. The colours were too bright for Dickens, who called this city 'insubstantial' like a stage prop for a marionette show. This is perhaps an optical illusion created by the haphazard placement of buildings, or arising from the fact that, then as now, for all of its old familiar sights Boston changes with extreme rapidity. The city's people also have a reputation for being colourful; their unmistakable brand of the New England accent is known and mimicked from coast to coast. President Kennedy delighted the nation whenever he uttered 'Hahvit' (his alma mater) or 'Cuber' (where the missiles were).

The city that once made its fortune from the codfish now thrives – and its economy is one of the healthiest of any in the northeast – on a single industry. Boston is the world's biggest college town, and every year about 250,000 students come to the metropolitan area's scores of institutions. The payoff has come for Boston not only from spin-offs like the booming electronics industry, but in the new ideas and cultural influences the students bring with them. Often they choose to stay in Boston, or in Cambridge, and their presence ensures that the city will never grow old. Right now (and you can see for yourself what this mob of educated youth is indulging itself in by looking through the pages of the *Boston Phoenix*) Boston seems to be enjoying a brief respite from its mental strife. You will still find a visit worthwhile, and probably wish – like the inscription on the 18th-century mug on display in the Old State House – 'SUCCESS, to the crooked but interesting town of BOSTON.'

**Arriving in Boston.** (1) *By air.* Logan International Airport, fortunately for travellers and unfortunately for the people who live around it, is located very near downtown Boston in East Boston. A taxi ride to central Boston is practical (about $6.50) but there are also airport limousines for half the price, and the Massport Shuttle Bus, which for a quarter will take you to the Airport stop of the subway.

(2) *By bus.* The Greyhound station is at 10 St James Avenue in the Back Bay. Trailways and local lines to points in Cape Cod and the rest of Massachusetts have a new station on Atlantic Avenue next to South Station.

(3) *By train.* Amtrak uses South Station on Atlantic at Summer Street (tel: 482-4400), also commuter trains to points on the North Shore and beyond. On the Boston and Maine, use North

Station on Causeway Street in the North End (tel: 227-5070).

**Getting around Boston.** (1) *By the subway.* Ever since Boston opened America's first subway in 1897, Bostonians have been alternatively cursing and making fun of it. One old song, revived by the folksingers of the 1960, is called 'The Man Who Never Returned', about poor Charlie who will ride forever 'neath the streets of Boston because he didn't have the nickle fare to get off. It's not as bad as Bostonians may tell you, though; the MBTA's four lines – Green, Red, Blue and Orange – will take you close to any of the sights in Boston or Cambridge, and though it's often a little slow, the system is pleasant, clean, colourful and easy to use. The four lines meet in a box of the Government Center, State Street, Park Street and Washington stations; tourists will mostly use the Green Line for the Back Bay and beyond and the Red Line for Cambridge. There are maps everywhere to help you, and you may pick up one for yourself at the *Information Booth* in Park Street Station on Boston Common (tel: 722-5700). As in New York, the fare is paid with a token, and you may find it convenient to buy some ahead of time in any of the stations. Unlike New York, the trains don't run all night: they stop at 1am.

In Boston the subway is called the 'T' and its stations are identified by a 'T' on a white disc. Because the 'T' goes everywhere, you probably won't bother with buses, but maps of the surface lines are available at the Information Center.

(2) *By car.* This is a fascinating subject. The traffic isn't as heavy as in New York or Washington, and the winding narrow sidestreets are less troublesome to motorists than to pedestrians, but you'll be sorry just the same if you take your car into Boston. Or perhaps you'll see it as a challenge, for there are no traffic rules; Bostonians see free-form driving as a means of self-expression.

In Boston, huge busy intersections have no traffic signals, while some traffic lights operate on sidestreets where there's never anyone to wait for them. Most traffic signs will tell you lies. 'One Way' often really means the other way; 'No left turn' is sometimes really 'No right turn' and the road that claims 'Concord 20 mi' may send you to Des Moines instead. One Bostonian offered the possible explanation that the patronage jobs in the traffic department of Boston and its suburbs are low-status and go to the last immigrants off the boat. As a result, exasperated motorists hurtle through the metropolitan area in every direction, and at high speed, ignoring the signals and trying to reach their destinations any way they can. Be careful. Another problem is the repetition of street names: there are two important thoroughfares in Boston called Washington Street, for example, and others in most of the towns on the periphery.

Parking is especially difficult in central Boston; in many neighbourhoods parking spaces are reserved for residents, and in the North End there is no room for cars at all. Cambridge, if anything, is worse than Boston. There are city-owned parking garages under Boston Common and in the Government Center. (3) *By taxi.* There are taxi stands all over central Boston, and all cabs are radio-equipped so that you may call for one at your hotel.

**Tourist Information.** On the Tremont Street side of Boston Common is the Tourist Bureau's *Information Booth* (weekdays 9am-5pm, or tel: 367-9275); near it is the *Park Street 'T' Stop* which dispenses information on public transit. There is another information centre in *City Hall,* and another in *Boston National Historical Park Visitors' Center* at 15 State Street, across from the Old State House (daily 8.30am-5pm; tel: 242-5642). In Cambridge the *Harvard University Information Center* is in Holyoke Center (Monday-Saturday 9am-4.45pm tel: 495-1573; and the *Cambridge Chamber of Commerce* at 859 Massachusetts Avenue (weekdays 9am-5pm; tel: 876-4100).

**Boston History.** In the early 17th century, both King James I and his son Charles I in turn lost patience with the growing number of religious dissenters, and were determined to 'harry them out of the land'. The Separatists, or Pilgrims, had already departed for the Netherlands and later Plymouth, and many of the Puritans – those who stayed in the English church but tried to 'purify it from within' – soon found it expedient to follow. In 1629 a group of them met in Cambridge, under the leadership of a wealthy Puritan attorney named John Winthrop, forming the principles and government for a New World colony, and founding the Massachusetts Bay Company for that purpose. They arrived in 1630 on eleven ships led by the *Arabella,* and made themselves quite at home in Salem and Charlestown.

Charlestown, however, had only a poor, brackish source of water that made Puritan stomachs fizz and howl, and the colony began casting envious eyes across the Charles River to a small island connected to the mainland by a narrow strip of land, at low tide, called Shawmut. Shawmut had a fine spring, but it also had a population, in the person of Reverend William Blackstone, the only serious member of an earlier crew of lazy adventurers who had experienced one New England winter and promptly sailed back home. Blackstone lived as a hermit on the island, stalking the woods in his clerical robes and walking his tame white bull. He invited the Puritans over to Shawmut, but when he realized what sort of crowd he was dealing with, he lit off for some other wilderness and never came back. And so Boston was founded (named after the Lincolnshire Boston, from which so many of the settlers had come), like ancient Syracuse, on a nearby island with its fountain of Arethusa, located off Washington Street where the department stores are now. And, also like Syracuse, it was a city meant to go far.

What we are to say about this Puritan colony? They founded the first public schools and the first university (Harvard, in 1636); they encouraged such enlightened policies as smallpox vaccination, and conducted their affairs, according to their mood, democratically. That's the good side. Most historians of the colony are themselves Bostonians and do not wish to offend anyone, but the Puritans continue to have a reputation – just as they had among their colonial neighbours – for dishonesty, cruelty and a fascinating moral perversity. What seems to have happened is that these pious, educated gentlemen, alone in the primeval forest with their Calvinist bogeys, lapsed quickly into a ritualized, Bible-thumping barbarism, combining greed and jealousy with terror, torture and mind control into a tiny 17th-century prelude to totalitarianism. Like Calvin's Geneva, this was a theocratic free city (for the founders had the presence of mind to sneak their royal charter illegally out of England) which was run by the governor and chief minister – originally Winthrop and John Cotton – and by the General Court, whose members were a small elite of Massachusetts Bay Company shareholders. Almost immediately they set up the first stocks on Boston Common, and tested them on the carpenter who built them – Winthrop said he charged too much.

Such offences as 'meddling', 'neglecting work' or 'dissenting from the rest of the jury' would land one in Boston's stocks; worse crimes, like kissing your wife in public or riding on a Sunday, were good for the whipping post, and for cursing the usual punishment was piercing the tongue with a hot iron. As the minions of the Devil were especially thick in Massachusetts, the ministers had to keep the citizens worked into a continual frenzy, resulting in the burning of several witches and the steady, grinding persecution of whatever Quakers and Baptists had the poor sense to try and settle there. Half the people who ever entered a Puritan jail died in it.

The founders had brought England's class system with them, without the titles, and the elite was as interested in commerce as in any kind of holy experiment. They amassed their fortunes on the trade of the growing port, and maintained their power by manipulating the rabble against their enemies, religious and civil. As for their commercial ethics, one British traveller, John Dunton, wrote from his experience in 1686: 'There Bostonians enrich themselves by the ruine of Strangers, and like ravenous Birds of Prey, strive who shall fasten his Tallons first upon 'em'. And for their morals: 'Nothing keeps 'em friends but only the fear of exposing one another's knavery. . . like Water-men, they Look one Way, and Row another.' No account of this grim little town would be complete without mention of Cotton Mather, preacher, scientist, scholar and leading spirit of late 17th-century Boston. He is remembered for the hilarious, hysterical prose of his histories and demonologies, and for his great achievement of being the nosiest, most sanctimonious and most bloody-minded of all the Puritans; he was the chief instrument of the witchcraft terror, and once wrote a letter to the King suggesting that they collaborate in conquering the Pennsylvania Quakers and selling them into slavery, splitting the profits between themselves.

How it happened that this moral cesspool of Boston should first provide the major impetus to American liberty and then become the most progressive and innovative corner of the new republic is one of the curiosities of our history. As Puritan meretriciousness won out over Puritan sanctity, the city grew so fast on the 'triangular trade' of rum, molasses and slaves, and on the sale of codfish to Europe's Catholics, that the founders lost control. When Boston first knew diversity, as men of different religion and nationality poured in, the 'city on a hill' was irrevocably and fortunately compromised. Boston before the Revolution was an unsafe and unhealthy place to live; John Bonner's famous Map of 1722 noted that the city had already suffered eight great fires and six smallpox epidemics, and government repression and mob violence were facts of everyday life, even after the original charter was revoked by the Crown in 1684. In the 18th century, it became the King's taxmen and not the Congregationalist ayatollahs who were the instruments of oppression, and turbulent, mercantile Boston now had a foreign enemy against whom to conspire. Bostonians had no desire to take part in England's imperial wars, such as the French and Indian Wars right in their backyard, and no desire to help pay for them, and so became the most troublesome spot in the English-speaking world. To the Sugar Act, the Stamp Acts, the Townshend Acts, all in the 1760s, and to every other attempt by London to make the colonies pay at least part of their share, Boston, in the midst of a long, hard economic depression, responded with riots, boycotts, ridicule and smuggling; often there was more smuggling than legal trading, and Bostonians like John Hancock made their fortunes from it. The 'Sons of Liberty' appeared, the very picture of a modern, tightly organized revolutionary cadre, and a new generation of leaders stirred the pot, such as James Otis, the brilliant, almost forgotten orator who had as much to do with the Revolution as any man, and Samuel Adams, a revolutionary tactician the equal of Lenin.

In the 1770s all America looked to radical Boston, the tinder-box of the colonies, to see if this struggle would break out in open rebellion. The Boston Massacre, which may have been orchestrated by the revolutionaries, occurred in March 1770, and the outrage swung the support of the population almost unanimously behind the radical leaders, who showed their sense of humour in December 1773 with the famous Boston Tea Party. The new tax on tea was an effort to shore up the British East India Company, but when the first shipment arrived at Griffin's Wharf, the revolutionaries – dressed as Mohawks, with their password 'Boston harbor a teapot tonight!' – whooped and giggled their way onto the ship, dumped its cargo overboard and then marched in drill formation, their axes on their shoulders, under the governor's window. This was the point of no return. The British closed the port and Boston became almost a ghost town as trade ceased; 17,000 of the city's population of 20,000 left, some as refugees, many as soldiers, while King George, determined to put an end to Boston's contentious ways, filled the empty houses with his troops. The events of 1775 broke the tension; two months after Paul Revere's Ride and the 'shot heard round the world' at Concord, the British first faced the new Continental Army at Bunker Hill in Charlestown, and won a costly victory. One month after that, the new commander of the patriot forces, George Washington, arrived and began his campaigns with the siege of Boston, which lasted until the spring of 1776 when Washington fortified Dorchester Heights and forced the British to evacuate. Boston was free, and started to rebuild even before the war was over.

With a little Yankee ingenuity, and with trade routes around the world no longer encumbered by British restrictions, Boston made its comeback. New districts were laid out, such as Beacon Hill, the first of the landfill projects was begun (at present, they have added 3,500 acres to the city) to make Boston no longer an island, or even a peninsula, and homes and public buildings were going up everywhere, many designed by the great Charles Bulfinch such as the Massachusetts State House. A new class of men directed the affairs of the city, merchants like John Hancock and Harrison Gray Otis. Although Massachusetts was the last state in the union to disestablish the church, the old theocracy was finally being eradicated. After the turn of the century, Boston underwent a quiet religious revolution as the mouldy Puritan straitness was swept away by the new liberal doctrine of Unitarianism, which eventually even the Brahmin elite began to accept. In politics, Boston was a centre of Federalism, sending John Adams and later John Quincy Adams to the White House and leading New England in opposition to the War of 1812 and to Andrew Jackson. At home, the city elected a reform mayor, Josiah Quincy, who built the Quincy Market, cleaned up the town – literally – and exiled the pigs.

If the worst of Puritanism was gone, the best of it survived – to Boston's and the nation's enduring benefit. A new Boston, committed to intelligence and education, was still seriously striving for spiritual and temporal excellence, and the flood of new ideas and achievements that issued from it astounded the world. Reform did not stop with matters of sanitation; Boston was improving and humanizing its government, its churches, its aesthetics, its jails, hospitals and schools. Under the great educator Horace Mann, the city and state created the finest public school system in the world, and set a pattern for eduction that dominates America's schools even today. By the 1850s, under the influence of such idealists as Ralph Waldo Emerson and his friend Henry David Thoreau, it was society itself that was to be remade.

The great movements of the time in Boston provide a parallel to the United States of the 1960s and '70s that is almost eerie in its completeness. Beards became fashionable again, and following the example of Thoreau young people went off to commune with nature. Health foods and various forms of religious mysticism were recurring fads, as were communal experiments like the famous Brook Farm. Margaret Fuller and other early feminists started the women's rights movement, and all the Boston intellectuals joined in a stout resistance to an immoral war – the slavers' and speculators' 1848 war with Mexico. The greatest effort of all, however, was abolitionism. What started with the publication of William Lloyd Garrison's *The Liberator* soon became the subject of all the city's passions. The mercantile elite, to whom Southern trade was important, at first succumbed to the slave owner's threats and tried to stifle the cause; some of its members actually tried to lynch Garrison. But on moral force alone, the movement captured the city. Just as it had started the Revolutionary War, Boston began to do its best to bring about the Civil War, as the centre of resistance to the Fugitive Slave Laws, and the place where men like Garrison and Wendell Phillips – himself a Brahmin and the son of a Boston mayor – incited the Southern slaves to escape or open rebellion. A curious sidelight of this was the first successful battle in America over school integration; in the 1850s, again foreshadowing the 1960s, Boston transferred pupils to integrated schools on Beacon Hill. When the war came, Boston contributed more than its share of men and arms, as well as the first black regiment (the Massachusetts 54th) and, through its citizen Julia Ward Howe, the 'Battle Hymn of the Republic'.

After all this, quite understandably, Boston was exhausted. The city's commerce and importance declined relative to New York and the new cities of the west, and in the postwar era of greed and tastelessness, she felt embarrassed and out of place. But there were problems too at home – namely, the Irish. They had been trickling into Boston ever since the troubles and famines of the 1840s, but now they were coming in waves, and their Catholic priests with them, taking over the North End, the old South End and making inroads everywhere else. The older Bostonians despaired for their city, and for a while responded to the threat by treating the Irish like dogs; 'NINA' in a newspaper advertisement meant 'No Irish need apply'. This state of affairs didn't last long. The Irish for their part discovered a talent they never knew they had, never having had the opportunity to find out. They learned how to vote, how to count votes, how to coax votes, how to buy votes, and occasionally how to conjure them up out of the grave. In a period when Boston was beginning to recover its confidence, with the creation of the Back Bay, the beautiful chain of parks called the Emerald Necklace, and new churches and public buildings, political control of the city gradually but surely fell into the hands of the once-despised Celts. Hugh O'Brien, in 1884, became the first Irish mayor, and proved an excellent one. For all but six of the last ninety-seven years, Boston's mayor has been an Irishman, an achievement made possible by such colourful types as Martin Lomasney of the West End, the great Mahatma, who once apologized to a candidate: 'I promised you one hundred and thirteen votes. You got only one hundred and nine. I will not rest until I find out what happened to those other four votes.' Other peoples, notably the Jews and Italians, were now pouring into Boston, and they too had to be cut in for a share of the action.

As the ward machines took over city politics, a different kind of Irish politician appeared. First came John Fitzgerald, 'Honey Fitz' as he was known, a spellbinding blarney-dispenser who regularly murdered the Brahmins and their 'Good Government Association' at the polls. After him there was James Michael

Curley, another from the same mould, who dominated Boston politics from 1920 to 1950, serving now as mayor, now as congressman, and who, in 1943, won an election from a jail cell; the Spencer Tracy movie *The Last Hurrah* was based on his career. It wasn't quite the last hurrah, though, even when the machines grew old and tired and most of their supporters left for the suburbs. Two of the last three Speakers of the US House of Representatives have been Boston Irish, and Curley's own Charlestown district, after the war, sent a young John F. Kennedy to Congress. Our first Catholic President, grandson of 'Honey Fitz' and son of the Boston Irishman whom Franklin Roosevelt sent as ambassador to the Court of St James, was the final remarkable flower of a century of Irish politicking in Boston.

Through all this sound and fury, however, the city hadn't been doing its housekeeping. Boston in the 1940s found itself filthy and falling to pieces, and like Philadelphia and Pittsburgh, went to work rebuilding itself at full speed. Unfortunately the job fell to a reform mayor named John Hynes, the worst of technocrats with the best of intentions. Under Hynes, the atrocity of the West End's total demolition was committed, the most destructive highway ever built in America was rammed through downtown, and huge ghastly building projects grew up like toadstools across the cityscape. Since then, the city's renewal efforts have improved – in fact they have become among the most intelligent in the nation – but the damage done in the '50s will take centuries, perhaps, to repair. In this period, Boston's sagging economy was also rebuilt; in the computer age, the area's great intellectual resources in the universities spun off hundreds of new high-technology concerns, most of them located around the circumferential Route 128 in the suburbs.

As the 'new Boston' of the '60s and '70s took shape (the Boston of revitalized old neighbourhoods and tens of thousands of young sophisticates who went to school there and liked it enough to stay) another ethnic political drama was playing at the new City Hall, in the federal courts and in every city neighbourhood. After thirty years of a steadily increasing black population in Boston, the courts ordered the city's schools to desegregate. Boston did it in the 1850s but couldn't do it now. Racial violence, perpetrated by young white punks in South Boston and other areas, shook the city and almost resulted in a white backlash candidate, Louise Day Hicks, being elected mayor in 1967. Race relations and the problems of Boston's blacks are still deplorable. The same angels and demons that arrived in 1630 still contend for the city's soul, but Boston hopes it can draw on its old reserves of energy and idealism to carry the day.

**Boston Streets.** This city's planners, as Emerson noted, were the cows. In fact, the Puritan belief in predestination extended even to urban design, and streets appeared wherever Providence chose to lay them, along cow paths, Indian paths, Blackstone's paths and crooked little alleys between them – a medieval city transplanted to America. You'll get lost, you'll stay lost, and collapse in despair just around the corner from your destination. Of course there are exceptions: the noble, formal plan of the Back Bay, and the simple grid of South Boston, but everywhere else in the metropolitan area, development has remained true to the founders. But if you do get lost, don't be shy; Bostonians themselves spend much of their time asking directions of each other.

**Boston Houses.** After five general conflagrations in the 18th century, Boston decided to build in brick. If Paul Revere's house, the only remaining wooden specimen, is at all representative, Boston in 1700 must have been rather sweetly quaint and picturesque, the kind of townscape you would see in the illustrations for a book of nursery rhymes. As the city grew wealthy, brick townhouses appeared that were as dignified as their counterparts in Philadelphia or New York, but less decorated. Only a few remain, mostly on Beacon Hill. When most people think of a Boston house, they think of the 'bow front' with a curved façade to increase window space and let more light into the tall, narrow structures. These are to be seen all over Beacon Hill, the Back Bay and the South End; we may see them as beautiful, ancient and wholly respectable but, as late as 1907, Henry James in his *American Scene* wrote of them as some kind of intrusion on the virtues of Boston's past. Conscious elegance may have conquered Boston completely, but never without misgivings.

The bow fronts were narrow because land was precious; until the great landfill projects Boston had little room to expand, and consequently built higher and denser than any American city, New York included. Boston's poor had their counterpart to Beacon Hill in the oldest neighbourhoods, with tall tenements of the same frontage as the townhouses of the rich, only housing a dozen families and shoehorned into winding narrow streets such as those you see in the North End. When modern transportation gave Boston room to breathe, it cheerfully reverted to the old New England manner of detached frame houses on open lots; the city's Irish, Jewish and Italian immigrants, as they improved their status, moved out to Boston's famous 'three-deckers' with a spacious porch on each floor. South Boston, Dorchester and such neighbourhoods are full of them.

**Downtown Boston.** *Boston Common* is a good place to start. Beacon Hill, the Back Bay and Downtown meet here, and the North and South Ends are only a short walk away. The Puritan settlers granted these forty acres to Reverend Blackstone, who immediately sold them back and set off for Rhode Island; then in 1634 they made the land America's first city park, as a common grazing land and site of the only public entertainment allowed in early Boston – whippings and hangings. Until the landfills, this was riverfront property and the Charles Street side was a sandy beach. Among its meadows and groves are a bandstand, the Frog Pond, a burial ground for the British who died on Bunker Hill, America's first subway station, on Park Street, and a *City Information Center,* facing Tremont.

Across Charles Street an extension of the park was created in the last century, the *Public Garden;* on its lagoon you may take a ride, as all Boston schoolchildren do, on the famous Swan Boats. The Public Garden is really a small arboretum, with monuments to such Boston notables as Channing, Sumner and Phillips under the shade of exotic Asian and North American trees.

On the other side of Boston Common, the *Massachusetts State House* stands on the slope of Beacon Hill; in front of it, you'll see memorials to Mary Dyer and Anne Hutchinson, and to Colonel Robert Gould Shaw and his 54th Massachusetts Regiment from the Civil War, the first black unit in the army, representing them marching through Boston on their way to near annihilation in South Carolina. The bas-relief is a 1900 work of Augustus Saint-Gaudens. The front door of the statehouse is opened only for governors departing at the end of their term of office; you'll have to go in the side.

Charles Bulfinch, Boston's architect, who virtually remade the city after the Revolutionary War with fine homes for the Brahmins and a score of public buildings, created here what many consider to be his masterpiece. Its gilded dome remains Boston's landmark, even with the platoon of modern towers that crowd it from the east; originally it was copper, done by Paul Revere. Massachusetts hasn't been kind to this building over the years. They've tacked on additions, performed numerous unfortunate redecorations including the present one, and until 1927 they kept it painted white like a New England farmhouse. During the last war, they painted the dome black so as not to attract any stray Nazi bombers. Inside, you may attach yourself to one of the periodic guided tours that leave from the Doric Hall, or pick up their informative booklet and do it yourself.

The block east of Park Street, in front of the State House, is some of the best of old Boston, dark brick and green trees unspoiled by modern fancies; there's the stately façade of the *Boston Athenaeum* on Beacon Street, a private library society founded in 1807; the *Park Street Church* that Henry James was so fond of and where Garrison began his abolitionist crusade with a fiery speech in 1829; and the *Old Granary Burial Ground,* on Tremont, where Revere, Hancock, Samuel Adams, the victims of the Boston Massacre, and Ben Franklin's parents rest. Somewhere, under a stone too faded to read, lies Elizabeth Goose, or Vergoose, or Vertigoose, a prolific spinner of verse for her many children. Boston's claims to being the hometown of Mother Goose seem rather thin; the evidence is on the side of the wife of Charlemagne, 'old goose-foot Mary'. The familiar stock of nursery rhymes we have was published and popularized in America before England, but Mrs Goose's volume has not survived in even a single copy – if indeed it ever really existed. Also, anyone wont of nights to fly through the air on a very fine gander in 17th-century Boston would be asking for trouble.

To the east, the old centre of Boston has become the modern business district. *Washington Street,* with department stores *Jordan-Marsh* and *Filene's*, the inventor of the bargain basement, has been done as a wonderfully attractive pedestrian mall called *Downtown Crossing*. The *Old Corner Bookstore* at School Street is now the circulation office of the *Boston Globe,* but in the 19th century when it was the office and bookstore of Ticknor & Fields, one of America's first great publishing houses, Boston's literary circles, including such luminaries as Hawthorne and Emerson, made it their second home. Across the street is the *Old South Meeting House* (1729) where Sam Adams and his friends plotted revolution, and where Boston's freshly painted Mohawks met for their famous Tea Party (open daily 10am-4pm; admission). West on School Street, the Victorian *Old City Hall* has been converted into shops and offices, next door to *King's Chapel* (1749) the first church in Boston to join the Unitarian movement (open daily 10am-4pm; free); in its adjacent cemetery are buried John Winthrop and William Dawes, and a lady named Elizabeth Pain whose suffering at the hands of Puritan prosecutors were reworked by Hawthorne into *The Scarlet Letter*. The old hotel just across School Street is the *Parker House,* famous not only for Parker House rolls, but for the fact that both Ho Chi Minh and Malcolm X, at different times, worked here as waiters.

Washington and State were the main streets of colonial Boston, and where they intersect stands the *Old State House,* perhaps the only 18th-century building anywhere with a subway station in its basement. Here, in the uneasy decade before the Revolution, the King's officials watched the storm gather outside their windows. Continually the radicals carried out what we could call today 'demonstrations'. One of these, on 5 March 1770, saw a pleasant afternoon's diversion of throwing snowballs at British troops turn into the *Boston Massacre,* with five civilians shot dead, including one black man, Crispus Attucks. News of the incident spread through the colonies as another tyrannous British outrage, but what really happened is unclear; the testimony of the commanding officer, who was promptly jailed by the civil authorities (and courageously defended by none other than John Adams), suggests that agents provocateurs in the mob had ordered 'Fire!' and the soldiers mistook the cry for their captain's. A circle on the pavement under the State House balcony marks the event. The Lion and Unicorn on the cornice, of course, were torn down after the Declaration of Independence was read to the people here. These replicas were put on long after the war was over. Inside, there's a small museum (open daily 10am-4pm; admission) of Boston's history and a good bookshop covering all things Bostonian. Across Court Street, the *Visitor's Center* of the National Park Service can get you started on the Freedom Trail and tell you what else is going on in town.

From 1830 to 1844, the Old State House served as City Hall; thus, within a few blocks you can see no less than three Boston City Halls, ending with the newest, dominating *Government Center.* Once this was Scollay Square, the city's Tenderloin, with its legendary establishments like the Old Howard Burlesque Theater, where Harvard boys and Irish dockhands could meet for the common purpose of ogling. When the district became rundown, the city simply wiped it out, as they did with the West End a few blocks away. In 1960, the city held a national design competition for a civic centre, the first such competition in America for over thirty years. Whatever you think of the result, be careful what you say; Bostonians are inordinately proud of it, even though a few malcontents have taken to calling the broad open plaza the 'Brick Desert'. The one old building the planners suffered to remain, the 1841 *Sears Crescent,* with its giant brass teapot and other early Boston shop signs, looks very uncomfortable next to the concrete bulk of *City Hall.* The architects here wanted to express 'openness in government' with a building that seems to sweep you right inside itself (this openness extends to everyone: half the bums in Boston spend their afternoons in the myriad little alcoves around the base), but the work is equally expressive of Boston's aggressive civic pride, with its Brobdingnagian size and its total lack of modesty. City Hall is already a landmark – most Americans would recognize it on sight – and elements of its idiosyncratic design are finding their way into other public buildings from coast to coast. Unfortunately, the other buildings of the ensemble are not up to the same standard, and the book is still out on whether Boston's metabolism will accept this newly transplanted heart.

*Faneuil Hall* sits tucked away behind the Government Center. You may pronounce it 'Fannel', 'Funnel', 'Fanyule' or even 'Faneel'; although it's been around since 1742, Bostonians do not seem to have arrived at a consensus. Merchant Peter Faneuil bestowed this gift on the city as a combination market and meeting house. It performs these functions even today, with produce on the first floor, politics on the second, and the famous golden grasshopper weathervane on top of it all. Boston calls this 'the Cradle of Liberty', for it was here that Otis and Samuel Adams, whose statue stands out in front of Dock Square, hatched their plots and won over the faint-hearted. Even in those times the building itself was a symbol of resistance, just a block away from the State House and royal authority. During their occupation, the British got a temporary revenge by turning it into a barracks, just as they used the Old South Meeting House as a riding school.

As part of the *Faneuil Hall Market,* Boston has something that's grey, 500 feet long and attracts more visitors every year than Disneyland: it's the *Quincy Market,* of course. In this case, instead of demolishing a past monument – and monumental is the word for this 1824 work of architect Alexander Parris – they have turned it into an instant carnival, with more trendy snack shops, trendy boutiques and trendies than City Hall has paperclips. Not that only trendies come here; in the few years since the Rouse Company, leading practitioners of the art, sprinkled their fairy dust over the place, Quincy Market has become the place to be in Boston. It's colourful, crowded and lots of fun; there's always something to see, from street musicians to a branch of the Museum of Fine Arts with changing exhibits (open Tuesday to Sunday 11am-6pm; donation) and, around the corner at 60 State Street, the city's fancy audio-visual show for tourists, called 'Where's Boston?' (hourly shows, $2.50).

This market district continues north with the little clutch of buildings and narrow alleys in the shadow of the freeway, known as the *Blackstone Block.* Young Benjamin Franklin lived here for a while; so did Louis Philippe, future Citizen King of France, who supported himself here, naturally, by teaching French. On Fridays and Saturdays it becomes the Italian *Pushcart Market.* To the south, State and Broad Streets lead toward the waterfront; 'State Street' in Boston has always been synonymous with the business district, close to the wharves where the money sailed in. One of the oddest sights in Boston is here, the 1834 Greek Revival *Customs House,* with a 496-ft tower, Boston's first skyscraper, popping right out of the roof. Why would they do such a thing? Well, it was built during World War I when building materials were allocated only for 'alterations', not for new construction. The fine 1890 Victorian *Grain and Flour Exchange* faces it on India Street.

From here you pass, not for the last time, under that damnable freeway to the *Waterfront* itself. Now that the big freighters dock in East or South Boston or in Charlestown, the city is seeking to redevelop the area; there's the new *Marine Park* at the foot of *Long Wharf,* once the biggest and busiest on the waterfront when it stretched almost a mile out into the harbour. State Street, both physically and symbolically, is an extension of it. Cruises around the harbour, to the harbour islands or to Nantasket Beach leave from here or from Rowe's Wharf a few blocks south. On Central Wharf, next to the new luxury apartment towers by I. M. Pei, there's the *New England Aquarium*(*). Atlantic Avenue follows the docks; a few blocks south it takes you to the *Boston Tea Party Ship and Museum* on Congress Street, a replica of the unfortunate brig *Beaver* with films and exhibits on the famous event (open daily 9am-5pm, until 8pm in the summer; admission). It isn't the exact site of the Tea Party – that would be a few hundred feet inland, right under the freeway, for all of the waterfront is on landfill. Nearby is *South Station,* for Amtrak lines, and just over the bridge across Fort Point Channel is *Museum Wharf.* Here, at the foot of the South Boston industrial district, an old warehouse block has been gaily painted and remodelled to house two attractions, the *Children's Museum*(*) and the *Museum of Transportation*(*). Out front, the big milk bottle is a relic of the 1930s. It served then as a dairy in a small Massachusetts town, and now as a snackstand for Museum Wharf.

Downtown Boston begins to fray at its southern fringes, and nowhere more than along Washington Street. South of the shopping district, it changes into the 'Theater District', a name more wishful thinking than reality since only two or three legitimate theatres remain, and then into the legendary *Combat Zone.* When the planners evicted vice from Scollay Square, they tried to concentrate it here, with unhappy results. The stretch of porno parlours and such is certainly seamy and dangerous, but in no wise interesting. Even sailors avoid it. Now the planners are once again set to make it disappear (they've already begun with one big hotel development), but first they need to find some other part of town to replace it. To the west along Tyler, Beach and Hudson Streets is a thriving *Chinatown,* surpassed in size only by those of New York and San Francisco. Among its restaurants is a branch office of the Kuomintang Party – not surprisingly, since Sun Yat-Sen himself lived here during his exile.

Finally, just before the railroad tracks and highway that mark the beginning of the South End, there's a tiny neighbourhood that most Bostonians don't even notice – at least, not since Prohibition, when most of the city's speakeasies were here. The homes in *Bay Village* are very much like those on Beacon Hill, only smaller; many of the workmen who built Beacon Hill built homes for themselves here.

**The North End.** In the Revolutionary era, many of Boston's wealthy lived here, on the northern tip of the Shawmut peninsula, as well as the city's black community. A large number of wealthy citizens turned out to be Tories, and left for England and Canada – which is not surprising, for though Boston was the most solidly radical corner of the colonies, many of its merchants' livings depended on trade with the mother country. With their departure and the trend for moving to Beacon Hill, the North End was handed down to successive waves of immigrants, first the Irish, then the Jews and finally the Italians, who still inhabit it. No American 'Little Italy' is more Italian, not even New York's; these narrow streets of high grey houses, old and dingy on the outside but immaculately kept within, could easily be in Naples. On Hanover Street there are a score of classic Italian cafés, with espresso machines and walls decorated with photographs of the football teams back home. The Italian tongue is still as common as English, for many of the North End's peoples are recent immigrants from Calabria or Sicily.

A walk through the North End is not to be missed, not only for the Mediterranean atmosphere (occasionally with snow on the ground) but for the remains of earlier Boston. The neighbourhood is neatly defined, cut off from downtown and from the Haymarket by the Fitzgerald Expressway. Near the waterfront, at Commercial Street, blocks of offices and warehouses from the 1850s have recently been recycled as trendy shops and apartments, *Mercantile Wharf* and the *Commercial Block*. Two blocks west, where North Street widens into North Square, Italian children kick the ball around in front of the *Paul Revere House* (open daily, 10am-6pm in the summer, 10am-4pm in winter; admission), the only remaining 17th-century building in Boston; before its restoration in 1905, it saw service as a grocery store and a candy factory. Long before the house was built, Cotton Mather lived on this spot; it was built in 1676, and Revere, his wife and his sixteen children moved here in 1770. Not surprisingly, it was the only house in the neighbourhood that the British couldn't use for quartering troops – there wasn't any room. Paul Revere was the typically industrious colonial. Besides being the indispensible courier of the Revolution and a famous silversmith, he cast America's first bells, founded industries, led military expeditions (very badly) and engraved the plates of the first American currency. His house windows, covered with broadsides and drawings on oiled paper illuminated from inside, provided a running chronicle of the time for his neighbours. We know him best from that rouser of a poem by Longfellow on his famous ride. Revere's colleague, Billy Dawes, deserved as much of the credit, if not more, but Dawes unfortunately does not rhyme with anything heroic. Next door, the *Pierce-Hichborn House* shows how Boston changed in a short time; built in the early 1700s it was one of the first brick homes in the city – after a few good fires, a law was passed in 1693 forbidding any more frame structures. Across the square, the *Sacred Heart Church,* a Sicilian parish, is one of the modern North End's institutions.

A block to the west, *Hanover Street* has most of the shops, cafés and restaurants (a good Italian restaurant is murder to find in America, but not here). At Clark Street is one of Bulfinch's finest buildings, *St Stephen's Church* (1806, formerly the New North Church), recently restored by the Catholic diocese. It faces *Paul Revere Mall,* a pleasant park constructed by the WPA in the 1930s and familiarly known in the neighbourhood as the *Prado.* The church at the other end is *Old North Church,* whose proper name is Christ Church; built in 1723, it's now maintained as a historical monument (open daily 9am-5pm; free). Its sexton, one Robert Newman, hung two lanterns in the belfry on that night on 18 April 1775 to tell Paul Revere that they were indeed coming by sea. Revere had secretly rowed over to Charlestown, his oars wrapped in a woman's petticoats to keep them silent, and there awaited the signal, to carry the news to every Middlesex village and farm. This steeple – a copy of the original, blown down by a hurricane – had already witnessed history. In 1757, a man named John Childs seems to have achieved America's first successful manned flight. Boston's annals record the event, though not what sort of contraption he was wearing when he jumped off Old North; they note only that the town fathers forbade him from doing it any more as it distracted the people from their work.

Old North Church faces Salem Street; it's hard to believe now, but not so long ago, when this part of the North End was Jewish, Salem Street was a miniature version of New York's Lower East Side, crowded with pushcarts, Hebrew-lettered signs and long

Semitic beards. Similarly vanished is the Irish North End, but John F. Kennedy's mother was born just off North Square on Garden Street; her father, Boston's famous mayor, 'Honey Fitz' Fitzgerald, held the North End as his strong political base. When the Irish had all gravitated to Charlestown and elsewhere, they still couldn't stay away – gangs of them would return to duke it out with the Italians in regular rambles on the Charlestown Bridge.

*Copps Hill Cemetery,* on Snowhill Street, offers not only a fine view of the harbour, but also some of the most interesting epitaphs anywhere, some over 300 years old. All the Mathers, Samuel, Increase and that old devil Cotton, who preached at Old North Church, are buried here, as well as a thousand or so members of Boston's earliest black settlement, 'New Guinea', which extended from here to the waterfront. A park, *Copps Hill Terrace,* covers that area today. On many of the gravestones in the cemetery you can see the marks of bullets; British troops apparently used them for target practice when they brought their artillery here to shell Bunker Hill. Back towards the south across the freeway, Commercial Street, which has looped around the neighbourhood along the docks, becomes Causeway Street; there are the old *North Station,* from which most of the commuter buses depart, and *Boston Garden.* The mighty Boston Celtics play basketball here, and their partisans are inclined to think it as much a Historical Site as Paul Revere's House.

On Commercial Street, on a cold day in January 1919, occurred one of the memorable events in Boston's history, something, perhaps, that could have happened only in Boston. Molasses in January, one would suppose, would be slow, but not this day. A giant tankful exploded, sending two and a half million gallons of the boiling, sticky stuff cascading across the North End in a tidal wave a hundred yards wide, sweeping away a firehouse, twenty-one people, and an elevated rail line. One young man named Anthony DiStasio became a local legend for his spectacular feat of body-surfing, riding the wave into the harbour and surviving – just barely.

Before the 1950s, Boston's *West End* was in appearance very much like the North End; its population was the most ethnically mixed in the city. Caught up in the fervour of the post-war revival of the downtown area, Boston's planners perpetrated an act of municipal vandalism unparalleled in this country; quite literally, they made the West End disappear, and haphazardly covered the space with ugly apartment blocks. The neighbourhood gamely resisted, but in vain – back in the '50s, everyone was still saying 'You can't stop progress.' All this was carefully chronicled by the famous sociologist Herbert Gans, who lived here at the time, in his book *The Urban Villagers.* The West End's experience and Gans's book have had a tremendous influence on how Americans look at cities. When Boston realized what it had done, a chill went through the city, and to its credit, subsequent renewal efforts have shown somewhat more consideration to the city's people.

**Beacon Hill.** Somehow, in the United States, any neighbourhood with 'Hill' in its name – Nob Hill, Society Hill, Capitol Hill and the rest – acquires connotations of exclusiveness, of utter social authority in its particular town. The trend started here in Boston, and still no other Hill stands so high on the social register. When the Brahmins recovered their fortunes after the Revolution, they wanted a new preserve that would be strictly residential, removed from the bustle of the city, and they found it here behind Bulfinch's brand new State House. They're still there; in the late 20th century perhaps they have no place else to go.

In the beginning there were three hills, not counting 'Mount Whoredom', Boston's colonial Combat Zone around Pinckney Street. Gradually, the landowners chopped about sixty feet off the tops of them, to sell as landfill, leaving the continuous ridge we see now; from the Charles, or from Boston Common, you'll see the famous skyline of gables and chimney pots, crowned by the golden dome of the State House. It's a lovely sight, and one dear to the Bostonians. A closer look will reveal old cobbled streets of elegant bow-fronts, and trees and flowers everywhere. To its inhabitants' minds, Beacon Hill is perfection, a small corner of the New World that no longer needs to strive or aspire; indeed, they intend not to change it at all. The neighbourhood's zealous architectural commission won't permit anything offensive, and back in the mindless '50s when the city wanted to come and pour concrete over their cobbles and brick walks, the ladies of Beacon Hill simply sat in their rocking chairs on the pavement and refused to let them.

The choicest part of Beacon Hill, the southern slope, starts at the edge of the Common on Beacon Street. No. 42 is the Somerset Club, lofty social citadel of the hill, and No. 45 next door is a townhouse by Bulfinch; more of his work may be seen on Chestnut (No. 13, 29A) and on beautiful *Mount Vernon Street,* (No. 85, the second *Harrison Gray Otis House)* and No. 55, the *Nichols House,* maintained as a museum (open Monday/Wednesday/Saturday 1pm-4.30pm; admission). Where Mount Vernon crosses Willow Street is *Louisburg Square,* the most celebrated and the most thoroughly satisfactory residential square in America; it is to Beacon Hill what Beacon Hill is to Boston. The narrow garden, like New York's Gramercy Park, opens only for the keys of the square residents. William Dean Howells and Louisa May Alcott, among dozens of other Boston celebrities, lived here. *Charles Street,* two blocks west, is the shopping street of Beacon Hill, lined with antique parlours and curiosity shops.

The crest of Beacon Hill follows *Pinckney Street.* You'll notice that there aren't many cross streets to connect to the southern slope, and this was by design. Pinckney Street and the northern slope were always the less desirable part of the Hill, with Mount Whoredom – until Mayor Quincy cleared it out in the 1820 – and the old black community around Jay Street. To complement the Freedom Trail, the *Museum of Afro-American History,* in the 1805 *African Meeting House* (8 Smith Court, off Joy; open by appointment, tel: 442-7400) has developed a *Black Heritage Trail* of neighbourhood sights, with a pamphlet available at any of the Boston information centres. The African Meeting House is the oldest black church in America; its parishioners constructed it because they were tired of being segregated into the balcony at Old North Church. For a while, after the black community moved on to Roxbury, it served as a synagogue. Smith Court and the streets and alleys around it are lined with the homes and institutions of what was, before the Civil War, the most important, most prosperous and best educated free black neighbourhood in America.

The summit of Beacon Hill used to be on Bowdoin Street, behind the State House; here the Sons of Liberty erected the beacon that gave the hill its name. After the Revolution, it was replaced by a Bulfinch monument honouring the heroes of the Revolution. This stood only a short time before the heirs of John Hancock, claiming the land it was built on, came in and carted away the earth beneath it for landfill, letting the monument collapse in a hole. Today *Bulfinch's Monument* has been salvaged, only to be reborn in the middle of the parking lot.

On Cambridge Street, the northern limit of Beacon Hill, No. 141 is the first *Harrison Gray Otis House,* restored to its 1796 appearance and furnishings (guided tours at 10am, 11am, 1pm, 2pm and 3pm; admission). To the west, streets like Revere and Phillips are dotted with picturesque hidden alleys and courts. *Rollins Place,* off Revere, is famous for the false housefront at the end disguising a brick wall; the Place's residents keep up the joke each Christmas by hanging a wreath on the brick door. *Massachusetts General Hospital,* on Cambrige at Anderson Street, keeps its original Bulfinch structure and the *Ether Dome* commemorating the first use of anaesthesia in an operation here. Near Charles

Street a pedestrian bridge (there's another near the Public Garden) will take you over the freeway to the *Charles River Embankment,* a park that runs the length of Beacon Hill and the Back Bay. Here are playgrounds, a marina, *Charles River Cruises* (tel: 727-5250 for schedules) and the *Hatch Memorial Shell,* where the renowned Boston Pops mounts its annual assault on music in July.

**Back Bay.** Boston's greatest contribution to urban design began in 1857 with its biggest landfill project. Gradually, as the new land appeared, streets were laid out alphabetically, Arlington, Berkeley, Clarendon, etc., with pretentious – in the 19th-century meaning of that word – homes in the best modern French and Renaissance styles. Cranky old Henry James, who called Mount Vernon Street on Beacon Hill 'the only respectable street in America', found this new elegance threatening; his word for the Back Bay was 'unknowable'. Today, after a period of modest decline, it is once more a fashionable residential area, though most of the mansions have been converted to apartments or to institutional uses.

*Commonwealth Avenue* is the central mall that makes the plan coherent. Among the many memorials on its long strip of greenery are those to Patrick Collins, one of the first Irish mayors, Garrison, and Domingo Sarmiento, Argentina's greatest president, who travelled as a young man to Boston to visit Horace Mann and to study the educational system he would later transplant to his homeland. In his 1847 *Travels in the United States,* he said such nice things about the Athens of America that the Bostonians were moved to erect this statue. The Avenue starts at Arlington Street, at the Public Garden. To the left, the *Arlington Street Church,* mother church of the Unitarians, shows how true Boston in 1867 remained to the architectural taste of 150 years before (Trinity Church on Copley Square, built in 1872, will in its turn show how fast things changed). Another interesting church, the *First and Second Church* on Berkeley at Marlborough, a descendant of the original 1630 church, was burned down in 1970 and its ruins were incorporated into the modern reconstruction by architect Paul Rudolph. Around the corner at 137 Beacon Street, the *Gibson House* has been restored to its Victorian origins and is open to the public (Tuesday to Sunday; 2pm-5pm).

On Commonwealth Avenue itself, the most impressive building is the Second Empire *Hotel Vendome* at Dartmouth Street. South of the Avenue, Back Bay becomes increasingly commercial. *Boylston Street* is a fashionable shopping area. At Hartford

Street a fine old police station has been converted into the *Institute of Contemporary Art*(*).

*Copley Square* and environs divides its space between culture and insurance companies; much of this area south of Boylston once was a railroad yard, redeveloped in the '50s with some of the city's tallest buildings in the huge Prudential Center project. Copley Square itself has three of Boston's landmarks; the first to be built, in 1872, was *Trinity Church,* the ponderous masterpiece of the Romanesque Revival and of its leading exponent, H. H. Richardson (another Richardson work nearby is the *First Baptist Church* at Commonwealth and Clarendon, with sculptural work by Frederic Bartholdi). There's some trickery involved in juggling the Romanesque styles of France, Spain, England and elsewhere in one building, but here it works; inside, some of the stained-glass windows are the work of William Morris's shop, from paintings by Sir Edward Burne-Jones.

Nowhere, perhaps, more than Copley Square did the Pre-Raphaelites get more of a chance to create public art, for directly across the square – behind McKim, Mead and White's façade of the great *Boston Public Library* – is a hall with suitably transcendent murals by Puvis de Chavannes and, upstairs in another room, Edwin A. Abbey's series of murals on the legend of the Holy Grail. Pick up one of the green cards on the centre table for Henry James's interpretation of this version of the Galahad legend. Behind the building, a 1972 addition by Philip Johnson houses most of the library's collections.

The third landmark, the *John Hancock Building* should never have been built; the weight of a 740-ft tower (Boston's tallest) on the Back Bay landfill caused the streets and pipes to buckle, and made Trinity Church start to sink. Although its architects claimed that its blue glass skin, reflecting the buildings around it, would make it practically invisible, it has ruined once and for all the aesthetics of a beautiful city square. For its arrogance, Providence repaid the John Hancock by making it, for a while, the world's first plywood skyscraper; hundreds of the large glass panes popped out every time the wind blew, so the holes were boarded up. Eventually all of the glass – several acres of it – had to be replaced. There's a wonderful view from the *John Hancock Observatory* at the top, with historical exhibits and shows; you can pick out Boston's landmarks on the horizon while the voice of Walter Muir Whitehall, historian and ardent lover of his city, explains them on tape (open Monday to Saturday, 9am-11pm, Sunday 10am-11pm; admission $2.00).

There was once a fourth monument on Copley Square, the massive, Gothic, original Museum of Fine Arts; when Gothic went out, it was abandoned for the Fenway. And before the square was built, the land was host to the biggest party Boston ever threw, the 1869 Peace Jubilee, brainchild of an Irish immigrant and America's favourite bandmaster before John Philip Sousa, the great Patrick S. Gilmore. A wooden coliseum was erected to seat 50,000; Johann Strauss's and everyone else's orchestra came for a week of concerts, some of which had over a thousand performers tooting and warbling at once. The Anvil Chorus from *Il Trovatore* was done with half the Boston Fire Department in full dress banging on anvils, and an orchestra of 600 played the William Tell Overture. They even made money on it.

Boston's second tallest building, the *Prudential Center,* also has an observation deck (open Monday to Thursday 9am-11pm, Friday to Saturday 9am-midnight, Sunday 10am-11pm; admission); its great advantage over its competitors is that, from here, you don't have to look at the Prudential Center. Every cliché of the monumental ugliness of the 1950s and '60s can be studied in this complex – it has everything but tailfins. Crossing Belvedere Street takes you from Boston's worst to Boston's best, the *Christian Science World Headquarters.* Around the dome of the 1894 mother church, this sect, now best known for their excellent national newspaper, the *Christian Science Monitor,* has constructed a colonnade and office tower, with a foundation and reflecting pool, all by I. M. Pei, with the effortless dignity of a Venetian piazza. Next door there's the *Massachusetts Horticultural Society,* and across the street the Boston Symphony plays at *Symphony Hall.*

**The Fenway.** This is another landfill project; before 1880 the little Muddy River flowed into the Charles through what were called the Back Bay Fens. Then, Frederick Law Olmsted, employed by the newly created Park Commission, incorporated them into his Emerald Necklace while keeping much of their swampy charm. The area is packed with colleges, large and small, hospitals and museums, and other institutions like the Boston Latin School, descendant of America's first high school, whose alumni include Benjamin Franklin and John Adams.

*Kenmore Square,* back of the Back Bay, is a typical Boston 'Square', meaning it isn't a square at all, but an intersection of two broad streets (Commonwealth and Beacon). This is a busy district, with clubs and restaurants mildly seedy in the way that the student clientele prefers. Along the river to the west stretches *Boston University,* biggest of all the city's colleges; its campus, like that of MIT across the river, is a permanent exhibition of some of the most adventurous contemporary architecture. South of the Mass Pike is another hallowed shrine, more venerated even than Revere's house or Boston Garden: it's *Fenway Park,* the paradisaical green pastures of the Boston Red Sox. If you can get a seat – it's old and small – this is the best place in the American League to watch a ball game. Across the Fens, where the Muddy still flows under stone bridges by Richardson, are several small colleges, the *Isabella Stewart Gardner Museum*(*) and the *Museum of Fine Arts*(*). The little street alongside the latter, Louis Prang Street, is named for the printer of the first Christmas card; Boston neglects none of her worthy sons.

Beyond the institutions, the Emerald Necklace continues, bordered by boulevards, the Riverway and the Jamaicaway, to the pretty *Jamaica Pond* in the neighbourhood of Jamaica Plain (where Curley lived). As with the Jamaica in New York, nobody can explain the name; some speculate that it came from the British capture of that island in 1655, or else that it has something to do with rum. Just west of all this is the large, independent suburb of *Brookline,* a wealthy, leafy place that has carefully managed to avoid being swallowed up by Boston for over a century. At 83 Beals Street, off Beacon, is the *John F. Kennedy National Historic Site,* where the President was born in 1917 (open daily 9am-4.30pm; admission). The old centre of Brookline is just north of Boylston Street; the *Puppet Show Place* at Station Street is the headquarters of the New England Guild of Puppetry, with shows every weekend.

**South End.** Washington Street was the original road to Boston over the neck to the peninsula. As Boston grew, this area just over the neck, off Washington and Tremont Streets, competed with the Back Bay to be the home of Boston's newly wealthy, and speculation ran wild in ornate row houses on newly built residential squares. Then a strange thing happened; the Panic of 1873 broke the speculative bubble, and the terrified elite began to pour out of the district as fast as they had poured in – status is such a fragile thing. George Apley's Brahmin father (in the book by J. P. Marquand) realized it was time to go when he saw a man in shirtsleeves sitting on his front steps. The South End rapidly became a polyglot neighbourhood of small flats and rooming houses. Its revival has come only in the last two decades, and the mix of the young middle class and blacks, Puerto Ricans, Arabs, winos and various others, has made it one of the most interesting parts of Boston. It is also one of the most politically aware neighbourhoods anywhere; it gained national attention in the 1960s during a tremendous struggle with the city and the

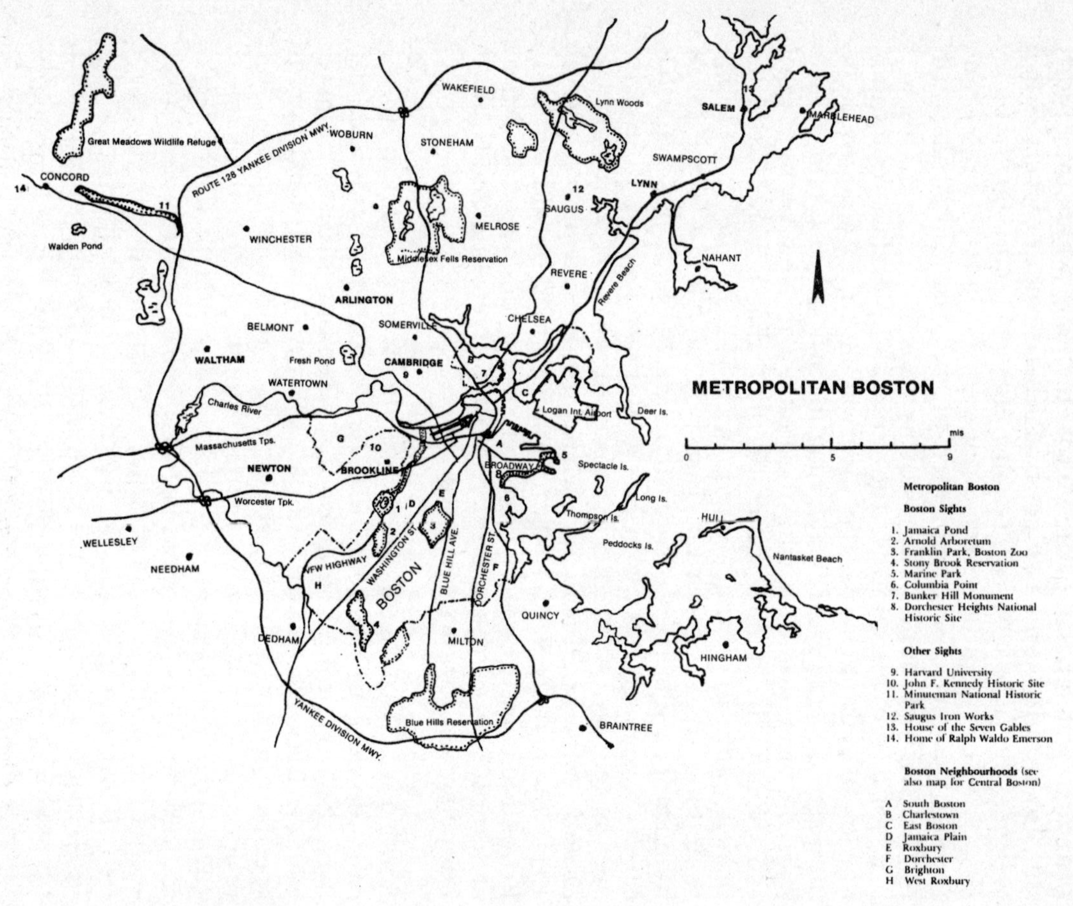
METROPOLITAN BOSTON
0
5
9
mls
Metropolitan Boston
Boston Sights
1. Jamaica Pond
2. Arnold Arboretum
3. Franklin Park, Boston Zoo
4. Stony Brook Reservation
5. Marine Park
6. Columbia Point
7. Bunker Hill Monument
8. Dorchester Heights National Historic Site
Other Sights
9. Harvard University
10. John F. Kennedy Historic Site
11. Minuteman National Historic Park
12. Saugus Iron Works
13. House of the Seven Gables
14. Home of Ralph Waldo Emerson
Boston Neighbourhoods (see also map for Central Boston)
A South Boston
B Charlestown
C East Boston
D Jamaica Plain
E Roxbury
F Dorchester
G Brighton
H West Roxbury
CONCORD
Great Meadows Wildlife Refuge
Walden Pond
ROUTE 128 YANKEE DIVISION MWY.
WOBURN
WAKEFIELD
STONEHAM
WINCHESTER
MELROSE
Middlesex Fells Reservation
Lynn Woods
SALEM
MARBLEHEAD
SWAMPSCOTT
LYNN
SAUGUS
NAHANT
REVERE
Revere Beach
CHELSEA
ARLINGTON
BELMONT
SOMERVILLE
WALTHAM
Fresh Pond
CAMBRIDGE
WATERTOWN
Charles River
Massachusetts Tps.
NEWTON
BROOKLINE
Worcester Tpk.
WELLESLEY
NEEDHAM
Logan Int. Airport
Deer Is.
BROADWAY
Spectacle Is.
Long Is.
Thompson Is.
Peddocks Is.
HULL
Nantasket Beach
HINGHAM
QUINCY
VFW HIGHWAY
WASHINGTON ST.
BOSTON
BLUE HILL AVE
DORCHESTER ST
DEDHAM
MILTON
Blue Hills Reservation
BRAINTREE
YANKEE DIVISION MWY.

Redevelopment Authority over new construction and the lack of good housing, which resulted in 'Tent City', a week-long squatter's party on a vacant lot. The neighbourhood's success has made it possible for it to remain, for the time being, a diverse community with room for rich and poor alike.

Apart from its diversity, the area's main attraction is its abundance of fine restored residential squares, built in the fashion of Louisburg Square. *Union Park,* and *Chester Square,* north of Tremont, *Rutland Square* and *Concord Square* are the best of them. On the other hand *East Berkeley Street* has some of the last surviving tenements in Boston. The *Piano Craft Guild* on Tremont and Northampton, once a piano factory, was once the largest building in the nation save only the US Capitol, and now it has been beautifully restored – as apartments. Also on Tremont, at Clarendon, the *Boston Center for the Arts* is headquarters for almost a dozen performing arts groups; its home includes the round 1884 Cyclorama Building, built to house the huge 'cyclorama' painting of the Battle of Gettysburg (now returned to Gettysburg) and the adjacent National Theater, a restored Vaudeville palace. The Syrian and Lebanese communities have their shops and social clubs a block south on Shawmut Avenue, and one more block south is Boston's Catholic see, the impressive *Cathedral of the Holy Cross.*

The South End has an interesting past, with the likes of John L. Sullivan, Edwin Booth, Alexander Graham Bell, Childe Hassam and Gelett Burgess (who wrote 'The Purple Cow' and invented the world 'ballyhoo') living or working here. Now, as long as its diverse inhabitants continue to work together, it also has a future.

**Charlestown.** Founded in 1629, Charlestown is a year older than Boston, though it was absorbed into the city well over a century ago. The years have not been kind to this neighbourhood; vast freeway interchanges have recently rendered much of it desolate. Many parts of it survive as that now rarest of American communities, the working-class Irish, and a stronghold of the anti-busing zealots. Many streets with some of the oldest and finest homes in Boston have been gradually restored in the last decade, and after a long decline Charlestown is on its way up again.

The *Charlestown Navy Yard*(*), now a National Historical Site with the famous 'Old Ironsides', once employed much of the neighbourhood from its beginning to its last gasp in World War II when the old yards cranked out almost a ship a week for Uncle Sam. Across the freeway are the lovely *Winthrop Square* and, south of Main Street, *Town Hill,* the oldest settlement in Charlestown, where the 18th-century *Harvard Place* and the 20th-century *Harvard Mall* (both just off Harvard Street) recall the benefactor of the great university, who was a preacher here. At Main and Winthrop is the *John Larkin House,* home of the church deacon who let Paul Revere borrow his horse.

Just around the corner, a long stately row of restored townhouses, *Monument Avenue* leads up to *Monument Square* on Bunker Hill, where, in a battle whose importance was more symbolic than strategic, the new American army first proved itself capable of standing up to the British. Any Schoolboy, that infamous know-it-all, will try and tell you this battle was really fought on Breed's Hill, but since both were summits of the same mount not much more than a block apart, it doesn't make much difference. On that morning of 17 June 1775, the colonials were just ending one of their favourite tricks, the instant midnight fortification, when the British caught on, and immediately gathered half their garrison in Boston for what they thought would be an easy capture. In successive waves of assault, marching up the hill in disciplined formation, the British were cut to pieces by the minuteman sharpshooters under the inspired leadership of Colonel Prescott and the hero of the day, Joseph Warren, a Boston physician turned general, who died in the eventual retreat. After the first few attacks, the badly outnumbered defenders were down to shooting nails, socks and their buttons, and Bunker Hill/Breed's Hill was finally taken. The patriots, too clever by half for General Howe, had accomplished their purpose; they had lost a few men, the British over a thousand. The final word on the Battle of Bunker Hill came from the American General Greene: 'I wish I could sell them another hill at the same price.'

The tall obelisk in the centre of Monument Square was erected in the 1820s to commemorate the fight; it offers a view of downtown Boston and the harbour, as well as exhibits relating to the event. Every year on 17 June the battle is re-enacted by local citizens. A final, offbeat Charlestown attraction is the 17th-century *Philips Street Burial Ground,* just a block south of Main Street. The cemetery is a miniature plan of the town, with everyone buried in the plot corresponding to their house lot. Among the interesting old headstones is the monument to John Harvard, erected by the city in 1828 over his grave.

Across the Mystic River from Charlestown, the northernmost part of the city, *East Boston* was once an island like Shawmut and Charlestown; now it's a predominately Italian neighbourhood with many of Boston's docks and *Logan International Airport* built out into the harbour on landfill. In the 1840s and '50s, East

Boston's shipyards were busy places, creating much of the city's prosperity. Boston was also turning out bold experiments in ship design, with the famous clippers of Donald McKay, an engineering genius and artist whose creations, such as the *Flying Cloud,* were not only the fastest sailing ships ever built but also the most beautiful.

**South Boston,** or 'Southie', as it is affectionately known to its inhabitants and to those who, at least on St Patrick's Day, wish they were. Southie's proper citizen, as the saying goes, is 'born on A Street, grew up on B Street, went to school on C Street . . . ' and if he's old and crazy he'll be a member of the L Street Brownies, who take a dip in the ocean each January if it's cold enough. No place could be more Irish (though among the other people who live here are a sizable number of Albanians), and no place has such a reputation for being an old-fashioned ethnic city neighbourhood with a sense of community. It has its warts, however; during the 1960s South Boston High School became known to Americans for its ugly and fierce resistance to integration.

With a great loss of population to the suburbs, South Boston has become somewhat rundown. Past Irish mayors took good care of the neighbourhood; Southie has its own little Emerald Necklace of parks and beaches on its ocean shore. On G Street is South Boston High School, and just behind it is Thomas Park. This is *Dorchester Heights,* where Washington planted the cannons that chased the King's troops from Boston in 1776. The cannons were captured at Fort Ticonderoga and dragged two hundred miles through the wilderness to Cambridge, where the Americans wrapped their wheels in straw and quietly rolled them up here at night – another nasty surprise for General Howe. A monument in Thomas Park marks the spot. 'Evacuation Day' in March is conveniently close enough to St Patrick's Day for South Boston to combine them for its annual festival, celebrated with a parade along Broadway, the main street of the district.

South of Southie, there's a small peninsula called *Columbia Point,* with a campus of the University of Massachusetts, the *John F. Kennedy Library*(*) and a huge, infamous 'instant ghetto' housing project of the 1950s, already largely abandoned. Beyond these are the three-decker neighbourhoods of Savin Hill and Dorchester sprawling out towards the city limits.

**Roxbury.** Roxbury too was one of the original Puritan foundations, the town on the other side of the Neck from Boston. The community grew slowly but gradually, and its hilly topography created a wildly meandering street plan. In the 1950s Roxbury became the home of Boston's most recent immigrants, poor blacks from the south, whose inability to gain a foothold in Boston's politics and economy has made this the city's most neglected neighbourhood. In the last decade, however, Roxbury has become one of the most organized and sophisticated of the nation's hard-core ghettos, and has shown impressive progress in redeveloping itself. The Roxbury Action Program, a community group that has provided a model for others across the country, and the National Center for Afro-American Artists are only two of the neighbourhood's modern success stories.

Among the bright new housing developments and crumbling commercial strips are some reminders of Roxbury's past. *Eliot Square,* on Roxbury Street between Washington and Columbus, has some fine old buildings, including the 1632 *First Church,* the oldest frame church in Boston, though it was rebuilt several times; a few blocks north, at the top of a hill offering a view over Boston is Highland Park, with a beautiful high-Victorian stone water-tower, the *Fort Hill Tower,* a landmark visible for miles around. The interesting *Roxbury Civic Center* (designed by the same architects as City Hall) has been constructed to serve as a new centrepiece for the neighbourhood.

The southern end of Roxbury is the northern edge of the biggest jewel in Olmsted's Emerald Necklace, *Franklin Park;* as in New York's Central Park, Olmsted's unfailing instinct for the picturesque is given full play. Everyone in Boston is awaiting the opening of the new, remade *Boston Zoo* in the park. It promises to take its place among the most innovative and well designed zoos of America, but for now only a few displays are open to the public (10am-4.30pm; free). The next link in the 'necklace' lies towards Jamaica Plain, the *Arnold Arboretum,* owned by Harvard and also laid out by Olmsted. If you're in Boston in May or June, when the thousands of flowers and trees are in bloom, don't miss it. Far beyond Roxbury, in the southwestern corner of the city, is West Roxbury. Here the Charles River, which seems so majestic and important from the Back Bay, gives away its secret; after wandering through the western suburbs it appears here again as a small shallow stream, among the ponds and brooks of West Roxbury and Dedham that are its source. Though not a trace of the site remains, the area here by the riverside was America's most famous communal experiment, *Brook Farm,* in the 1840s. Much of the Transcendentalism's inclination to woolly-mindedness found an outlet here. Founded by George Ripley as a combined working farm and philosophical academy, Brook Farm attracted most of the leading Boston intellectuals to stay, or at least to visit. Arcadian virtue flourished, but even with Nathaniel Hawthorne keeping the books, he who was the terror of every ship's captain when he worked in the Boston customs house, it never achieved financial success. A fire in 1846 destroyed the main building, which the residents had built themselves, and brought the experiment to an end; those who had lived there, with an unaffected joyfulness and 'leisure to live in all the faculties of the soul', trickled back to Boston.

## Cambridge

If Boston is not the intellectual capital of the nation, then Cambridge is, for the presence of Harvard University and, increasingly, for the Massachusetts Institute of Technology. But there is more to Cambridge than these; it is a city of 100,000 people, with working-class districts of Italians, Poles and Portuguese. Thirty years ago, much of the city was tired and decaying, but now, with the spectacular growth of the university communities, everyone wants to live here. Cambridge has become a crowded, colourful mix of students, former students, ethnics and the loose ends of the eastern states and several nearby continents. Cambridge is like California for its diversity, its tolerance, and for being a few jumps ahead of the rest of the nation, but Cambridge is a California with substance.

The Red Line of the MBTA passes through Kendall Square (MIT), Central Square and Harvard Square, and is presently being extended westwards; this is how you should go to Cambridge, for traffic and parking are even more discouraging than in Boston. Massachusetts Avenue is the main street. After crossing the broad Charles River Basin at the Back Bay, it follows the subway line across Cambridge from east to west.

Cambridge is just as old as Boston. John Winthrop founded it as 'Newtowne', on a defensible inland site, to serve as capital for the Massachusetts Bay Colony. The leader of the church in Newtowne was Thomas Hooker, whose disagreements with the colony's rulers caused him to leave it in 1635. Taking almost all of Newtowne's population with him, he settled at New Haven and founded Connecticut; thus did Cambridge become the mother of an American state. With no one left behind to transact business, the Puritans moved the seat of government back to Boston, gave Newtowne its modern name – after the town where many of them had attended university and where they had planned their colony and drafted its laws – and founded the first American university, for the training of future Puritan clergymen. The statue of John Harvard in Harvard Yard refers to him as the founder of the school, but that isn't quite true. John Harvard had nothing to do with the founding, but he left his library and half his sizable fortune to the new school, and so it was named for him. In 1775, Cambridge served as headquarters for the patriot forces besieging Boston, and here George Washington took command of the new army.

The great *Massachusetts Institute of Technology,* on the northern bank of the Charles Basin, makes a perfect balance to Harvard. It is younger, and no ivy clings to its steel and concrete walls. MIT first gained prominence before and during World War II, under its president Carl Compton, as it leaped into the vanguard of scientific and technological advance, and it has contributed much to the government's nuclear and aerospace programs. Anyone who thinks MIT is all business, however, should note the marks painted across the Harvard Bridge over the Charles; these measure the bridge in 'smoots', a new unit of length developed at this school when the physicists of tomorrow tanked up Smoot, a 5′9″ freshman, put a football helmet on his head and rolled him, end to end, the length of the bridge, tallying 369.4 'smoots'. MIT students, with their calculators in belt holsters like six-guns, are as celebrated for their silliness as for their advanced research accomplishments. The sprawling campus contains some first class contemporary architecture, notably the *Kresge Auditorium* by Eero Saarinen and Alvar Aalto's undergraduate dormitories on Memorial Drive on the riverside.

North of MIT is the ethnic enclave of East Cambridge and, to the west, *Harvard Univeristy,* two miles down Massachusetts Avenue in the old centre of Cambridge. While touring Cambridge, you may stop and let Cambridge come to you at *Harvard Square* (Massachusetts at Peabody), easily one of the most interesting and delightful urban settings anywhere. All around are some of America's finest bookstores, shops and popular student restaurants, and all manner of street folk, people with a religious or political cause to sell, and – especially at night, when it's marginally quieter – musicians in the 'T' shop entrances and storefronts offering both the familiar and exotic. The new glass block facing the square is *Holyoke Center,* where the *Harvard University Information* can fill you in on the sights and coming events. Everything north and east of the square is *Harvard Yard,* a properly leafy academic background. Here, in the 1726 *Wadsworth House,* facing Massachusetts Avenue, was Washington's headquarters in 1775. Behind it, the oldest buildings of Harvard line the Green; *Massachusetts Hall* (1718), *Harvard Hall* (1764) and *University Hall* (Bulfinch, 1813), in front of which stands, or rather sits, the statue of John Harvard to whom the faculty in procession each Commencement Day doff their hats. Another green waits behind University Hall; here are *Sever Hall,* another lovely work by H. H. Richardson, and *Widener Library,* the biggest library of any kind in the United States, with over nine million volumes.

Along Quincy Street to the east are the *Fogg Art Museum*(*) and next to it the *Carpenter Center for the Visual Arts,* Le Corbusier's only work in America. Until the 1940s, when Walter Gropius came to teach here after his exile from Germany, Harvard was never very adventurous in its architecture, but since 1949, when Gropius designed the *Harvard Graduate Center* (on Everett Street), not only has Harvard collected an example of seemingly every possible experiment in design, but Cambridge itself has become the architectural centre of the US with over fifty firms. One of the experiments stands a block north on Quincy, the glass half pyramid of *Gund Hall.* Something very different across the street is the Victorian fantasy of *Memorial Hall,* with drama and concerts in its Sanders Theater. The *Busch-Reisinger Museum*(*) of German art is at the end of Quincy, with the *Harvard University Museums*(*) just behind it on Oxford Street.

The small teardrop-shaped *Cambridge Common* on Massachusetts at Concord Street is almost as old as the town itself; this is the site where Washington took command of the patriot troops, a year and a day before the Declaration of Independence. The 1760 *Christ Church,* the cemetery of the early settlers, and the small, pretty yard of *Radcliffe College* are all on Garden Street, the southern border of the Common. In the days when sexual segregation was thought to be essential to education, Radcliffe was the female counterpart of Harvard, but today the courses and student bodies of the two schools are integrated. A walk directly across Radcliffe Yard will take you to *Brattle Street,* the high-rent district of colonial Cambridge, which for the proclivities of its residents in the Revolution earned the name Tory Row. A number of colonial mansions remain, as well as some of their Victorian-era counterparts. The oldest of them is at No. 105, the *Henry Wadsworth Longfellow House* (1759) where America's favourite 19th-century poet lived for 45 years (a National Historical Site; open daily 9am-4.45pm; admission). Longfellow taught languages at Harvard for many years. From the house, the remains of the original estate, now Longfellow Park, stretch down to the river. Longfellow's 'spreading chestnut tree' by the way, stood just down the street at No. 54.

Back towards Harvard Yard, the area south of Massachusetts Avenue is filled with the university's huge quadrangle dormitories. At 54 Brattle Street is the *American Repertory Theater,* one of expected, is full of innovative theatre, and also one of the best places on the East Coast to catch the movies, domestic or foreign that will never come to your home town. On Mount Auburn Street, or rather in the middle of it, stands a wonderful fake neo-Dutch confection, the *Harvard Lampoon Castle,* home of the wits for whom the term 'sophomoric humor' was probably invented and who would probably gracefully accept it.

## Museums in Boston and Cambridge

**Boston Fire Museum:** 20 Eustis Street, Roxbury (open Monday to Friday 9am-5pm, weekends 10am-4pm; free). Firemen, like your favourite aunt, never throw anything away. Boston has had its great firemen, in their droopy moustaches, also a dozen Great Fires, the last in 1872. Old equipment, mementos and models are displayed in a restored 1819 firehouse.

**Busch Reisinger Museum:** 29 Kirkland Street, Cambridge (open Monday to Saturday 9am-4.45pm; free). A unique museum specializing in art of Germany and Central Europe, with a small collection of very high quality. The Middle Ages are covered particularly well, with the 11th-century doors from St Michael's church in Hildesheim and other expensive German medieval sculpture. There are several rooms of Renaissance and Baroque German art, but the museum is proudest of its collection of 19th and 20th-century German painting, the most extensive in America, where you can be introduced to, or reacquainted with, artists like Barlach and Feininger, often neglected in American museums.

**Charlestown Navy Yard:** just across the Washington Avenue Bridge in Charlestown (open daily 9am-5pm, 9.30am-4.30pm in the winter; admission). From 1799 until its closing in 1975, as part of the government's policy of moving all military installations to the Sunbelt, the Charlestown Navy Yard built ships for every American war. The buildings are maintained as a National Historic Site, and you may tour the old drydocks, the quarter-mile-long rope walk built in 1834, and the various workshops. Of special interest are the two ships maintained as part of the museum, the World War II destroyer *Cassin Young* and America's most famous warship, the USS *Constitution*, built in 1797. Throughout the War of 1812, this vessel regularly mugged the Royal Navy, whose sailors gave it its nickname 'Old Ironsides' from its stout oaken hull that made cannonballs bounce. You may inspect the ship, which has now been rebuilt three times after periods of neglect, and visit the Constitution Museum on shore, devoted to the ship's long proud history.

**Children's Museum:** Museum Wharf (open Tuesday to Sunday 10am-5pm, Fridays until 9, daily 10am-6pm in July and August; $3.50). In an old warehouse, just behind the giant Milk Bottle, is a colourful, fun place much like the Children's Museum in Brooklyn, to participate in, not just look at, exhibits from fond old things to up-to-date technological gadgetry.

**Fogg Art Museum:** Quincy Street, on the Harvard campus (open Monday to Friday 9am-5pm, Saturdays, 10am-5pm, Sundays 2pm-5pm; free). From its huge collection, including Impressionists, Italian painting and classical works, the Fogg chooses changing exhibits in co-ordination with Harvard's art classes. This is the largest college art museum in the country.

**Isabella Stewart Gardner Museum:** 280 Fenway (open Tuesday 1pm-9.30pm, Wednesday to Sunday 1pm-5.30pm; admission). This is the house that 'Mrs Jack' built, a genuine 'Eye-talian' palace packed with some great art and an infinity of clutter. Mrs Jack, a New York girl who married a wealthy Boston merchant, became the great lady of Boston in spite of being a beer-drinking Buddhist with a pet lion and a life filled with amorous sins, in repentance of which she annually scrubbed the steps of a neighbourhood church. There's nothing that says an eccentric widow can't be a clever art collector, especially if she has a few million to spend on it; she got her start after a nervous breakdown, when her doctor advised her to take up a hobby. In her palace are superior works of Titian, Vermeer, Botticelli, and others, also many of the greatest 19th-century American artists, though you'll need to search carefully among the rooms crowded with antiques, bric-a-brac and forgettable paintings. Every item is exactly where Mrs Jack placed it; if anything is ever moved, according to her will, the entire collection must be sold and the money given to Harvard.

**Harvard University Museum:** Oxford Street, off Kirkland on the Harvard campus (open Monday to Sunday 9am-4.30pm, Sundays 1pm-4.30pm; admission). Four museums in one: the *Peabody Museum of Archaeology*, with cultures of the world represented; the *Mineral and Geological Museum*, the *Museum of Comparative Zoology*, with dinosaurs and mastodons, and the *Botanical Museum* with a famous collection of glass flowers.

**Institute of Contemporary Art:** 955 Boylston Street, near Prudential Center (open Tuesday to Saturday 10am-5pm, Sundays 12pm-5pm; admission). Temporary exhibitions, concerts and films.

**John Fitzgerald Kennedy Library:** Columbia Point, Dorchester (open daily 9am-5pm; admission). Lately, America's tribute to her past presidents has taken the form of such depositories of Presidential documents and memorabilia. There's a film, and exhibits.

**Museum of Fine Arts:** Huntington Avenue at the Fenway (open Tuesday to Sunday 10am-5pm; admission). This is a great comprehensive collection; though not as large as its counterparts in New York, Philadelphia or Washington, it has a number of specialities that make it worth a visit, notably American painters; Gilbert Stuart, and Bostonian John Singleton Copley, and American decorative arts. Paul Revere, when he wasn't rousing the countryside, was the most skilled silversmith in the colonies, and many of his works are here. The Egyptian and Greek collection are outstanding, and those of Chinese and Japanese art are among the best to be found anywhere. Japanese art got its introduction to Boston, and to America, soon after that country was reopened to trade, when two Harvard zoologists on an expedition became enthralled with the beauty of Japan's painting and costume and began sending some home.

**Museum of Science:** on the Charles River Dam, between Boston and Cambridge (open Monday to Thursday 9am-4pm, Fridays 9am-10pm, Saturdays 9am-5pm, Sundays 10am-5pm; $4.00). Formerly the Museum of Natural History, it now combines exhibits on the world's flora and fauna with expositions of the sciences. There's lots of gadgetry to play with, including a giant Van de Graff generator to make your hair stand up.

**Museum of Transportation:** at Museum Wharf, in the same building as the Children's Museum, 300 Congress Street (open daily 10am-5pm; $3.50). This museum began with the antique car collection of a wealthy Bostonian named Larz Anderson, who bought one every year starting in 1898 and kept them all. Besides the cars, there are examples and exhibits covering every means a Bostonian has used to move around for the past 350 years, some of which they'll let you ride on.

**New England Aquarium:** Central Wharf, near the end of State Street (open Monday to Thursday 9am-5pm, Friday 9am-9pm, weekends 9am-6pm; $4.00). A brand new building, and one of Boston's most popular attractions. Seven thousand fishes want to tell you their stories, along with penguins, seals and otters. Exhibits spiral upwards around a huge glass-walled tank three storeys tall, where you can watch an intrepid diver feed the sharks and sea turtles, and trained seal and dolphin shows in a big tank on a barge docked next door. Don't sit in the front two rows unless you're wearing a raincoat.

## Events in Boston

**Late January to early February:** *Chinese New Year,* in Chinatown.
**17 March:** *St Patrick's Day Parade and Evacuation Day,* South Boston, on Broadway.
**Third weekend in April:** *Boston Marathon*, the world's most famous footrace, 26 miles from suburban Hopkinton to Prudential Center; also, on 19-20 April, the *Re-enactment of Paul Revere's Ride* and the *Ancient and Honorable Artillery Company parade*, through the North End, all as part of the *Patriot's Day* celebrations.
**Third weekend in May:** *Cambridge River Festival*, at City Hall, in Cambridge.
**Last weekend in June:** *street fairs* in the Back Bay, Bay Village, and *Chinese Cultural Week.*
**15-17 June:** *Bunker Hill Day Parade* in Charlestown.
**July and August:** *Parish festivals* in the Italian North End; usually one every weekend.
**December:** *Christmas Lighting* of Boston Common.
**16 December:** *Boston Tea Party Re-enactment*, Congress Street Bridge.
**December:** *Christmas Revels* at Memorial Hall, Harvard, a medieval celebration and concerts; also Christmas carolling in Louisburg Square, Beacon Hill.

### Boston Restaurants

Locke-Ober***, 3 Winter Place; Café Budapest***, 90 Exeter Street (in Copley Square Hotel); Ritz Carlton***, Arlington & Newbury (also in hotel); Maison Robert***, 45 School Street; Bay Tower Room***, 60 State Street; Legal Sea Foods**, 64 Arlington; Genji**, 327 Newbury Street; Davio's**, 269 Newbury Street; Union Oyster House**, 41 Union Street; Brandy Pete's*, 82-84 Broad Street; No-Name*, 15½ Fish Pier; Shanghai*, 21 Hudson Street; Ida's*, 3 Mechanic Street;

Regina's*, 11½ Thatcher; Jacobs Wirth's*, 31 Stuart.
**In Cambridge:** The Voyagers***, 45½ Mount Auburn; Harvest***, 44 Brattle; The Peacock**, 5 Craigie Street; Wursthouse**, 4 Boyleston; Lucky Garden*, 282 Concord; Autre Chose**, 1105 Massachusetts Avenue; Averof*, 1924 Massachusetts Avenue; Elsie's Deli*, 71a Mount Auburn; Rendezvous*, 24 Holyoke.

## South of Boston

Contiguous with Boston's sprawl, **Quincy** (pronounced 'Quinzy') was a farming village when John and Abigail Adams bought a house in 1787, believing they would retire in it after John left his post as minister in Britain. As it was, they retired in it after his presidency, as did his son, John Quincy Adams; members of the Adams family lived in and added to it until 1906. Now the *Adams National Historical Site* (135 Adams Street) and maintained by the National Parks Service, it is one of the finest mansions in the state, with many family heirlooms and the priceless Adams library (guided tours daily 9am-5pm, 19 April to 10 November; small admission). John Hancock, 'Prince of Smugglers', was born not far away at 8 Adams Street, now the site of the *Quincy Historical Society Museum* in a former boys' academy raised by John Adams's estate. Built of Quincy granite (as are a number of structures in Boston, including the Bunker Hill Monument), its exhibits deal with the colourful history of the town (open Tuesday to Saturday 1pm-4pm).

Surrounded by commercial activity at Franklin and Independence Avenue, the *Birthplaces of John and John Quincy Adams* maintained their appearance when our second and sixth presidents were born there in the 18th century (open 9am-5pm 19 April to 1 October, closed Mondays; admission). On Quincy Square (from Boston) stands the church of the Adams family, *First Parish* (founded 1636; present structure, of Quincy granite, built in 1828). Beneath it in a crypt lie the tombs of John and John Quincy Adams and their wives.

Perhaps more famous today than any of the notable Adams family is another son of Quincy, Howard Johnson, whose orange roofs and ice cream are a mainstay of the American family vacation scene (it all began in 1925, in a Quincy drugstore).

**Hingham,** west on the Bay, claims the oldest wooden church in America still in use, the 1631 *Old Ship Church* on Main Street. Because its roof beams curve like a hull, some believe they came from an old ship (open July to Labor Day, Tuesday to Sunday 12pm-5pm, Sunday for services the rest of the year). A long state beach, **Nantasket** extends several miles out in Boston Bay, with the village of **Hull** at the tip where the first night baseball game was played in 1880 under electric lights (invented in 1879). Attractions include the old *Paragon Park*, Boston's Coney Island, with a Tunnel of Love (open end of May to Labor Day). In the summer there is a passenger and bike ferry to Nantasket beach from Boston (tel: 723-7800).

More fun for children and adults, the South Shore Music Circus in nearby **Cohasset** features summer celebrity performances (tel: 383-1400 for information). One of Boston's finest bedroom communities, Cohasset's lovely homes surround a splendid common. South along the shore we have **Scituate**, with its old homes, summer cottages, and the *Lawson Tower*, a 150-ft shingled watertower built in 1902 by an eccentric financier.

Inland, south of Boston, **Milton** lies on the edge of the metropolitan area and the *Blue Hills Reservation*, where activities include skiing, riding, swimming, hiking and camping. Canton and Adams Avenues have many fine homes and, on 215 Adams, the *Museum of the American China Trade,* in a mansion built by merchant Robert Bennet Forbes in 1833. This tells the fascinating story of the fortunes behind many of a Brahmin family, who sold opium to the Chinese in exchange for tea, silk and later porcelain, which was used as ship's ballast until its quality attracted notice (open Tuesday to Saturday 2pm-5pm; adults $4, under twelves $1.50). Be sure to see the view of Boston from Governor Hutchinson's Field across the street. Nearby **Canton** was named during the early days of the China trade, when someone noticed it was exactly on the other side of the globe from Canton, China. Engineer Whistler, father of painter James McNeil, built the *Canton Viaduct* (Neponset Street) in 1834, still used by trains today.

The eclectic *Kendall Whaling Museum*, at 27 Everett Street in **Sharon** (south of Canton), houses whaling memorabilia from Holland, Japan, England and elsewhere, making it an interesting side-dish to New Bedford's museum on local whaling (open Monday to Friday 1pm-4pm; admission). Industrial **Brockton**, the shoe city and home of heavyweight Rocky Marciano, may be reached via Route 27 from Sharon. It has a lovely park (*D. W. Field*) and the *Brockton Art Center* on Oak Street, with American Art Impressionists, changing exhibits and loans from the Museum of Fine Arts in Boston (open Tuesday to Sunday 1pm-5pm; admission).

**Whitman**, on the east side of Brockton, has an inexpensive amusement park, *King's Castle Land*, designed with the very young child in mind (open 10am-6pm, May to October) and a landmark of every American's childhood, Whitman's *Toll House* (1709), restaurant and birthplace of chocolate chip cookies, which you can buy here (junction of Routes 18 and 14).

Back towards the coast is **Marshfield**, no longer marshy, last home of New Hampshire lawyer Daniel Webster, who is buried here as well. In his little white *Law Office* Webster and Lord Ashburton settled the Aroostook War in 1842 by drawing the boundary between Canada and Maine. Nearby, the *Winslow House* (1699 and 1750) rates as one of Massachusetts' finest historic houses, with innumerable authentic furnishings, (both located on Webster & Careswell; open July to Labor Day, 10am-5pm, closed Tuesdays; admission).

Just south, on Plymouth Bay, **Duxbury** was founded by three well known Pilgrims: Myles Standish, John Alden and William Brewster. Standish's Cellar remains at *Myles Standish State Reservation* on Crescent Street, along with a 116-ft monument dedicated to him on Captain's Hill.

The *Duxbury Art Complex*, in an avant-garde glass building on Alden Street, contains Japanese ceramics and Shaker furnishings and changing exhibits (open Friday to Sunday 2pm-5pm; free). At no.105 *The John Alden House* (1653), lived in by his heirs into the 20th century, has been refurbished in 17th-century style (open July to Labor Day, 10am-5pm, closed Mondays; admission). About 150 years after Alden, the Aristotle Onassis of the Federal period, Ezra (King Caesar) Weston, shipbuilder and richest man in America, built his mansion at Powder Point, on King Caesar Road. Today the *King Caesar House* (1807) is a museum, with well preserved parlours (open mid June to Labor Day, 2pm-5pm, closed Mondays; admission).

The main attraction in the area, with both worthwhile and tacky offerings, is, of course, **Plymouth**, on Plymouth Bay where it all began when the Pilgrims landed in December 1620. That first winter the dead were buried on Coles Hill in the middle of the night, so the Indians wouldn't know how few remained; the Indians, however, welcomed them, and taught them how to survive. The Plymouth colonists ill-repaid the kindness of their friend Massasoit, when after his death they imprisoned his eldest son, who died in captivity; in revenge, his brother Philip began the war that ended Plymouth Colony's expansion. A short time later it was incorporated into Massachusetts Bay Colony.

Plymouth partly atoned for its mistreatment of the Indians when it gave 94 acres to former slave and Revolutionary War hero, Cato Howe, and three other black veterans to found the free settlement of **Parting Ways**, one of the first free black villages in America (1792-1840). Located near Kingston, you can still see the foundations of their homes and their graves. As an old summer resort, with a twenty-mile beach, Plymouth today claims to be 'Cranberry Capital' of the world. America's largest cranberry co-operative and retailer, Ocean Spray, has rehabilitated an old clam factory as the *Cranberry World Visitors' Center* (on Water Street) which, along with nearby *Plymouth Rock*, is notable as the only free site in town. Cranberry World, by a small working bog, has the inside dope on the tangy red berries native to this corner of the country, as well as a free sample (open daily June to September 10am-5pm; Wednesday to Sunday April to November). In between cranberries and Rock is an English-built replica of the tiny *Mayflower*, called *Mayflower II*, which sailed across the Atlantic like its predecessor in 1957. The guided tour gives an inkling of the misery on board (open July and August 9am-8pm, April to November 9am-5pm; admission).

Other sights near Plymouth Rock, in the clutter of souvenir stands, include the *Pilgrim Hall Museum* at Chilton and Court Streets, founded in 1824 and displaying original Pilgrim possessions, including Myles Standish's sword and furniture (open June to October 9.30am-5pm; admission); the *Antiquarian House*, 126 Water Street, built by a wealthy merchant in 1809 and furnished to the period with a toy and costume collection (Memorial Day to mid September 10am-5pm; admission); *Coles Hill*, up the steps from Plymouth Rock, where you'll find a statue of Massasoit and a view of the harbour; the *Plymouth National Wax Museum*, with 26 wax tableaux of Pilgrim History (March to November, 9am-5pm; July to Labor Day until 9.30 pm; admission), and the *Spooner House*, behind it on North Street, home of a prominent Plymouth family for 200 years (Memorial Day to mid September, 10am-5pm; admission). Other historic houses in Plymouth are nearby: *Harlow Old Fort House*, 119 Sandwich Street, built in 1677 from beams of the old Pilgrims' fort, with demonstrations of 17th-century crafts; *Howland House*, 33 Sandwich Street, also built in 1677, the only house in town that a Pilgrim actually lived in; and *Richard Sparrow House*, 42 Summer Street, built in 1640, with pottery demonstrations (all open Memorial Day to mid September, 10am-5pm; admission).

Probably the best place to get a feel for the life of the Pilgrim is the *Plimouth Plantation*, three miles south of Plymouth on Route 3A. A complete replica of the Pilgrims' village circa 1627, it takes you back via folks dressed like Pilgrims, doing Pilgrim chores, and chatting in Pilgrimese; children love it because you can touch everything, sit on the chairs and pet the pigs (open April to November 9am-5pm; adults $4, children $2).

If you come in the autumn, by no means miss a side trip to **Carver**, home of Massachusett's largest cranberry bogs. Around the beginning of October the bogs are flooded for the harvest, creating lakes of brilliant red by the fall foliage and blue autumn sky – Mother Nature's fauvist masterpiece. Through this runs the stream *Edaville Railroad* (Route 58, South Carver) on a five-mile track; other attractions here include a museum of train memorabilia, fire engines, petting farm, rides, barbecues etc (open daily June to Labor Day 10am-5.30pm; April Sundays; May weekends and holidays; Labor Day to October, Monday to Friday 10.30am-3pm, weekends and holidays 11pm-5am; mid November to first Sunday in January: Christmas Festival, 4pm-9pm weekdays, 2pm-9pm weekends; admission).

Along with Bridgeport, Connecticut, **Middleborough**, near Carver, is the place to go for midget memorabilia. Lavinia Bump Warren, wife of General Tom Thumb (of P.T. Barnum fame) was born here; after Tom died, she returned to Middleborough with a midget Italian Count as her new husband and ran a refreshment stand. The *Middleborough Historical* on Jackson Street contains memorabilia of her life, as well as local items (open Sunday/Wednesday/Friday 1pm-5pm, July and August).

'Silver City' **Tauton**, west of Middleborough, was founded by a women, Elizabeth Poole in 1637. Some of its famous silverware and an attic-like collection of other antiquities may be viewed at the *Old Colony Historical Society*, 66 Church Green (open Tuesday to Saturday 10am-4pm; admission). While you're here, ask directions to *Dighton Rock State Park*, south on the other side of the Tauton River. Dighton Rock, which has been puzzling scholars ever since Cotton Mather wrote of it in *The Wonderful Works of God Commemorated*, is a great hunk of sandstone carved with mysterious pictographs. Cotton thought they were the work of local Indians; later scholars have hypothesized Carthaginians, Phoenicians, Norsemen and Portuguese explorers as the authors. The various theories and their proofs line the walls of the building now sheltering the Rock, so you can decide for yourself which, if any, are correct.

Like nearby Rhode Island, **Attleboro** makes jewellery; it is also the headquarters of the Massachusetts Archaeological Society and their *Bronson Museum* above the Attleboro Trust Bank (8 North Street), containing prehistoric Indian finds from the state (open Monday/Wednesday/Thursday 9am-4pm; in summer Monday to Friday 9am-4pm; free).

**Fall River,** a small city on Mount Hope Bay, was a leading textile town from 1817 to 1930 when it had a hundred mills in operation; in the Depression abandonment and a great fire forced the city into bankruptcy. Today largely Portuguese, the home of small manufacturers and factory outlets, Falls River has three offerings for the visitor: *Battleship Cove*, well signposted, home of the battleship *Massachusetts*, the submarine *Lionfish* and the destroyer *Joseph P. Kennedy* (daily 9am-5pm; admission). Adjoining (same admission) is the *Marine Museum* on Water Street, with models and exhibits featuring great passenger ships of the past. At 451 Rock Street the *Fall River Historical Society*, in an 1843 granite mansion used as a stop in the Underground Railroad, has a large collection of items chronicling local history and the famous Lizzie Borden murders (open Tuesday to Friday 9am-4.30pm; Saturdays 9am-12pm, Sundays 2pm-4pm; free). *St Anne's Shrine* on Main Street is held in particular esteem by this country's French Canadians.

Between Fall River and New Bedford runs Route 6; just off it stands Paul Rudolph's *Southeastern Massachusetts University campus,* of futuristic design; several beaches line the south shore, among them *Demarest Lloyd State Park* (parking fee).

Fans of *Moby Dick* will instantly recognize **New Bedford** as the old whaling capital of North America, and although its fleet – New England's largest – may chase after more puny fare these days, New Bedford is still a salty town. Fortunately, when whaling ended in America, the town's waterfront was abandoned and commercial activity moved uphill, preserving it for the city fathers to fix up again; it's a charming, lively area, not a museum piece. The *Whaling Museum* (Johnny Cake Hill) contains a number of unique exhibits – the world's largest model whaling ship, in perfect half scale, and a quarter-mile long painting by a local artist depicting a whale chase in the Arctic – as well as paintings, figureheads, some very unusual harpoons and other tools of the trade, and one of the best scrimshaw collections anywhere (open Monday to Saturday 9am-5pm, Sundays 1pm-5pm, closed Mondays in off-season). Across the street, the *Seamen's Bethel* described by Melville in *Moby Dick* is still very much a fishermen's church, with plaques honouring those lost at sea. In the *Warfinger Building* by the State Pier, early risers can watch the scallop (6am) and the fish (7am) auctions every morning. New Bedford's 175 fishing boats bring in the third most valuable catch in the United States. On *County Street* parallel to Water Street are the grand mansions of the merchant princes of whaling.

Another New Bedford industry, art glass (almost as well known as its whales), has its museum as well. The *Glass Museum*, in a Federal-style mansion on Elm Street, houses a collection of locally made Pairpoint and Mount Washington Glass (open June to September, Monday to Saturday 9am-5pm, Sundays 1pm-5pm, closed Mondays and Tuesdays rest of the year). Retired firemen run the *Fire Museum* at Bedford and South Sixth Streets, and have made it particularly fun for children (open daily 9am-5pm; admission). The *New Bedford Free Public Library*, a fine granite, Greek Revival pile, has an extensive whaling collection, including a first edition of *Moby Dick* and some good paintings (City Hall Square).

From Leonard's Wharf, New Bedford, you can take the passenger ferry to **Cuttyhunk Island** (daily round trips in the summer, twice a week other times). One of the thirteen Elizabeth Islands, Cuttyhunk is the only one with a village, public transportation and a few places to stay; the other islands belong to wealthy Bostonians, all forming the town of Gosnold. Forty people live on Cuttyhunk, site of the first white settlement in Massachusetts, in 1602. Most tourists come to Cuttyhunk today for the superb game fishing.

East along the coast towards Cape Cod are **Mattapoisett** and **Wareham**, resort towns on Buzzards Bay. In the former, an added attraction is the *Mattapoisett Historical Society Museum* is an old church, with a good collection of just about everything, including whaling memorabilia (open July and August, Tuesday to Saturday 10am-12pm, and 2pm-4.30pm, at 5 Church Street). Wareham is famous for a Victorian summer colony at **Onset**, where you may stay in one of the old houses, or visit the *Cranberry Museum* (Routes 6 and 28) and learn about the history of the 'crane berry', named for the crane's neck shape of the blossoms (open end of June to Labor Day 9am-3.30pm; September to mid October weekends; admission).

**Restaurants.** *In Nantasket Beach:* Jake's Seafood**. *In Cohasset:* Red Lion Inn**, 71 Main. *In Scituate:* Harbor View*, 194 Front. *In Middleborough:* Tamarack**, Route 105. *In Plymouth:* The Vintage House***, Route 3A; Souza's**, Town Wharf; Bert's*, Warren Avenue. *In Whitman:* Toll House**, Routes 18 and 14. *In Fall River:* Sagres**, 181 Columbia Avenue. *In New Bedford:* Louie's***, 1776, Wharf; Freestones***, 41 William Street; Me & Ed's**, 30 Brook Street. *In Mattapoisett:* Mattapoisett Inn**, on the water.

## Cape Cod and Nantucket

Whence the great popularity of Cape Cod and its islands? Before World War II it was a backwater, its whaling days long gone, its famous Sandwich Glass industry closed sixty years, its population in rapid decline, while those who stayed fished and worked the cranberry bogs. After World War II, Cape Codders began to rent rooms to make ends meet, it was 'discovered' and real-estate values have been skyrocketing every since. Although it has gone commercial, it hasn't gone highrise, and there are certainly many spots left where you can soak up the atmosphere of quaint villages and sandy shore (particularly in the off season). Since 1961 much of the famous Great Beach, where Thoreau once wandered, is now the Cape Cod National Seashore, open to all and protected from development.

Outside the State Campground in Nickerson State Park, which takes campers on a first-come, first-served basis, note that it is virtually impossible to find any kind of accommodation on Cape Cod in the summer without a reservation. A point to remember when reserving a place, or when navigating on the Cape, is that each of the fifteen towns contains several villages, so look to your map.

The **Cape Cod Canal,** built by the Army Corp. of Engineers at Buzzards Bay (1909-14) divides the Cape from the mainland and enables ships to bypass the dangerous waters off Provincetown. On Academy Road in **Buzzards Bay** there is an information centre for the canal; when you cross it, keep an eye out for the beautiful railroad bridge – one of the largest vertical lift bridges in the world.

Route 6 is the main highway to Provincetown, passing through the middle of the Cape, while scenic Route 6A meanders along the north shore, facing *Cape Cod Bay*. This cold water 'Bay Side' of the Cape is the least commercial side, although it was the first settled. Westernmost of the towns along Route 6A, **Sandwich**, founded in 1637 and the oldest on the Cape, produced the famous Sandwich coloured glass, examples of which are often seen in museums, historic houses and antique shops, since the last glass was made in 1888. If you've never seen it, hie to the *Sandwich Glass Museum* on Main Street (open 9.30am-4.30pm daily, April to 1 November; admission). Children's author and naturalist Thorton W. Burgess, another unique product of this lovely town, is the subject of the nearby *Thorton W. Burgess Museum* (4 Water Street), stocked with a large collection of his works and their original illustrations (open May to September 10am-4pm, Sundays, 1pm-4pm; free). Other sites within easy walking distance in central Sandwich include *Hoxie House* on Water Street, the oldest on Cape Cod (1637), with period furnishings (open mid June to September, 10am-5pm, Sundays 1pm-5pm; admission); *Dexter's Mill*, built in 1654, where a miller demonstrates the workings of a gristmill (Main Street: open mid June to September, 10am-4pm, Sundays 1pm-5pm; admission); and *Yesteryear's Doll and Miniature Museum*, also on Main Street, featuring dolls from all countries and many centuries (open end of May to mid October, 10am-5pm, Sundays 1pm-5pm; admission). A whole day could easily be spent at *The Heritage Plantation of Sandwich* (Route 130), former estate of rhododendron-hybridizer Charles O. Dexter. Dexter's rhododendrons bloom from May to June; other features of the Plantation are a replica of a round Shaker Barn housing antique autos, an original 1800 windmill, museums featuring military items and miniatures, flags, folk art, a working antique carousel and Currier and Ives lithographs. Jitney buses provide transport within the plantation (open mid May to mid October 10am-5pm; adults $3, children $1.00). Several beaches in Sandwich are open to the public, among them *Scusset State Beach*, just on the other side of the canal.

To the east is **Barnstable**, largest town on Cape Cod, incorporating Hyannis and other villages on Nantucket Sound. On Bay Side, **West Barnstable** is the home of the Congregational *West Parish Meeting House,* on Route 149. Built in 1717 by New England's oldest parish (founded 1616), it is one of the grandest churches in the state. Barnstable itself has many large homes, once owned by codfish barons. They and other aspects of Barnstable's salty heritage are the subjects of the *Trayser Memorial Museum* (Route 6A) in a 1856 Customs House (open July to mid September, Tuesday to Saturday 1.30pm-4.30pm; admission).

**Yarmouth** and its various villages have become Cape Cod's retirement community; most of its attractions lie south on Nantucket Sound. Among the many old houses in Yarmouth proper, several have become museums, all on Route 6A in Yarmouthport. **Dennis**, next to the east, was the scene of Cape Cod's once profitable salt works; today, besides its beaches, the *Cape Playhouse* with summer 'name' entertainment (tel: 385-8000 for information) is the big attraction here; the *Cape Cinema* next door claims 'the largest ceiling mural in the world' (both are on Route 6A).

**Brewster** with its fancy homes has developed several commercial attractions, all on 'Cranberry Highway' (Route 6A). These are: *Sealand of Cape Cod*, with performing dolphins and sea lions (open daily 10am-9pm, closed Wednesdays 1 October to 1 June; admission; tel: 385-9252 for schedules); *New England Fire & History Museum*, starring a diorama of the Great Chicago Fire (open 10am-5pm; weekends only May to Memorial Day and mid September to Columbus Day; admission); *Cape Cod Museum of Natu-*

*ral History*, with local critters and a trail (open Monday to Saturday 10am-5pm, Sundays 12.30pm-5pm; in winter Tuesday to Saturday 9.30am-4.30pm; admission); and the *Drummer Boy Museum*, with lifesize painted scenes of the Revolutionary era (open 15 May to mid October, 9.30am-5pm; admission). The *Old Grist Mill*, on Stony Brook Road, grinds corn for visitors during July/August (open Wednesday/Friday/Saturday 2pm-5pm); upstairs is a small historical museum and nearby there is an alewife fish ladder, which the fish climb in the spring. *Nickerson State Park* by East Brewster mainly has activities for campers.

**Orleans**, transportation hub of the eastern 'Lower Cape' has a tad more history than most. A port of call for the 11th-century Vikings, relay station from 1879 for messages to New York from France, and the only town in the western hemisphere to suffer at the Kaiser's hands in World War I (a U-boat sank four coal barges just off shore), it is now one of the fastest growing towns in the Cape. The *French Cable Museum* (Route 28 and Cove Road), housed in the 1890 station building, contains an interesting collection on the relay station's history – it was used until 1959 (open July to 15 September, Tuesday to Saturday 2pm-4pm; admission). Orleans' *Nauset Beach*, part of the *Cape Cod National Seashore*, is one of the loveliest as well as the best for surf fishing. The National Seashore extends much of the length of the 'Lower Cape' from Provincetown to *Monomoy Island*, a National Wildlife Refuge.

In **Eastham** the *Salt Pond Visitor Center* offers a good orientation for the seashore (open daily 8am-6pm, and in the winter Thursday to Monday 8.30am-4.30pm). On Eastham's *First Encounter Beach* the Pilgrims came ashore on 6 December 1620, only to be chased off by the Indians. Another beach, belonging to the National Seashore, is *Marconi Beach*, just north in **Wellfeet**, from where Marconi laid the first trans-Atlantic cable in 1903; there is an interpretative site here explaining the feat. Wellfeet also has an *Audubon Wildlife Sanctuary* (open 8am to 8pm; admission charged for non-members) and the beginning of the *Great island Trail* through a primitive corner of the Cape. Dune-bound **Truro**, the next town north, is the site of two towers: the *Highland Lighthouse*, built on a sheer 150-ft cliff and one of the strongest lights on the coast, and the *Jenny Lind Tower*, brought here in 1927 from Boston, once part of an old train station. The Swedish Nightingale sang from here when Barnum oversold her concert, so everyone could hear.

At the tip of the cape, **Provincetown** was the first landing place of the Pilgrims, but settled by privateers and pirates who called it

'Cape Cod'; today everyone refers to it as 'P-town'. It has several identities; it is a well-preserved 18th-century village, inhabited by Portuguese fishermen; it is 'the whale-watching capital of the East' from where daily boats offer eyeball-to-eyeball encounters with humpback and right whales; it is the post-World War I 'Greenwich Village North' of intellectuals and writers, including Eugene O'Neill, whose works first played in the now-famous Provincetown Playhouse; it is today artsy-craftsy in the more affluent, post-hippie fashion, and attracts a sizable gay crowd.

Provincetown remembers its Pilgrim claim-to-fame with the *Pilgrim Monument and Museum* on Monument Hill (with fantastic views). The museum contains a wide variety of items, including souvenirs of MacMillan's Arctic expeditions (open mid June to mid September, 9am-9pm; in winter 9am-5pm; admission). The *Provincetown Heritage Museum* at Center and Commercial features local history (open June to October 10am-10pm; admission). Commercial, the main street, also has the *Provincetown Art Association and Museum* at no.460, where works by artists of the local art colony, in existence since 1900, are the main exhibits, with constant activities (open Thursday to Saturday 11am-5pm and 8am-10pm and Sunday 2pm-5pm in summer; donations). At no. 72, the *Seth Nickerson House*, built in 1746 by a ship's carpenter, incorporates items found from shipwrecks, with some unique results (open June to October 10am-5pm; admission).

The *Provincetown Playhouse*, on a wharf by the Town Hall, performs new plays and revivals, mainly of O'Neill, in a new building – the original was burned down in 1976. An adjoining museum houses memorabilia from the life of Eugene O'Neill, who lived in a garret in Provincetown before it become fashionable (for performance information, tel: 487-1750). The *Dolphin Fleet Whale Watch* leaves MacMillan Pier twice daily in the summer (off season, tel: 255-3857). On Race Point Road, the *Province Lands Visitor Center* has a number of exhibits, activities and information about this northernmost part of the National Seashore – the constantly shifting dunes are eerie and fascinating.

The shore of Nantucket Sound, the warmwater '*South Side*' of Cape Cod, sprawls along congested Route 28. Here are most of the resorts, motels and the like, and easternmost, by Monomoy Island, the town of **Chatham**, untouched by commercial activity (due to a strict ordinance). The 'elbow of Cape Cod', as Chatham is sometimes known, has a very scenic lighthouse and pier, and two museums: the *Atwood House*, a 1752 sea captain's home crammed full of antiques (open June to September, Monday/Wednesday/Friday 3pm-5pm; admission), and the *Railroad*

*Museum* in a 100-year-old depot, with all manner of train memorabilia (open late June to early September, Monday to Friday 2pm-5pm; free).

**Harwich**, next town to the west, is the Cape's main cranberry producer; items from the hard, bad-old-days of cranberry harvesting, and other antiques are in the *Brooks Academy Museum* on Main Street (open July and August, Monday/Wednesday/Friday 1.30pm-4.30pm; free). **South Dennis's** *Congregational Church* (1835) has a fine interior with Sandwich glass globes (open 2pm-5pm), on Main Street; the village is also home to the kinky-sounding *Curious Forms of Colonial Punishment Exhibit* at Route 134 and Access Road (open daylight hours). Dennis's once prosperous saltworks are recalled among the exhibits at *Jericho House*, a restored old mansion in **West Dennis**, on Trotting Park Road (open end June to mid September Wednesday/Friday/Saturday 2pm-5pm; free).

**West Yarmouth**, the next village east on Route 28, has two places to take the kids: *Aqua Circus*, with dolphin shows and a small zoo (open February to November 9.30am-9pm; 10am-5pm in winter; admission), and *Treasure Island Attractions*, a carnival-like assemblage of activity and rides (open June to September daily 10am-5pm; admission). **Hyannis**, commercial and transportation hub, with ferries to the islands, owes much of its fame to America's royal family, the Kennedys, who spend their summers in the fenced-off Hyannis Port Kennedy Compound (off-limits to papparazzi and everybody else). On Ocean Street there is a *John F. Kennedy Memorial*.

Old **Cotuit**, synonymous with oysters (harvested in September), lies to the west; **Mashpee,** originally lands given to the Wampanoag Indians, has been encroached on by an ambitious condominium development, New Seabury, and by the Otis Air Force base, even as the local Indians attempt to regain their lands in court. In 1674, the parish of *Old Indian Meetinghouse* was established, and the church itself constructed in 1684, making it the oldest church on the Cape and the oldest Indian church in America (Route 28; open end of May to mid September).

**Falmouth** occupies much of the southwest corner of the Cape; its village green, lovely and peaceful, is home of the *Falmouth Historical Society's* two buildings. The Headquarters Museum, in a fine 1790 mansion, contains furnishings and a formal garden from that period, and the Conant House Museum, with whaling and sea memorabilia (open 15 June to 15 September 2pm-5pm; admission). Near here, the *Katherine Lee Bates Birthplace*, at 16 Main, honours the authoress of 'America the Beautiful' with articles associated with her life (open 15 June to 15 September,

Monday to Friday 2pm-5pm; admission).

**Woods Hole**, a village to the south, has the only year-round ferry to the islands, and is famous for its marine biology research in the National Marine Fisheries Service. Open to the public is their *Woods Hole Marine Aquarium* with educational exhibits explaining the life of the lobster and haddock and other sea creatures of the northeast Atlantic (open 10 June to September, 10am-4.30pm; free). Looking towards the future, *The New Alchemy Institute* in **Hatchville** uses experimental energy sources, farm and fishing techniques to grow vegetables and raise fish (for a Saturday visit, tel: 563-2655).

**Bourne**, at the southern end of the Cape Cod Canal, has a replica of the Pilgrims' trading post of 1627, where they traded wampum for beaver hides with Indian and Dutch trappers. Located at 24 Aptucxet Road, the *Aptucxet Village Trading Post* also features a Dutch windmill, an Indian Village, saltworks and President Cleveland's special railroad station, which he used when he vacationed on Buzzards Bay (open April to November Monday to Saturday 10am-5pm; closed Mondays from April to June; admission).

## Martha's Vineyard

Population 8,000 for ten months of the year, 45,000 in July and August, Martha's Vineyard has been a summer destination since 1835, when the Methodists staged a camp meeting at Oak Bluffs. Several decades later this became 'Cottage City', as little gingerbread summer houses sprang up, many built by whaling captains as whaling declined on the island. Tourism began in a big way only when Cape Cod was 'discovered' but, as an island, it has retained its peculiar charm. Its six towns are individualistic and easily accessible by rented bicycle.

Largest island in New England, Martha's Vineyard once had numerous vineyards (today but one) taking advantage of the warm sea currents that moderate the island's climate. Thomas Mayhew bought it in 1640, and his direct descendants still live there along with members of the Wampanoag tribe, who 'owned' the island before Mayhew acquired it. Both the Indians and the white settlers worked the island's whaling fleet until catering to the Methodists became more profitable. Camp meetings had been held on Cape Cod from the beginning of the 19th century in places like Wellfeet and Truro; they were the main summer social events for the isolated Cape Codders, and grew more and more popular and elaborate. At first the families brought great picnics, listened to rousing sermons all day, then slept in one great tent at night. In Oak Bluffs, family tents were replaced by elaborate cottages in the 1860s and '70s, when single meetings would draw up to 12,000 people. The circus tents used for preaching were replaced by a permanent iron and glass tabernacle in 1879. Today, **Oak Bluffs'** cottages, many on old tent platforms, are located around the *Weslyan Grove Camp Ground* in Trinity Park. The *tabernacle*, also here, holds interdenominational services on summer Sundays. Children love the *Flying Horses Carousel* on Circuit Avenue, operative since 1876, nowadays in a shelter.

Oak Bluffs and nearby **Vineyard Haven**, part of the town of **Tisbury**, are the ports of Martha's Vineyard (Oak Bluffs, summer only). Near the Steamship Authority ticket office in the latter, the *Seamen's Bethel* is now a small historical museum (open May to October, Wednesday to Monday 10am-5pm). Tisbury is the commercial hub of the island, and has a small beach. **Edgartown**, southeast on the other side of the State beach, is the oldest town on Martha's Vineyard, and the fanciest, with its old captains' mansions and shops. Once a major whaling port, Edgartown is now a fashionable resort that remembers its history in the *Duke County Historical Society* on Cooke Street. In a 1765 house shaped like a whaling vessel, it exhibits whaling memorabilia and items relating to the island's history (open summer 10am-4.30pm; winter Thursday to Friday 1pm-4.30pm, Saturdays 10am-4.30pm; admission). There are two beaches near Edgartown and a ferry to **Chappaquiddick Island** and its two wildlife preserves (the *On Time* ferry from Dagget Street). The typical New England village, **West Tisbury**, a farming community, has the vineyard on the island, although ironically of recent origin. Hilly **Chilmark** to the west is best known for *Menemsha Harbor* and its beach; the shanties, lobster traps and fishing boats here compose an oft-photographed scene. Chilmark centre has one of the East Coast's pungent names – Beetlebung Corner – recalling the days when residents utilized tupelo trees to make barrel bunghole plugs. **Gayhead** at the far corner of the island has the most spectacular natural feature of Martha's Vineyard, the *Gayhead Cliffs*, multicoloured and 150 ft high, made of clay embedded with exotic fossils of prehistoric camels. Because of erosion, visitors are not permitted to climb them any more, and must be content to view them from the beach down below or from a terrace on top, where descendants of the Gay Head Indians sell souvenirs.

**Nantucket**, an Indian word meaning 'the faraway land', takes three hours to reach by ferry from Woods Hole, two hours from Hyannis in the summer. Its large sheltered harbour made it a natural for seafaring occupations, and in the 1840s, until a fire destroyed Nantucket town in 1846, it rightfully claimed the title of 'whaling capital of the world' with over seventy ships and numerous spermaceti candle factories. 'The Nantucketer, he alone resides and riots on the sea,' wrote Melville, who devoted an entire chapter of *Moby Dick* to the island; when you visit Nantucket today, with its sea-weathered homes and old captains' mansions, its lonely heath and sands, its fog and salty breezes and its powerful sense of the past, you see much of what Melville saw, minus the whaling ships and the stink of whale oil and blubber. Strict laws forbid any modern intrusions.

Like Martha's Vineyard, Nantucket belonged to Thomas Mayhew, who sold it to nine Proprietors in 1659. By 1672 Nantucketers caught their first whale; in the island's heyday its whalers were known as the most adventurous on the Atlantic coast. The population of Nantucket was double what it is today in the mid 19th century, when it ranked third in commercial activity in Massachusetts. Today this heritage is relived in the *Whaling Museum* on Broad Street, located in a factory that once made spermaceti candles. This belongs to the *Nantucket Historical Association*, as do numerous other sites, all open 10am-5pm, from mid June to mid October. They offer a discount season pass to all, or you may pay separate admission for each. Among their properties are the *Peter Foulger Museum* near the Whaling Museum, featuring the non-whaling aspects of Nantucket's history; *Hadwen House* (1845) on Main and Pleasant, the richly furnished home of a whale oil merchant prince; the 1723 *Nathaniel Macy House*, typical of the period on Liberty Street; the *1800 House* on Mill Street, with domestic exhibits and interesting furnishings; the *Old Gaol* on Vestal Street, built in 1805 of oak logs, containing the old stocks and pillories; the *Old Mill* at Mill and Prospect, built from wood salvaged from shipwrecks, still grinding corn today; the *Greater Light*, a former barn converted into a residence by Hannah Monihan in the 1920s with imaginative furnishings and stained glass, on Walnut Lane; and the *Jethro Coffin House* on Sunset Hill, the oldest house in Nantucket, built in 1686 and featuring period furnishings and antique china. Another NHA site is the *Lightship Nantucket* at Straight Wharf, once docked at South Shoals. Not included in the pass, it is open daily in the summer, 11am-8pm.

Nantucket was the birthplace of Maria Mitchell (1818), one of America's fiirst woman astronomers, professor at Vassar and discoverer of Mitchell's Comet. Her home, the *Maria Mitchell Birthplace* on Vestal Street, is open Monday to Friday 10am-12pm and 2pm-5pm, Saturdays 10am-12pm; admission; on Wednesday nights you can gaze at the heavens from the Liones

Observatory (1912), built in her honour. On Polpis Road is a replica of the local 1874 lifesaving station, the *Nantucket Life Saving Museum*, contains antique equipment (open mid June to Labor Day 2pm-5pm).

Outside Nantucket town, the island consists of summer colonies, beaches and wild lands, including an enormous cranberry bog, maintained by the Nantucket Conservation Foundation; their holdings include several beaches, and the harbour's barrier beach. Both bus and bike trails lead from Nantucket harbour to **Siasconset**, an old New York summer colony and the largest on the island, with fine homes and a scenic *Bluff Walk*.

**Restaurants.** *In Sandwich:* Eli's Cape Shore**, Route 6A. *In Falmouth:* Flying Bridge**, Scranton Avenue; Coonamessett Inn**, Jones Road & Giford. *In West Barnstable:* Ojala Finnish Restaurant***. *In Barnstable:* Mad Duck**, Route 6A. *In Yarmouth:* Old Yarmouth Inn***, Route 6A; Cranberry Goose**, 43 Main Street. *In Dennisport:* Swan River Seafood*, Lower County Road. *In Brewster:* Chillingsworth***, Route 6A; Inn of the Golden Ox***, Main & Tubman. *In Orleans:* Cap'n Linnel House***, Skaket Road; Orleans Inn**, Route 6A. *In Wellfeet:* Sweet Seasons***, at Inn at Duck Creek; Lighthouse*, Main Street. *In Provincetown:* Circo & Sal's***, 4 Kiley Court; Front Street***, 230 Commercial; Tip for Tops'n***, 334 Commercial; Cookie's*, 133 Commercial. *In Chatham:* Christopher Ryder House***, Route 28; Captain's Table**, 580 Main. *In Harwich:* Thompson Brothers Clam Bar**, Snow Inn Road. *In Hyannis:* Beachwood Inn**, 415 Main. *In Oak Bluffs:* Captain's Table**. *In Vineyard Haven:* Black Dog Tavern***, Beach Street. *In Edgartown:* Lawry's**, Main Street; Seafood Shanty***, Dock Street. *In Menemsha Harbor:* Home Port**. *In Nantucket:* Jared Coffin House***, Broad Street; India House**, 37 Pearl. *In Siasconset:* Chanticleer Inn***.

## North of Boston: West to Concord and Lowell

In the northwest suburbs of Boston, **Watertown** was the first inland town founded in America, in 1630; today it has Massachusetts' largest Armenian population, who, among other things, publish two newspapers in the city. Watertown's most famous institution, the *Perkins School for the Blind*, was endowed in 1829 by a Boston merchant after a public demonstration of blind children reading, taught by Dr Samuel Gridley Howe, who invented a raised alphabet. Annie Sullivan, a teacher at the school, taught the blind and deaf Helen Keller, the first of the many multi-handicapped children educated at Perkins.

**Waltham**, to the west, was the site of Francis Cabot Lowell's first textile mill in 1812 and the Waltham Watch Company, in 1854 the first to make watches with machines. Today the elite, Jewish-founded *Brandeis University* (1948) has changed Waltham's tenor from industry to education – the main thing to see here is the *Rose Art Museum* (open Tuesday to Sunday 1pm-5pm) at 415 South Street with permanent and changing exhibits. On 2 Thornton Road the *American Jewish Historical Society* maintains a museum on the history of Jewry in the United States (open Monday to Friday 9am-5pm, Sundays 2pm-5pm; free). Home of a former governor, *Gore Place* (52 Gore Street) is considered one of the most beautiful Federal homes in America (open mid April to mid November, Tuesday to Saturday 10am-5pm, Sundays 2pm-5pm, admission).

'Stand your ground. Don't fire unless fired upon. But if they mean to have a war, let it begin here,' Captain John Parker said to the farmers on Lexington Green on 19 April 1775 who had come to 'observe' the British. The British moved to disarm them; the militia began to disperse, and the British nervously fired, killing eight militiamen. Word quickly spread. The war had indeed begun, and as the Redcoats continued their march to Concord, they were fired on by snipers from every side. **Lexington** commemorates the fateful encounter with a bronze statue of Captain Parker on *Lexington Green*; here its historical society maintains the *Buckman Tavern* where the farmers gathered before the bloody encounter, and where the wounded were taken after the fray (open 15 April to October, Monday to Saturday 10am-5pm, Sundays 1pm-5pm; admission).

Just south of the Green, at 33 Marrett Road (Route 2A) the Scottish Rite of Freemasonry's *Museum of Our National Heritage* exhibits the work of American craftsmen (open Monday to Saturday 9.30am-4.30pm, Sundays 12pm-5.30pm; free). West of town, Route 2A becomes the *Battle Road*, where the British marched that day in April to Concord; the *Battle Road Visitors'Center* a couple of miles west of Lexington has a multi-media recounting of the events and general information (open daily 8.30am-5pm in summer, closed Mondays and Tuesdays in winter). The Battle Road continues to **Concord**, and the *Old North Bridge*, where the American militia rebuffed the British after their search for the hidden military supplies in Concord. An information centre at the *Buttrick House*, off Monument Street, can help you figure out what happened where; it is near North Bridge (the fifth) and the famous *Statue of the Minuteman* by Daniel Chester French, inscribed by Emerson's equally famous verse on 'the shot heard around the world'.

But the legendary place that Concord holds in American history is due not only to the incident at Old North Bridge, but also to its role in 19th-century thought and literature – besides Ralph Waldo Emerson, Thoreau, Nathaniel Hawthorne, Bronson and his daughter Louisa May Alcott, Daniel Chester French and Margaret Sydney, all lived here and are buried in *Sleepy Hollow Cemetery* just outside town on Route 62. Near North Bridge on Monument Street *The Old Manse*, built by Emerson's grandfather, was the home of Nathaniel Hawthorne and his wife after their wedding; Hawthorne later wrote *Mosses from an Old Manse* about their life here (open late April to mid November weekends, 1 June to 15 October daily 10am-4.30pm, Sundays 1pm-5pm; admission). The *Emerson House* on Route 2A, operated by the philosopher's descendants, contains many of his personal items and writings. Curiously, it has become a kind of shrine for Japanese visitors who all encounter Emerson when first reading English in school (open mid April to October, Tuesday to Saturday 10am-4.30pm, Sundays 2pm-4.30pm; admission). Other Emerson and also Thoreau memorabilia are on display in the *Concord Antiquarian Society*, at Lexington and the Cambridge Turnpike, along with Paul Revere's lantern and other unusual New England artifacts (open April to November, Monday to Saturday 10am-4.30pm, Sundays 2pm-4.30pm; admission).

*Orchard House*, across the street at 399 Lexington, was the home of the Alcott family from 1858 to 1877, and although *Little Women* was actually set in The Wayside next door, this is the place to come for dioramas and items relating to the lives of the Alcott girls, on whom the novel was modelled (open mid April to mid November weekends, June to 15 October daily 10am-4.30pm, Sundays 1pm-5pm; admission). The *Wayside*, built by militiaman Samuel Whitney, was another Alcott residence. Later Hawthorne lived out his last years here, and Margaret Sidney, the author of *Five Little Peppers*, also resided here (open April to October 10am-5pm; admission). This is not to be confused with the subject of Longfellow's *Tales of the Wayside Inn*, which lies south of Concord in **Sudbury** (Route 12 to Route 20) and is still a popular restaurant today. Along Route 126, not far from Concord, **Walden Pond** has a plaque where Henry David Thoreau built his hut in his famous retreat from society, 1845-47; now part of Walden Pond State Reservation, it is one of the prettiest spots in the state. At 156 Belknap Street in Concord the *Thoreau Lyceum* contains a small museum and a replica behind it of Thoreau's Walden Pond home (open all year 10am-5pm, Sundays 2pm-5pm; admission).

Directly north of Boston, no.90 Elm Street in **Woburn** was the birthplace of Count Rumford, born Benjamin Thompson in 1753. In his eclectic career he invented the double-boiler and the drip coffeepot, served as a colonel in the King's Dragoons in New York City, was knighted for his pains by George III, became Grand Chamberlain of Bavaria, was made a count of the Holy Roman Empire ('Rumford' was his wife's home in New Hampshire) and a member of the Institute of France. For the whole story, visit his home (open daily except Mondays, 1pm-4.30pm; free). In **Saugus,** the *Saugus Iron Works National Historic Site*, at 244 Central, commemorates the first integrated ironworks in America, founded in 1646. The furnace, the forge, the rolling and slitting mills here are reconstructions; the ironmaster's home was restored in 1915 (open April to October 9am-5pm, winter 9am-4pm). **Revere,** south on the coast, has Boston's most easily accessible beach, although not its most attractive. There are other beaches at shoemaking **Lyon** and on the **Nahant** causeway.

In **Swampscott** Mary Baker Eddy performed the healing miracles with Bible readings that led her to found the Christian Science Church. The story is told at the *Mary Baker Eddy House* at 23 Paradise Road (open 10am-5pm, Sundays 2pm-5pm; winter Tuesday to Saturday 10am-3pm; free). Swampscott was once a fashionable resort; **Marblehead** to the north still is, with its lovely colourful old town on a hill overlooking the harbour that made the town wealthy in the slave and rum trade before the Revolution. Fishermen from Cornwall founded it in 1629, and even today Marblehead turns its face to the sea, claiming to be 'the Yachting Capital of the World'. Cars are cumbersome and unnecessary – take the boat from Salem and avoid the traffic on the twisting, narrow, hilly streets. There are three buildings open to the public: *Abbott Hall* on Washington Square, where one of A. M. Willard's three copies of the *Spirit of '76* hangs in the Selectman's Room. This famous painting of wounded patriots drumming, fifing, and bearing the flag was painted in 1876. The 1768 *Jeremiah Lee Mansion*, at 161 Washington, once belonged to a wealthy shipowner, who furnished it with imported wood and wallpaper (open mid May to 12 October, Monday to Saturday 9.30am-4pm; admission). The *King Hooper Mansion*, at 8 Hooper Street, is unusually tall for a 1728 structure; now it houses exhibits of the Marblehead Arts Association (open Tuesday to Sunday 1pm-4pm; admission).

'Come to Salem for a Spell' the **Salem** tourist board invites, although it is eager to stress that there is more to Salem than the witchcraft trials of 1693. Salem, from the Hebrew 'Shalom', for peace, was the first settlement of the Massachusetts Bay Colony, making it older than Boston. One of its first churchmen, Roger Williams, was exiled for heresy and founded Rhode Island. A later one, Reverend Samuel Parris was largely responsible for the witchcraft hysteria that cost the lives of nineteen people in nearby Danvers (then part of Salem). The Puritans were quick to show that they had no room for the Devil in the New World but the witch hunts ended as abruptly as they began when the wife of the governor of Massachusetts was accused by the 'bewitched' girls, one of them the daughter of Reverend Parris. None of this prevented Salem from becoming one of the leading ports during the China trade, specializing in Sumatra pepper. Great fortunes were made, including that of America's first millionaire, Elias Hasket Derby, known as 'King' Derby. Young Nathaniel Hawthorne, who grew up in Salem, worked in the Customs House and watched the port slowly decline from its heyday in the 1810s and '20s. His novel *The House of the Seven Gables* evokes a sombre image of Salem which seems distant on a sunny summer day, but true to form when it's gloomy.

The actual House of the Seven Gables, more a character than a setting, is the most visited historic house in New England. Located near the harbour at 54 Turner Street, it was built in 1668 with a secret room and a hidden stair. Admission includes *Hawthorne's birthplace* and the 17th-century *Hathaway House* (open 9.30am-6.30pm July to Labor Day, 10am-4.30pm rest of the year). The Department of the Interior maintains the *Salem Maritime National Historic Site,* which encompasses the restored *Customs House* (where Hawthorne worked and wrote part of *The Scarlet Letter* when business was slow), the *Bonded Warehouse*, the *Derby House* and *Derby Wharf* and the *West India Goods Store*, stocked with typical imports of the 19th century. The wharf is the centrepiece here; built before the Revolution, it was the departure point for voyages to the other side of the world, many owned by 'King' Derby. His fine brick house, built in 1762, costs fifty cents to see, but everything else is free (open 8.30am-7pm in July and August, 8.30am-5pm the rest of the year).

Another complex of buildings, the *Essex Institute* at 132 Essex Street, features a large museum housing domestic, China trade and military items, and six restored and furnished homes from different periods covering 150 years up to 1818 (open June to mid October, Monday to Saturday 9am-4.30pm, Sundays 2pm-5pm; closed Mondays and Sundays the rest of the year; admission). The houses have varying hours and separate admission, with combination tickets available. Another museum, at 161 Essex, the *Peabody Museum of Salem* has been open since

1799, making it one of the oldest in America. Its enormous collection includes marine items, South Pacific ethnological exhibits, natural history and thousands of other objects (open Monday to Saturday 9am-5pm, Sundays and holidays 1pm-5pm; admission).

Yet another museum, the *Salem Seaport Museum* at Pickering Wharf, features a multi-media account of the voyage of the *India Star* and other items relating to the heyday of Salem's port (open 10.30am-5.30pm, Sundays 12pm-5pm; June to Labor Day Thursday to Saturday till 8.30pm; admission). *Ye Olde Pepper Companie*, at 122 Derby Street, claims to be America's oldest candy company, and manufactures such colonial goodies as 'Black Jacks' and 'Gibraltars'.

There are three sites that attempt to evoke the Salem witchcraft madness: the *Salem Witch Museum*, in a castle at 19½ Washington Square North, near the Essex Institute, with a multi-media show guaranteed to scare little kids (open 10am-5pm, July/August 10am-7pm; admission); the *Witch Dungeon*, 16 Lynde Street, with live witch trials, and a replica of the dungeon and Old Salem (open May to October 10am-5pm; admission); and the *Witch House* on Essex Street where Jonathon Corwin, a judge at the trials, lived and held preliminary hearings (open March to November, 10am-5pm; admission).

Next to the latter the *First Church* is home of the oldest Protestant parish in America (1629). *Chestnut Street*, parallel to Essex, has been declared a Historic District for its beautiful old homes, one of which, the *Stephen Phillips*, is open, furnished with the fruits of Salem's exotic trade. The house belonged to an old sea captain (open 29 May to 17 October, Monday to Saturday 10am-4.30pm; admission). In Salem's Forest River Park *Pioneer Village* is a replica of the earliest settlement, when Salem was called 'Naumkeag' (open June to Labor Day, 10am-5pm). A modern Salem institution, *Parker Brothers Games* on Bridge Street, offers factory tours weekdays for free, but you must reserve a place (tel: 744-5951).

**Danvers**, formerly Salem Village, where the witch trials actually took place, is primarily known today for its dark old mental hospital. Of the several historical houses here *Glen Magna Farms* at 57 Forest Street is the most lavish. Built in 1790, the grounds later landscaped by Frederick Law Olmsted, it was originally built for Elias Hasket Derby, the millionaire merchant of Salem. The 1678 *Nurse Homestead*, at 149 Pine, was the home of 70-year-old Rebecca Nurse, one of the accused witches hung at Gallows Hill; her family stole her body at night to bury it near the house (open June to September, Wednesdays and Sundays

1pm-5pm, Saturdays 10am-5pm).

More history awaits the visitor in posh **Beverly**, next to Danvers but attainable by bridge from Salem. One of the several 'birthplaces of the American Navy', it claims the *Hannah* was armed in September 1775 and caught a British prize almost immediately; George Cabot of Beverly was the first Secretary of the Navy, appointed by John Adams. Later Beverly was famous for its gargantuan United Shoe Machinery Company. Today the crowds come for the *North Shore Music Theater*, with a variety of summer performances, often starring celebrities (tel: (617) 922-8500 for details). The Beverly Historical Society operates three sites: the *Balch House* (488 Cabot Street), built in 1636 and the oldest frame house in America; the *Hale House* (39 Hale Street), the 1694 home of the Reverend John Hale, who helped stop the witchcraft trials in Salem (both open 15 June to 15 September weekdays 10am-4pm, admission), and the *Cabot House* (117 Cabot Street), built in 1781, containing period furnishings and a museum reflecting the town's sea trade and privateering heritage (open 15 June to August, Tuesday to Saturday 10am-4pm; other months Wednesday to Friday). For a more lively time, head north on Route 1A to Hamilton and the *Myopia Hunt Club* for the weekly Sunday (3pm) polo match; the club's peculiar name was given it by its founders, four near-sighted polo players.

**Manchester**, west on the coast toward Cape Ann, is famous for its *Singing Beach* of fine, 'acoustical' sand that hums when you walk on it; if you come by train, it stops very near it. Manchester, Pride's Crossing and Magnolia were once summer colonies of the Brahmins, the latter having *Norman's Woe Rock*, of Longfellow's poem 'Wreck of the Hesperus'.

*Rafe's Chasm*, 200 ft deep, is near here, but only visible from the sea. Surrounded by a moat, the *Hammond Castle* (1926) in Hesperus Avenue belonged to John Hays Hammond, medieval fancier, inventor of remote control radio and the incendiary bomb. It features arts and crafts from the 13th-15th centuries, and a 8,600 pipe organ designed by Hammond, on which concerts are given Saturday evenings in the summer (open December, February and March 10am-3pm, closed Mondays, and open daily 10am-4pm from April to November; admission).

Over an old canal lies **Cape Ann**, an unknown compared to popular Cape Cod; it is smaller, but certainly not without interest. **Gloucester,** the largest town on the Cape, is synonymous with fish, pulling in America's greatest lobster catch. Gloucester was founded by fishermen and earned its place as a leading fishing port with its development of the schooner. The famous

*Statue of the Fisherman*, erected in 1923 for Gloucester's Tricentenniel, has a Biblical inscription: 'They that go down to the sea in ships.' In August a memorial service is held here in honour of the thousands of Gloucestermen lost at sea; flowers are tossed into the tide. Today the town's fishing fleet totals some 185 different craft, many manned by Portuguese, and most of the fish they catch are quick-frozen. The burning issue in town today is whether or not the followers of Reverend Moon should buy up the town; 'Don't let the moon set over Gloucester' read the bumperstickers.

Famous seascape artist Fitz Hugh Lane lived in Gloucester; he built his house on the Harbour Loop, now the *Chamber of Commerce Information Center*, and 33 of his paintings form the nucleus of the collection of the *Cape Ann Historical Association*, located at 27 Pleasant Street in a 1800 Federal-style mansion. Many of the other exhibits relate to marine subjects (open Tuesday to Saturday, closed February; admission). For the inside view on the history of fishing, visit the *Gloucester Story Museum*, with films and exhibits (at Rogers and Porter, open 10am-4.30pm, Sundays 12pm-4.30pm; admission), or the colourful port itself.

**Rockport**, named for its old granite quarries, is a charming village and art colony. A picturesque lobster shack on picturesque Bearskin Neck has been the subject of so many paintings it has a name: Motif No. 1. It blew down in the great blizzard of 1978 but will be reconstructed for the benefit of future generations of artists. The other fishing shacks on Bearskin Neck have been converted into trendy shops. At 12 Main Street, the *Rockport Art Association* displays works by members in a 1830 tavern, open daily in the summer. Local history, including Rockport's granite saga, are the subject of the *Sandy Bay Historical Museum* at 40 King Street (open July to August, 2pm-5pm; free). Almost everything in Rockport is within easy walking distance (fortunately, because there's no place to put your car), but the *Paper House*, in Pigeon Cove, is a couple of miles away, on 52 Pigeon Hill Street. Begun in 1922, by a Swedish immigrant named Elis F. Stedman who read so many newspapers he didn't know what to do with them, it is a masterpiece of folk art composed of 100,000 newspapers, pressed and chemically treated to endure. Even the furnishings, even the fireplace, clock and piano, are made out of newspaper. The walls are 215 pages thick (open June to September, daily 10am-5pm; admission).

**Essex,** sometimes considered part of Cape Ann, but on the other side of the canal, was long renowned for its shipbuilding activity, mainly for the Gloucester schooners. On Main Street the *Essex Shipbuilding Museum* contains memorabilia, tools and models (open mid April to mid October weekends 1pm-5pm; free). Route 133 in Essex is lined with antique shops.

**Ipswich**, home of 'the sweetest clams in the world' – harvested nowadays by Greeks – was founded in 1633 and still has many fine 17th and early 18th-century homes clustered around the *Meeting House Green*. The prize here is *The John Whipple House* at 53 S. Main, built in 1640 and containing fine furnishings and a herb garden (open April to November, Tuesday to Saturday 10am-5pm, Sundays 1pm-5pm; admission). The Congregational Church is surrounded by peculiar marks in the rocks, locally called 'Devil's Footprints'. The main thing at Ipswich, besides clams, is the *Crane Reservation* and Crane's Beach, with lovely dunes, considered the finest on the North Shore (parking fee).

A few miles inland, **Topsfield** boasts the lovely 1681 *Parson Capon House* on the Common, perhaps the finest Elizabethan style house in the country, with an interior to match (open 18 June to 11 September, 1pm-4.30pm; admission). Another village off the coast, **Wenham** has one of the largest doll collections in the world and other toys and tools in the *Wenham Historical Society* at 132 Main Street (open Monday to Friday 1pm-4pm, Sundays 2pm-5pm; admission).

**Plum Island**, stretching south from the Merrimack River, is mainly occupied by the *Parker River Wildlife Refuge*, with bogs, dunes, bird watching towers, and a beach with excellent surf casting. In **Newbury**, an old village on Plum Island Sound, the *Old Town Hill Reservation* near the Parker River has a scenic winding path to the top of a hill, with views as far as Maine. **Newburyport**, like Salem and other once wealthy seaports in the Commonwealth, has undergone a restaurant-and-boutique-shop-type revival and refurbished its beautiful Federal era mansions on High Street, former homes of sea captains and merchant princes. The centre of Newburyport's revival efforts is *Market Square* on the waterfront, originally built in the early 19th century, and the *Custom House Maritime Museum*. The Custom House, built of Rockport granite in 1835 and designed by Robert Mills, served a variety of uses before recently becoming a museum, dealing with Newburyport's sea trade and its native son, novelist John P. Marquand, whose book *Point of No Return* describes his home town (open 29 May to 12 October, Monday to Saturday 10am-4.30pm, Sundays 2pm-5pm; admission). Newburyport produces fine silverware; one company, *Towle Silvermiths*, have a showroom at 262 Merrimac Street in a 17th-century house (open daily, 9am-12pm and 1pm-4pm). The Unitarian and Presbyterian churches in town both have bells cast by Paul Revere. **Salisbury**, the last shore town before New

Hampshire, has a popular beach, a boardwalk and amusement parks and arcades.

The Merrimack River skirts the southern border of New Hampshire before plunging north at Lowell. Inland from Salisbury, on the northern bank of the Merrimack, **Amesbury** was the home for 46 years of John Greenleaf Whittier; the *Whittier Home* at 85 Friend Street contains many of the personal belongings of the poet-abolitionist (open March to December, Tuesday to Saturday 10am-4pm). Outside of town on Route 110, the *Rocky Hill Meeting House* with its large Palladian window and unusual design makes a pretty site (open June to October, Wednesday to Saturday 1pm-5pm; admission).

**Lawrence**, one of New England's great mill towns, ran the gamut from benevolent paternalism to the low wages and wretched tenements and the Great Strike of 1912. At one time it claimed to be 'the worsted center of the world', as immigrants from half the countries in the world laboured in the mills. Today many of the remaining mills house small manufacturing firms, some still dealing in textiles; many new and second and third-generation ethnic groups still live in town. The *Merrimack Valley Textile Museum,* 800 Massachusetts Avenue, in **North Andover** nearby, has exhibits tracing the history of cloth manufacture (open Monday to Friday 9am-5pm, weekends 1pm-5pm).

Did you ever go into Lowell, Oh! rackett,
Good Lord what a buzzing it makes,
Like fifty live crabs in a bucket,
And what a darned sight of cotton it takes.

(1849 playbill)

**Lowell**, founded in 1822 on the Pawtucket Falls by the 'Boston Associates' and their Merrimack Manufacturing Company, was named for Francis Cabot Lowell of Boston. In 1811 Lowell had toured England, studying the mills and social effects of the Industrial Revolution there. The latter he detested and was determined not to repeat in the mills he built in Massachusetts, the first was in Waltham, where he and mechanic Paul Moody designed a power loom and transformed cotton to cloth in a single factory. Lowell died in 1817, but his work and the foundation of a mill town on the Merrimack were carried out by the 'Boston Associates' – Patrick Jackson, Nathan Appelton, Paul Moody and Kirk Boott. Boott created the model manufacturing town of Lowell, planning both the physical aspects and the employee policies. James B. Francis, hydraulic engineer, built the power canals from the Merrimack and Concord Rivers to run the mills, some of which are very complex, innovative firsts in hydrology.

The first workers in Lowell's mills were Yankee farmgirls, eager to leave the narrow confines of their home life to earn some money for their dowries, or to send home to indigent parents. Their lives were strictly controlled; they lived in boarding houses, their every hour regulated by a bell. They managed, however, to support churches, schools, lectures and contribute to their very own literary magazine, *The Lowell Offering*, published 1840-45, which 'compares advantageously with a great many English Annuals' according to Charles Dickens, who was quite impressed with Lowell during his American visit. He compared the Lowell experiment with working-class life in England, as the contrast between 'Good and Evil'. However, not long after Dickens's visit, working conditions deteriorated – strikes and walk-outs were hardly effective with a seemingly endless supply of immigrant labour, first from Ireland, then French Canada, Greece, Portugal, Eastern Europe and Armenia. In the '30s the mills closed, many of the workers moved on, and Lowell's important place in American industry became just another subject for the history book.

In 1978, however, Lowell was designated a National Historical Park, and an interesting (and free) three-hour tour has been devised, using canal boats and old trolley cars as transport between the various sites. You can either take the guided tour (reserve a place at National Park Headquarters, 171 Merrimack Street; tel: 459-1000) or take a self-guided tour, reversing the same route as the guided tour. Besides the canal locks and the Pawtucket Falls, the tour includes the *Lowell Museum* at 560 Suffolk Street (open October to March 9am-5pm, closed Mondays) with photographs and artifacts from the mills. In a house built for a mill agent, James McNeill Whistler was born; today it houses the *Parker Gallery*, which includes some of Whistler's etchings and works by contemporary local artists (243 Worthern Street; open September to June, Tuesday to Sunday 2pm-4.30pm).

**Restaurants.** *In Concord:* Colonial Inn**, Concord Green; Café L'Orange***, 86 Thoreau Street. *In Sudbury:* Longellow's Wayside Inn**. *In Swampscott:* General Glover Inn**, Salem Street. *In Marblehead:* Atlantic**, 40 Atlantic Avenue; Rosalie's**, 18 Sewall; Dill's*, 141 Pleasant. *In Salem:* Lyceum***, 43 Church; Bistro Le Bistingo**, 8 Front. *In Manchester:* 7 Central**, Union Street. *In Gloucester:* White Rainbow***, 65 Main; Gloucester House** Route 127; Ernie's Cape Ann Diner*, 216½ Main. *In Rockport:* Oleana-by-the-Sea**, 27 Main Street; Peg Leg**, 18

Beach Street. *In Essex:* Woodman's**, Route 133. *In Ipswich:* Riverside Inn**, 4 S. Main; 1640 Hart House**, 31 Linebrook Road. *In Newburyport:* Scandia***, 26 State; Grog House**, 11 Middle. *In Lowell:* The Spear House**, 525 Pawtucket; Old Worthern Tavern**, 5 Worthern; Club Diner*, 145 Dutton.

## Central Massachusetts

Heading west of Boston on Highway 9, you pass by way of **Wellesley,** home of the famous women's college of the same name, with its *Jewet Art Center* (open September to June). Business college *Babson Institute* is also in Wellesley, and boasts the world's largest revolving globe, weighing 25 tons. The New England Wildflower Association has its headquarters in *Garden in the Woods,* on Hemenway Street in **Framingham,** west of Wellesley. The Garden features a vast collection of plants native to the northeast, with over 400 species, all labelled. It is both educational and beautiful, particularly in May and June (open April to October 8.30am-4.30pm, closed Sunday; admission). The recently established *Danforth Museum* at 123 Union has frequently changing multi-media exhibits (open Wednesday to Sunday 1pm-4.30pm; free).

North of here, towards Hudson and Maynard are Massachusetts' apple orchards. **Harvard** holds an apple-blossom festival; it was also the home of Bronson Alcott's Transcendental Community of *Fruitlands,* which he founded in 1843. Vegetarianism and the refusal to use any animal product, including wool, made life in the community difficult and soon caused it to disband. Now a museum, the old farmhouse contains memorabilia of Transcendentalist leaders like Emerson, Alcott, Thoreau and Margaret Fuller. Another Fruitlands museum contains Indian crafts; yet another houses 19th-century American paintings, including a wide selection by the Hudson River School. A *Shaker House* has been restored, displaying items made by that curious sect (all open 30 May to 30 September, Tuesday to Sunday 1pm-5pm; admission).

North of Harvard, in the Groton area (where FDR spent his school days) there are several ski resorts; to the southwest the little town of *Lancaster* was made famous by an Indian massacre during King Philip's War, and by author J. Greene Chandler, who wrote *Chicken Little.* The *John Greene Chandler Museum* contains an excellent collection of toys, doll houses, children's books; adjoining it is the *Toy Cupboard Theater,* with puppet shows (57 East George Hill Road; tel: 365-9519 for performance information; the museum is open daily in July and August 2pm-

6pm, closed Monday; admission). On Lancaster Green the 1816 *Fifth Meeting House,* designed by Charles Bulfinch, is perhaps the finest church in the state, open for services on Sunday.

If Chicken Little evokes no fond childhood memories, *Sterling,* just to the west, surely will: here Mary Sawyer's little lamb followed her to school one day – there's a statue of the lamb on the town green. The actual schoolhouse visited by the lamb was purchased by Henry Ford and brought to his Greenwich Village east, in Sudbury, by Longfellow's Wayside Inn. Johnny Appleseed, né John Chapman, another favourite of children, was born in nearby **Leominster** in 1774. He wasn't quite the dimpled character that children know via Walt Disney, but an eccentric Swedenborgian who wandered about scantily clothed and wearing his cooking pot on his head. He did, however, plant thousands of apple trees, mainly in Ohio. His statue stands in Leominster today. Leominster has long been Massachusetts' plastic city, and the *Leominster Historical Society and Plastics Museum* (School Street) will give you the straight story on the subject. **Fitchburg,** the larger of these two closely related towns, has more Finns per capita than almost anywhere in America, many who came to work in the paper mills. It also has a small but good *Art Museum* at 25 Merriam Parkway, with a basic American collection (open September to June, Tuesday to Saturday 9am-5pm, Sunday 2pm-5pm; free). East of Fitchburg, *Whalom Park* in Lunenburg has 33 rides and other old fashioned amusements (open Memorial Day to Labor Day, weekends in the spring and in September).

This area of the state, often called **Montachusett,** is hilly and scenic, similar to the adjacent region of New Hampshire. There are waterfalls near Athol, *Doane Falls* at Mill Road and *Royalston Falls* off Route 68, near the New Hampshire border. Swift water and a wealth of forests made **Gardner,** west of Fitchburg, 'Chair City' until Grand Rapids, Michigan, stole the honour. Gardner, however, was the first to massproduce chairs in America and in honour of the Bicentennial the town erected a giant chair on Elm Street. Another town in the Montachusett region, **Winchendon,** is still called 'Toy Town' for the wooden toys once manufactured here; a Trojan-horse-like wooden rocking horse (10½ feet high) in one of the parks recalls the former major industry.

The largest town in central Massachusetts, **Worcester** claims to be 'The Heart of New England', at least geographically. It supported one of America's first newspapers, *The Massachusetts Spy,* put out by patriot printer Isaiah Thomas, who was the first to read the Declaration of Independence in New England on 17 July 1776 in Worcester Common. In the mid 19th century Worcester was a hotbed of Yankee ingenuity, its inventors producing the first liquid-fuel rocket, the carpet loom, the envelop-folding machine, the calliope etc. This led to Worcester becoming and remaining a major industrial centre and residence of a large number of immigrants from Sweden, Finland, Italy, French Canada, Ireland and the carpet-making countries of the Middle East, like Armenia and Albania. Like Boston, Worcester has a very intense 'Little Italy' neighbourhood; the other ethnic groups are almost as closely knit, giving the city a diversity so typical of New England today.

There are several exceptional things to see in Worcester, although nowadays the city seems proudest of its plexiglass covered *Worcester Center* with a shopping mall, theatres, offices, restaurants and a parking garage, all next to the historic common. Isaiah Thomas himself founded the *American Antiquarian Society* in 1812. Now located at 185 Salisbury Street, it specializes in printed matter, containing an excellent library with two-thirds of all the books and pamphlets printed in the US prior to 1820; exhibits include Isaiah Thomas's original printing press and other early American artifacts (open Monday to Friday 9am-5pm). The *Worcester Art Museum* at 55 Salisbury Street has a remarkably fine collection spanning 42 galleries, with art from ancient Egypt to the moderns, and such unusual features as a reconstructed 12th-century French monastery, mosaics from Antioch, medieval sculpture, a beautiful Flemish tapestry, and early American art (open Tuesday to Saturday 10am-5pm, Sunday 2pm-5pm; admission). Most unusual of all, however, is the *Higgins Armory Museum* at 100 Barber Avenue, with the finest collection of medieval armour in the western hemisphere, accumulated by steel manufacturer John Woodman Higgins, who wanted to relearn medieval secrets of fine steel. The museum has some unique pieces among the hundred suits of armour, made for everybody from king to dog. Other memorabilia from the days of chivalry, the Classical and Stone Ages round out this fascinating collection (open Tuesday to Friday 9am-4pm, Saturday 10am-3pm, Sunday 1pm-5pm, closed Mondays; admission). Yet another museum is the *Worcester Science Center* designed by Edward Durell Stone on Harrington Way, with a zoo, minature trains to ride, and numerous 'hands on' exhibits (open Monday to Saturday 10am-5pm, Sunday 12 noon-5pm; admission). A variety of performances are held in the recently refurbished *Mechanics Hall* at 321 Main; you can swim in the nearby *Quinsigamond State Park* just east of town.

Around Worcester are a number of old mill towns; in Paxton's *Moore Memorial State Park* are the ruins of an 18th-century mill town. **Auburn** to the south may claim to be the country's first Cape Canaveral, for here Robert Goddard launched the world's first liquid-fuel rocket in 1926, in what is now *Goddard Rocket Park.* Its centrepiece is a model of the rocket. **North Oxford** boasts the *Clara Barton Homestead* where the great reformer and founder of the American Red Cross was born (Ennis Road, off Route 12). The house contains some original furniture and tells the story of Clara Barton (open July and August, Tuesday to Sunday 1pm-5pm). **Webster,** near the Connecticut border, has a lake with the longest name in America – Lake Chargoggagogg-manchauggagoggchaubunagungamau, a gift to the white man from the Nipmuc Indians; its name translates as 'I fish on my side, you fish on your side and nobody fishes in the middle.' **Sutton,** to the east of North Oxford, draws visitors, good and evil alike, to its *Purgatory Chasm,* an awesome abyss with a trail to the floor.

**Southbridge** to the west claims to be the birthplace of the American optical industry; the now enormous American Optical Company was founded here in 1833; today it is the world's largest maker of optical lenses and instruments. Albert Wells, whose family controlled American Optical, was an avid collector of Americana, so much so that it outgrew his home – and thus *Old Sturbridge Village* was born. One of the largest outdoor museums in the country, it covers 200 acres with forty old buildings to represent a New England farm village of the early 19th century. Guides perform typical chores and craftsmen perform typical crafts; there are gardens, galleries, films, etc, in an attempt to give the visitor a sense of the past. Located on Route 20 in Sturbridge, Old Sturbridge Village is open daily (closed Monday in the winter) 9.30am-5.30pm; adults $5.50, children $2.00, under fives free. There is a daily Peter Pan bus direct from Boston to Sturbridge at 10.30am (Trailways Station), with the fare including admission to the village.

**Barre** to the north has a lovely big town green, surrounded by fine buildings, and on Route 122, *Rockingham Park,* with an odd boulder formation left by a passing glacier. West of here, the *Quabbin Reservoir* is by far the state's largest lake; it's used for drinking water. There are a number of entrances to Quabbin, one of them in **Ware,** the city of bargain factory outlets, at the junction of Route 9 and 32. Here Quabbin is administered; here also, on Quabbin Hill, there's a lookout tower with wide-ranging views.

**Restaurants.** *In Framingham:* Ken's Steak House**, 95 Worcester Road. *In Worcester:* El Morocco**, 73 Wall Street; Maxwell's

Toolhouse**, 25 Union; Boulevard Diner*, 155 Shrewsbury. *In Fitchburg:* Old Mill**, Route 2A. *In Sturbridge:* Publick House***, Route 131; Rom's*, Route 131. *In Southbridge:* Broke Wheel**, Elm Street. *In Spencer:* Toupin's*, Main Street. *In West Brookfield:* Salem Cross Inn***, Route 9.

## The Pioneer Valley and Western Massachusetts

The Pioneer Valley was a tourist promotion name that stuck, referring to the counties along the Connecticut River. The soil of the Connecticut Valley, richer than any other in New England, attracted settlers early on. In 1636 Puritans from the coast founded Springfield, but future development of the valley was suddenly curtailed in King Philip's War – Springfield and other valley villages suffered the most during the conflict, almost all burned to the ground, the whites who escaped the tomahawk fleeing to Boston. When they dared to return, they prospered, not only by farming but in transportation on the river and various canals. Mills soon followed, and education – the Pioneer Valley is the home of Mount Holyoke, Smith, Amherst, and the University of Massachusetts.

**Springfield,** the largest city in the Valley, grew up around the armoury founded there in 1777; munitions factories soon followed, and in the 19th century the famous Springfield rifle was developed. The city's close links with the war industry are explored in the *Springfield Armory National Historic Site* on Federal Street; the museum here contains the world's largest military collection (open Monday to Friday 9am-5pm, Saturday 10am-5pm, Sunday 1pm-5pm; admission). The Armory was only demilitarized in 1968 – many of the buildings now belong to a college. Besides rifles, Springfield is known as the birthplace of that uniquely American sport, basketball; in 1891, Dr James Naismith formed the first B-ball teams in a Springfield gym and told them to throw the ball through a peach basket. The *Naismith Memorial National Basketball Hall of Fame* on the campus of Springfield College (263 Alden Street) includes movies, etc, tracing basketball's history and shrines to past greats in the sport (open July and August 9.15am-6pm, June 10am-5pm, Sunday 1pm-5pm; admission). What Springfield is proudest of, however, are its rehabilitated neighbourhoods, its downtown area (although this is confusing to navigate and often seems strangely deserted) and the *Quadrangle,* downtown on State Street, a campus of big league culture unmatched in New England outside Boston. Four museums, the city library and an Episcopal Church surround a green square (all are free). Most unusual is

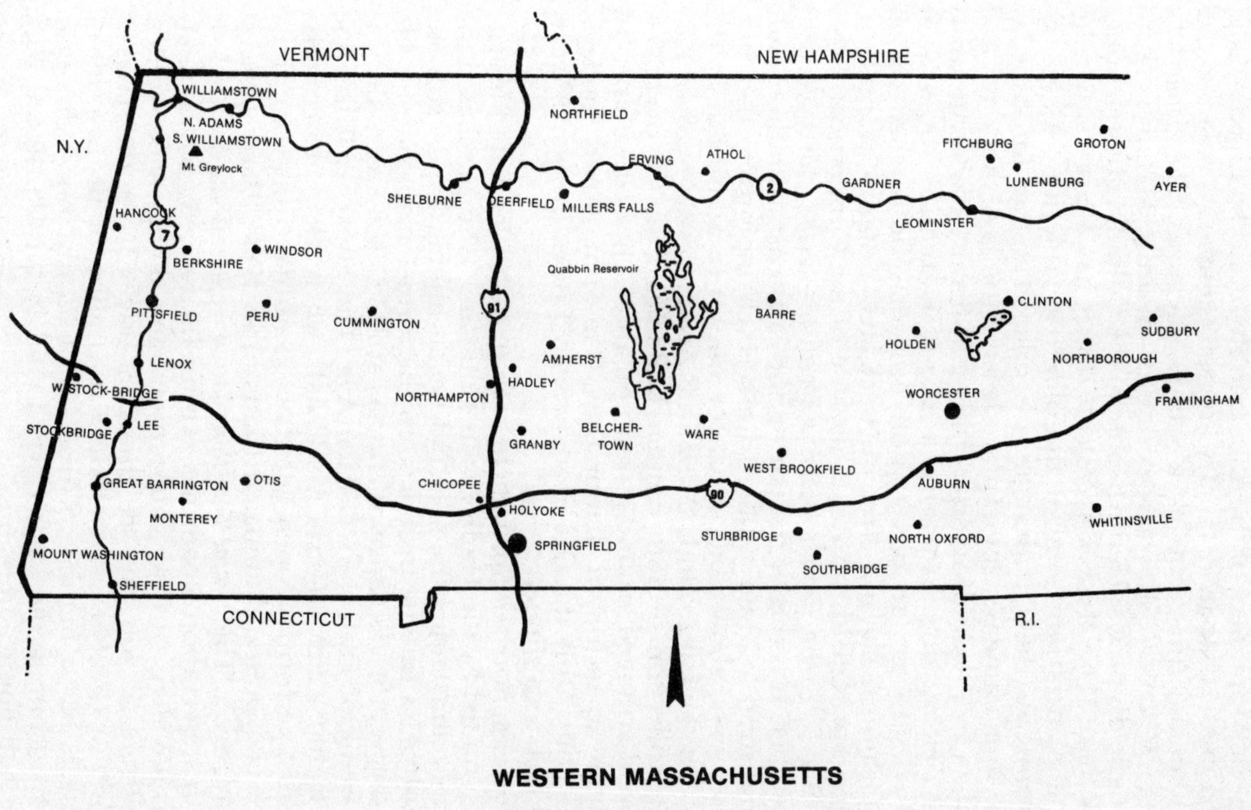
VERMONT
NEW HAMPSHIRE
N.Y.
WILLIAMSTOWN
N. ADAMS
S. WILLIAMSTOWN
Mt. Greylock
NORTHFIELD
ERVING
ATHOL
FITCHBURG
GROTON
LUNENBURG
AYER
SHELBURNE
DEERFIELD
MILLERS FALLS
GARDNER
LEOMINSTER
HANCOCK
WINDSOR
BERKSHIRE
Quabbin Reservoir
CLINTON
PITTSFIELD
PERU
CUMMINGTON
BARRE
SUDBURY
LENOX
AMHERST
HOLDEN
NORTHBOROUGH
W STOCK-BRIDGE
STOCKBRIDGE
LEE
NORTHAMPTON
HADLEY
WORCESTER
FRAMINGHAM
GRANBY
BELCHER-TOWN
WARE
WEST BROOKFIELD
GREAT BARRINGTON
OTIS
CHICOPEE
AUBURN
MONTEREY
HOLYOKE
SPRINGFIELD
STURBRIDGE
NORTH OXFORD
WHITINSVILLE
SOUTHBRIDGE
MOUNT WASHINGTON
SHEFFIELD
CONNECTICUT
R.I.
2
7
90
91
WESTERN MASSACHUSETTS
mls
0
10
20
30

the *George Walter Vincent Smith Art Museum* in the Italianate palazzo, containing one man's collection from various countries and various periods, but the picture you'll remember best is the 'Historic Monument of the American Republic' by Erastus Field, a Thomas Cole-like fantasy of monumental palaces and monumental Americans on a wall-sized canvas. The *Connecticut Valley Historical Museum* contains mainly artifacts from Springfield's past, including some of the Columbia bicycles once made here. The *Museum of Natural History* has a large aquarium and a planetarium, one of the oldest in America. (All of the museums in the Quadrangle are open Tuesday to Saturday 1pm-5pm, Sundays 2pm-5pm, closed Mondays, holidays and Sundays in July and August.) The main feature of downtown is *Court Square,* dominated by a 300-ft Florentine tower with carillon. On top an observation deck may be reached via an old-fashioned elevator (free on weekdays, 2.30pm-3.45pm).

**West Springfield,** on the other side of the Connecticut, hosts the 'Big E' – the *Eastern States Exposition* – every third week in September. It is the largest fair on the east coast, with thousands of industrial and agricultural displays, championship matches, amusements, shows, etc, most for one-price admission at the gate. On the fairgrounds (Memorial Avenue) is *Storrowtown Village,* a collection of 18th-century buildings from all over New England arranged around a common and furnished with period antiques (open May to Labor Day, 1pm-5pm, closed Sundays; admission). Only the Old Storrowtown Tavern is open all year, for lunch and dinner.

**Holyoke,** north of Springfield, was an early planned industrial city, founded by the Hadley Falls Company, who purchased the canal circumventing the falls and began milling paper, still one of Holyoke's leading products. In the former mansion of a silk mill owner, the *Wistariahurst Museum* at 285 Cabot Street, there is a diorama of Holyoke's Golden Age. The house itself has fine details and a French-style music hall, where chamber concerts are often performed (open Tuesday to Saturday 1pm-5pm; free). There is a pretty illuminated fountain in *Water Power Park* on Lyman Street. The *Mount Tom Reservation,* reached via Routes 5 or 141 to Reservation Road, has extraordinary views of the Connecticut Valley, bird-watching towers and skiing in the winter. Off Route 5, you can see dinosaur tracks from the Triassic period; the *Granby Dinosaur Museum* in Granby, on the east side of the river, has a number of displays of locally found dinosaur tracks, including the largest ever found in the US (Route 202; open 9am-6pm; admission).

Near Granby, **South Hadley** is home of *Mount Holyoke College,* founded in 1837 and the oldest women's college in America. The core of the campus was designed by Frederick Law Olmsted; it has a fine art museum. From South Hadley, you can either take Route 47 for *Skinner State Park,* where you can drive up Mount Holyoke to its ruined summit house for the panoramic view, or take Route 116 for *Nash Dinosaur Land,* with more tracks and one of the country's prime dinosaur quarries (open April to November, Monday to Saturday 8.30am-5pm, Sunday 9am-6pm; admission).

On the other side of the famous Connecticut River 'Oxbow' is the curious town of **Northampton,** where an uncle and niece, Oliver and Sophia Smith, left their mark in Smith charities, founded by Oliver, which give every bride in town a dowry, and Smith College, founded by Sophia in 1871, today the largest women's college anywhere. Northampton heard the fire-and-brimstone sermons of Calvinist Jonathan Edwards, and tasted the first Graham crackers in the world, thanks to Sylvester Graham. Calvin Coolidge lived here for 38 years and was even elected mayor once; the *Forbes Library* at 20 West Street has a large collection of Coolidge memorabilia.

At the top of Main Street, the campus of *Smith College* has a notable art museum, with many 20th-century masters (open 15 September to June, Monday to Saturday 9am-5pm, Sunday 2.30pm-4.30pm; in summer open Tuesday to Friday 11am-12 noon and 2pm-4.30pm). The *Northampton Historical Society* at 58 Bridge Street operates three houses built in 1658, 1792 and 1812, as well as an 1840 barn, full of antiques and other fond mementoes of the past (open Wednesday/Friday/Sunday 2pm-4.30pm; admission). The society also has maps of Northampton that point out interesting buildings in town, like the *Clarke School for the Deaf,* founded by Alexander Graham Bell.

Cross the Connecticut on Route 9 and head for another college town, lovely **Amherst,** which poetry lovers will recognize as the home of recluse Emily Dickinson; here she was born and here she wrote most of her verses. (Her house at 280 Main Street is privately owned, so you must telephone ahead to see it: ( (413) 542-2321.) She lived near *Amherst College,* one of the East Coast's nobbiest schools, with the excellent *Mead Art Building,* its collections ranging from a complete medieval dining hall to 19th-century paintings. Another college museum, the *Pratt Museum of Natural History* contains dinosaur skeletons and tracks, a huge mastodon and minerals (open Monday to Friday 10am-5pm, Saturday 1pm-5pm, September to May).

The *University of Massachusetts* is to the north of town, its enormous campus sprawling over 1,100 acres. For the visitor, its main attraction is the *University Gallery,* containing almost exclusively 20th-century American art (open Tuesday to Friday 11.30am-4.30pm, weekends 1pm-4pm, closed summer). Yet another college, *Hampshire College* is in the south of Amherst, giving the town a combined student population of 30,000, outnumbering residents. One non-college thing to see in the pleasant, tree-shaded town, the *Jones Library* at 43 Amity Street has special Emily Dickinson and Robert Frost rooms with their letters and works.

Between Amherst and Northampton, the pretty village of **Hadley** was saved at least temporarily from destruction in King Philip's War by Colonel Goff, ex-commander of Cromwell's elite Invincibles, who had been in hiding from the wrath of King James in Hadley. When the Indians were about to get the better of the settlers, he suddenly appeared like a ghost out of the past and rallied the defenders. It was only much later that the locals learned their saviour wasn't heaven-sent. Hadley has one of the finest historic houses in Massachusetts, the *Porter-Phelps-Huntingdon House,* at 130 River Drive; built in 1752 and unaltered since 1799, it is beautifully furnished (open 15 May to 15 October 1pm-4.30pm; admission). Note the long tobacco barns here and to the north along the valley.

In **Leverett** north of Amherst live a number of craftsmen who work, sell and demonstrate their various arts, from blacksmithing to photography, in the *Leverett Craftsmen and Artists' Center* (open 1pm-5pm, weekends 12 noon-5pm). In nearby **Shutesbury** there are two of the strange stone huts that seem to be outposts of Mystery Hill (see 'Salem, New Hampshire'). They may be found off Sand Hill Road.

North along the Connecticut we come to **Deerfield,** site of the Bloody Brook Massacre, the worst in King Philip's War, marked by an obelisk on Main Street. *Old Deerfield,* a National Historic District, was the actual location of the early settlement; after the massacre, some courageous settlers returned, only to suffer a devastating Indian raid in 1704 costing 50 lives – the survivors were taken into slavery. The village recovered, but quietly, and when it went into decline its homes were converted into museums, which may be toured (open Monday to Saturday 9.30am-4.30pm, Sunday 1pm-4.30pm; admission). On the Village Green is the elite school for boys, Deerfield Academy, founded in 1797; its first building, the *Memorial Hall Museum* holds a wide selection of Indian artifacts and antiques of every description (open mid May to mid November, 9.30am-5pm, Sunday 1.30pm-5pm; admission). **Miller's Falls,** on the eastern side of the Connecticut, may be reached via the beautiful, high-arched *French King Bridge,* its name derived from the French King Rock, a border of the lands claimed by French explorers for Louis XV. The very scenic **Mohawk Trail,** following an old path used by Mohawk raiding parties, heads west of Miller's Falls towards **Shelburne Falls** with its beautiful war memorial: the *Bridge of Flowers,* a 400-ft old inter-urban trolley bridge bedecked with shrubs and flowers. The *Potholes* here are not the street craters that plague most American towns, but depressions left by ancient flooding (signposted). **Charlemont,** a small resort town, has skiing and, close by, the *Mohawk Trail State Forest* with hiking, swimming and camping facilities. North of Zoar up to the Vermont border stretches the lovely **Deerfield River Gorge.**

From 1850 to 1875, almost 200 workmen died making the 21 million dollar, $4\frac{1}{2}$-mile-long *Hoosac Tunnel,* linking Boston and the west, passing by way of **North Adams,** an old mill town where the *Hoosac Tunnel Museum,* in a 1926 train car by the North Adams Inn, tells the history of the tunnel with exhibits and a slide show (open June to August; admission). North of town the *Natural Bridge,* the only natural marble bridge in North America, may be reached on Route 8; you have to pay to see it, but admission includes a spectacular gorge and ancient rock formations (open 30 May to 30 October). On the other side of North Adams, Route 2 to Notch Road stands the tallest mountain in Massachusetts, *Mount Greylock* (3,491 ft), with a 93-ft War Memorial on top, which you may drive to for the not surprising fantastic views; some people get an even better panorama by hang-gliding from the summit.

The northwesternmost town in the state, **Williamstown,** has yet another of America's top-ranking colleges, *William College,* endowed by a Colonel Ephraim Williams who died in the French and Indian War; his will, however, made it a condition that Williamstown be part of Massachusetts (New York coveted it). Today it is a popular resort among New Yorkers, the main centre of the northern Berkshires, and the site of two art museums: the *College Museum of Art* at Williams, with works from all periods (open Monday to Saturday 10am-12 noon and 2pm-4pm, Sundays 2pm-5pm; free) and the *Sterling and Francine Clark Art Institute* on South Street, founded by the heir of a sewing machine fortune, with an outstanding collection of medieval to 19th-century masters. In the entrance hall a voluptuous nude will catch your eye; this notorious painting, by Bouguereau, once hung in the Hofman House tavern in New York City, and somehow epitomizes the taste of the upper class in the Gilded Age. (The museum is open Tuesday to Sunday 10am-5pm; free.) North of town on Route 7, the *Sand Springs Mineral Springs* was a popular bathing spa for the Indians; a warm outdoor pool and a sauna are available for modern visitors.

From Williamstown south along the New York border you are in the **Berkshires,** the beautiful hills of Massachusetts, famed as an all-round resort with skiing in the winter and culture in the summer. Originally settled by the Dutch instead of the Calvinists, it has always had more rapport with New York than Boston. Its artistic patrimony began in the 19th century, when writers like Melville and Hawthorne spent relaxing summers in the hills. In 1934 the Boston Symphony began playing at Tanglewood. It has been trendy ever since.

Like North Adams, **Adams** itself was once an important mill town – if the old mills didn't give it away, the statue of President McKinley in the square, frozen in the act of debating for a tariff on imported textiles, would tell all. Susan B. Anthony was born here, and the town is proud of her, although everyone else in the country seems mad at her for the unpopular dollar coin her likeness adorns.

To the south, **Pittsfield** is the metropolis of the Berkshires; it's the county seat and birthplace of the General Electric Company in William Stanley's 19th-century lighting plant; today General Electric employs about a fifth of Pittsfield's residents. At **Arrowhead,** just outside Pittsfield, Herman Melville lived for thirteen years and wrote *Moby Dick* – the rolling Berkshire hills from his window are said to have reminded him of the sea. Built in 1780, the house at 780 Holmes Road is furnished as it was when Melville lived there (open May to October, Monday to Saturday 10am-5pm, Sunday 1pm-5pm, closed Tuesday; admission). Holmes Road is named for Oliver Wendell Holmes, whose summer house was nearby. In downtown Pittsfield, the *Berkshire Museum* at 39 South Street has collections of ancient art to Norman Rockwell to science and history (open Tuesday to Saturday 10am-5pm, Sunday 2pm-5pm, open Mondays July and August; free). The *Berkshire Athenaeum*, in the Pittsfield Public Library at 1 Wendall Avenue, contains a special Melville room with papers and portraits of the author (open on request during library hours). At weekends from June to October the old Coolidge estate south of Pittsfield is the scene of the *South Mountain Concerts* (tel: (413) 442-0130). Also to the south, the *Bousquet Ski Area* was one of America's first ski slopes – America's second ski tow and the first one to be lit at night.

West of Pittsfield, **Hancock**, a long narrow village near New York once had a thriving Shaker colony, founded in 1790; when the last of the Shakers was going to sell the property to a racetrack, a group of Pittsfielders rallied to save it and have since restored eighteen buildings, most famously, the round *Stone Barn.* Collectively known as *Hancock Shaker Village* it is a good place to learn of one of America's most successful communal experiments, that failed due to its rules of celibacy (open June to 1 November, daily 9.30am-5pm; $3.00 adults).

East of Pittsfield on Route 9, **Dalton** was the home of Zenas Crane's first paper mill before the Revolution; Zenas' son convinced the government to print paper money, and the Cranes have been supplying the special money paper ever since, made of rags, not of trees. The *Crane Museum,* located in an 1844 mill, features the history of paper and a collection of paper currency (open June to September, weekdays 1pm-5pm; free).

One of America's greatest contemporary poets, Richard Wilbur, lives in **Cummington** to the east; a former poet and editor of the *New York Evening Post,* William Cullen Bryant, was born here and in later years returned every summer. The *Bryant Homestead,* a fourteen-room white clapboard house built by Bryant's grandfather in 1783, contains books and memorabilia, and many of the souvenirs the poet brought home from his travels (open 14 June to 14 October, Friday to Sunday and holidays 1pm-5pm; admission).

South of Pittsfield is **Lenox,** home of *Tanglewood,* where the Boston Symphony's *Berkshire Music Festival* takes place from July to August (for information tel: (413) 637-1600 in Lenox, or (617) 266-1492 in Boston). The name 'Tanglewood' is in tribute to Nathaniel Hawthorne, who lived for several years on the estate where the 'Music Shed' stands today; here he wrote *The Wonder Book* and planned the *Tanglewood Tales.*

Lenox in the 19th-century was the summer home of Boston's literary elite, followed as usual by the very wealthy, whose elaborate 'cottages' earned Lenox the nickname 'the inland Newport'. When, as in Newport, World War I and income tax burst the bubble of the Gilded Age, Lenox suffered accordingly – until it was chosen as the summer home of the Boston Symphony. *The Mount,* novelist Edith Wharton's summer residence that she built in 1902, is now the home of *Shakespeare and Company,* which presents outdoor performances there in July and August, and gives summer weekends tours of the Mount (1pm-4pm; admission).

Of **Stockbridge,** where he had a studio, sculptor Daniel Chester French once said: 'I live six months of the year in heaven. The other six months I live, well – in New York.' Many consider Stockbridge to be the archetypal New England town, a belief certified by the fact that Norman Rockwell chose to move here from Vermont. He painted so many magazine covers – since reproduced on calendars, tea trays and greeting cards – of scenes in Stockbridge that many Americans who visit the town get a queer sense of déjà vu. The history of Stockbridge, however, is not ordinary. In the early 18th century it was founded with the sole purpose of educating and 'civilizing' the Mohican Indians in the company of several white families, who were to be their models. The Stockbridge Mohicans were the only tribe to serve in the Revolution, for which they were the first to receive citizenship, but gratitude ended there. When whites outnumbered the Indians, the Indians were sent to the Mid West. In the 19th century New Yorkers of means began to summer here, and the literati still do, like Robert E. Sherwood and Norman Mailer. Arlo Guthrie filmed 'Alice's Restaurant' in Stockbridge.

One of the few relics of the Indian period, the *Mission House* on Main Street was built by the first missionary to the Indians, Reverend John Sergeant, in 1739, the period to which the house is furnished (open 28 May to 15 October, closed Mondays; admission). One of the summer cottages built by the wealthy, *Naumkeag,* was designed in 1885 by Stanford White for Joseph Hodges Choate, a famous lawyer – the gardens are lovely (located on Prospect Hill, open in the summer, closed Mondays). On Main Street, the 18th-century Georgian *Old Corner House* contains a large number of Norman Rockwell paintings and town memorabilia (open 10am-5pm, closed Tuesdays; admission). In an alleyway off Main is the charming *Village Restaurant* seen in 'Alice's Restaurant'. On East Main Street the *Berkshire Playhouse,* a long established summer theatre, presents plays in an old casino designed by Charles McKim, from June to Labor Day (tel: (413) 298-5536 for details). Near here, on Route 183 is the lovely studio of Daniel Chester French, *Chesterwood;* here he designed the statue of Lincoln in Washington DC's Lincoln Memorial. The grounds are exceptionally lovely (open May to 5 November 10am-5pm; admission). At the junction of Routes 183 and 102 are the botanical gardens of the *Berkshire Garden Center* (open April to November).

**Lee** to the east is the only town in the state still quarrying marble, some of it used for the capitol in Washington. Further east, in **West Becket** (Routes 20 and 8) the *Jacob's Pillow Dance Festival* in the Ted Shawn Theater presents renowned international dance companies in summer performances (tel: 243-0745).

**Great Barrington,** the centre of less mountainous, gently rolling South Berkshire, was the first town in the world to be lit by alternating current, thanks to William Stanley, who later opened a lighting plant in Pittsfield. NAACP founder, W. E. B. DuBois grew up here on a farm on Route 23; Erica Anderson, film-maker and assistant of Albert Schweitzer, built the *Schweitzer Friendship Center* with the money he left her. The Center, located a couple of miles outside town at 7 Hurlburt Road, shows a film that Ms Anderson made of the doctor in his Gabon clinic (open daily in the summer, winter weekends). In June and July baroque ensembles perform the *Aston Magna concerts* in Great Barrington's St James Church and other locations (tel: 528-3747 for information).

**Sheffield,** an antique-buyer's paradise south of Great Barrington, has two covered bridges, the original 'upper bridge' dating back from 1853, and the 'lower bridge' a replica built in 1952. Further south, near the Connecticut line stands the 1735 *Colonel John Ashley House,* a finely restored house with an interesting history (open June to mid October; admission).

**South Egremont,** west of Great Barrington, is a New England village turned into a trendy ski resort; **Mount Washington,** the southwesternmost town in the state, is confusingly situated at the foot of Mount Everett, 2,624 ft high. The hardy can follow the trail in the Mount Washington State Forest to the 200-ft *Bash-Bish Falls* or to *Sages Ravine,* a 700-foot chasm reached from Salisbury Road. **Tyringham,** east of Great Barrington, is almost as remote. It went from Shaker community to summer community in the 19th century, and today it's best known for the Storybook *Tyringham Galleries,* designed by Henry Hudson Kitson, who sculpted the contoured roof (open daily; admission).

**Restaurants.** *In Springfield:* Student Prince and Fort**, 414 Fort Street; Ichabod's*, 8 Worthington Street. *In West Springfield:* Storrowtown Tavern***, at the fairgrounds. *In Holyoke:* Delaney House***, 1 Country Club Road; Mel's, 490 Pleasant. *In Northampton:* Wiggins Tavern**, 36 King Street; Miss Florence Diner*, Route 9. *In Amherst:* The Grist Mill**, Route 116; Goten of Japan**, Old Amherst Road. *In Greenfield:* Bill's Famous Restaurant**. *In Pittsfield:* Rainbow**, 109 First Street. *In Lenox:* The Candlelight Inn**, Main Street; Wolf's Log Cabin**, Route 7A. *In Stockbridge:* Red Lion Inn***; Village Restaurant*. *In Lee:* Morgan House**, 33 Main Street. *In Hancock:* Hancock Inn**. *In Great Barrington:* 20 Railroad Street*. *In North Egremont:* The Old Mill**, Route 71. *In South Egremont:* Swiss Hutte***.

## Annual Events in Massachusetts

**March:** Maple sugaring in the west.

**The Sunday after 17 March:** St Patrick's Day Parade in *Holyoke,* third largest in the country.
**19 April:** Re-enactment of the Battle of Concord, pre-dawn and daytime, *Concord.*
**Late May:** Spring Festival of the Portuguese Heritage Foundation, *Fall River.*
**First Saturday in June:** Johnny Appleseed Day, *Leominster.*
**Mid June:** Swedish Midsummer Festival, *Shrewsburg.*
**Last Saturday in June:** Three-day St Peter's Fiesta, *Gloucester.*
**Week before 4 July:** Village Fair, *Chatham.*
**Last Saturday in July:** Yankee Homecoming, *Newburyport.*
**Lask week in July:** *Marblehead* Race Week (sail boats); also New England Morgan Horse Show, *Northampton.*
**First week in August:** *Quincy* Bay Race Week.
**August Fridays:** Pilgrims' Progress (at 5pm) in *Plymouth.*
**Early August:** Feast of the Blessed Sacrament, *New Bedford.*
**Mid August:** *Marshfield* Fair.
**Week before Labor Day:** Three-County Fair, *Northampton.*
**Early September:** Cranberry Festival, *Harwich.*
**Ten days in late September:** Eastern States Exposition, *West Springfield.*
**Late September:** Northern Berkshire Fall Foliage Festival, *North Adams.*
**Early October:** National Invitational Women's Rowing Regatta, *Holyoke.*
**Columbus Day weekend:** Bourne Bay Scallop Festival, *Buzzards Bay.*
**October:** Cranberry Harvests throughout the southeast; also, Harvest Days at Plimouth Plantation, *Plymouth.*
**Late October:** *Worcester* Music Festival.
**Halloween:** Parades in *Salem.*
**Thanksgiving:** Celebration in *Plymouth.*

## Accommodation in Massachusetts

**In Boston** (area code: 617)
Ritz-Carlton, Arlington & Newbury St, tel: 536-5700. Deluxe; on the public garden.
Copley Plaza, 138 St James Ave, tel: 267-5300. Deluxe.
Colonnade, 120 Huntington Ave, tel: 424-7000. Deluxe; by Prudential Center.
Boston Park Plaza, Arlington at Park Square, tel: 426-2000. Very expensive.
Copely Square, 47 Huntington, tel: 536-9000. Moderately expensive; good location.

Lenox Hotel, 710 Boylston, tel: 536-5300. Expensive; near Prudential Center.
Parker House, 60 School St, tel: 227-8600. Expensive.
The Midtown, 200 Huntington, tel: 262-1000. Moderate.
Eliot, 370 Commonwealth, tel: 267-1607. Moderate.
Northeast Hall, 204 Bay State Rd, tel: 267-3042. Inexpensive; charming old home in the middle of Boston U; tea served in room.
Milner, 78 Charles St South, tel: 426-6220. Moderately inexpensive.
YMCA, 316 Huntington, tel: 536-7800. Inexpensive; for men and women.
YWCA, 40 Berkeley St, tel: 482-8850. Inexpensive; women only, must belong to Y.

**In Cambridge**
Harvard Motor House, 110 Mount Auburn, tel: 864-5200. Moderate; next to Harvard Square.
Hotel Sonesta, 5 Cambridge Pkway, tel: 491-3600. Expensive, on river.
Kirkland Inn, 67 Kirkland St, tel: 547-4600. Near Harvard Square, cheap.
YMCA, 820 Massachusetts Ave, tel: 876-3860. Inexpensive; men only.
YMCA, 7 Temple, tel: 491-6050. Women only; inexpensive.

**In Brookline**
Beacon Inn, 1087 Beacon St, tel: 566-0088. Inexpensive.
Strathmore House, 45 Strathmore Rd, tel: 566-8936. Youth hostel.

**South of Boston** (area code: 617)
Kimball's By-The-Sea, 87 Elm, tel: 383-6650, *Cohasset*. Moderately expensive; on the harbour.
The Governor Carver, 25 Summer St, tel: 746-7100, *Plymouth*. Fairly dear.
Cold Spring Motel, 188 Court St, tel: 746-2222, *Plymouth*. Moderate.
Alpine Motel, Route 28, tel: 947-0710, *Middleborough*. Inexpensive.
Skipper Motor Inn, 110 Middle St, tel: 667-1281, *Fairhaven*. Moderate; near New Bedford.
4-D Motel, US-6, tel: 678-9071, *Falls River*. Inexpensive.

**Cape Cod, Martha's Vineyard and Nantucket** (area code: 617)
*Write to the Cape Cod Chamber of Commerce for their Resort Directory (Jct. Rt 6 and 132, Hyannis, Mass. 02601) for complete listings. You must make a reservation if you expect to stay during July or August, otherwise it's easy to find a place. A few which stay open all year are:*
Bay Hill Inn, Rip Van Winkle Way, tel: 759-4434, *Buzzards Bay.* Old inn and motel; expensive.
Daniel Webster Inn, Main St, tel: 888-3622, *Sandwich.* Fairly expensive.
Sandy's Motor Lodge, Rt 6A, tel: 888-2275, *Sandwich.* Moderate.
Old Yarmouth Inn, Rt 6A, tel: 362-3191, *Yarmouth Port.* Charming old inn; moderate prices.
The Willows, 79 Seaside Ave, tel: 385-3232, *Dennis.* Expensive; near beach.
Linger Longer By the Sea, Linnell Landing, tel: 896-3087, *East Brewster.*
Cow Motel, Rt 23, tel: 255-1203, *Orleans.* Moderately expensive; on Cove.
Mid-Cape Youth Hostel, near Routes 6 and 28, tel: 255-9762, *Orleans.* Open 26 May to Labor Day; card and reservations required.
Cove Bluffs Motel, Rt 6, tel: 255-6514, *Eastham.* Moderate; by beach.
Gull Cottages, Rt 6, tel: 255-4644, *Eastham.* Moderately expensive; one/two bedrooms.
Richmond Inn, 4 Conant St, tel: 487-9193, *Provincetown.* Inexpensive.
White Wind Inn, 174A Commercial St, tel: 487-1526, *Provincetown.* Not to expensive.
Bradford Gardens Inn, 178 Bradford, tel: 487-1616, *Provincetown.* Moderately expensive; deluxe breakfasts.
The Town Inn & Lodge, 11 Library Lane, tel: 945-2180, *Chatham.* Moderate to expensive.
Moorings, 326 Main St, tel: 945-0848, *Chatham.* Moderately priced motel.
Red River Motel, Rt 28, tel: 432-1474, *South Harwich.* Moderate.
Snug Harbor Motor Lodge, Rt 28, tel: 775-4085, *West Yarmouth.* Inexpensive.
Yellow Door Guest House, 6 Main St, tel: 775-0321, *Hyannis.* Inexpensive.
Hyannis Inn Motel, 473 Main St, tel: 775-0255, *Hyannis.* Moderate.
Cotuit Inn, tel: 428-5000, *Cotuit.* Reasonably inexpensive.
Schofield's Guest House, 335 Grand, tel: 548-4648, *Falmouth Heights.* Cheap; on Nantucket Sound.

Coonamessett Inn, Jones Rd, tel: 548-2300, *Falmouth*. Moderate, good food.

**Martha's Vineyard**

Dagget House, N. Water St, tel: 627-4600, *Edgartown*. Expensive, but worth it.
Edgartown Inn, N. Water St, tel: 627-4794, *Edgartown*. Moderate.
Menemsha Inn, Menemsha Rd, tel: 645-9530, *Menemsha*. Moderately expensive.
Manter Memorial Youth Hostel, Edgartown Rd, tel: 693-2665, *West Tisbury*. Open 1 April to 30 November; card and reservations required.
The Wesley House, Lake Ave, tel: 693-0135, *Oak Bluffs*. Moderate.

**Nantucket**

White Elephant, Easton St, tel: 228-2500. Deluxe old establishment.
Jared Coffin House, Broad & Center, tel: 228-2400. Expensive; converted old mansion.
Star of the Sea Youth Hostel, Surfside, tel: 228-0433. Open 15 June to 5 September; card and reservation required.

**North of Boston** (area code: 617)

Colonial Inn, Concord Green, tel: 369-9200, *Concord*. Fairly expensive inn.
Hawthorne Inn, 462 Lexington Rd, tel; 369-5610, *Concord*. Moderate guesthouse.
Catch Penny, 440 Bedford St, *Lexington*. Very cheap.
Pleasant Manor, 264 Pleasant St, tel: 631-5843, *Marblehead*. Moderate.
Hawthorne Inn, Salem Green, tel: 744-4080, *Salem*. Moderate, fine old hotel.
High Cliffe Lodge, 181 Atlantic, tel: 283-0680, *Gloucester*. Expensive.
The Blue Shutters, Nautilus Rd, tel: 283-7600, *Gloucester*. Moderate.
Turk's Head Motor Lodge, 283 South St, tel: 546-3436, *Rockport*. Moderate to expensive.
Morrill Place, 209 High St, tel: 462-2808, *Newburyport*. Moderate inn.
YMCA, 40 Lawrence St, tel: 686-6191, *Lawrence*. Men only; cheap.

**Central Massachusetts** (area code: 617)
Framingham Motor Inn, 1600 Worcester Rd, tel: 879-8400, *Framingham.* Moderate to expensive.
Coach House Inn, Lunenburg, tel: 582-9921, near *Fitchburg.* Moderate.
Holiday Inn, North Main, tel: 587-1661, *Leominster.* Moderate.
Days Lodge, 50 Oriol Dr, tel: 852-2800, *Worcester.* Moderate.
Pleasant Valley Motor Lodge, Rt 146, tel: 865-5222, *Worcester.* Moderate to expensive.
YWCA, 2 Washington, tel: 791-3181, *Worcester.* Women only.
YMCA, 766 Main, tel: 755-6101, *Worcester.* Men only.
Publick House, Rt 131, tel: 347-3313, *Sturbridge.* Moderate to expensive inn.
Sturbridge Coach Motor Inn, US-20, tel: 347-7327, *Sturbridge.* Moderate.

**Western Massachusetts** (area code: 413)
Stonehaven, 70 Chestnut, tel: 781-8030, *Springfield.* Moderate; downtown.
YMCA, 275 Chestnut, tel: 739-6951, *Springfield.* Men and women; new; inexpensive.
Yankee Peddlar Inn, 1886 Northampton St, tel: 532-9494, *Holyoke.* Moderate with restaurant.
Autumn Inn, 250 Elm St, tel: 584-7660, *Northampton.* Moderate; finely rated.
North King Motel, 504 N. King St, tel: 584-8847, *Northampton.* Inexpensive.
The Lord Jeffery Inn, 30 Boltwood, tel: 253-2576, *Amherst.* Moderately expensive, on the Common.
Green Mountain Guest House, 94 High St, tel: 773-8748, *Greenfield.* Inexpensive.
The Sheraton North Adams Inn, 40 Main St, tel: 664-4561, *North Adams.* Expensive; indoor pool.
Le Jardin, Cold Spring Rd, tel: 458-8032, *Williamstown.* Moderately expensive inn.
The Springs Motor Inn, US-7, tel: 458-5945, *Pittsfield.* Moderate.
YMCA, 292 North St, tel: 445-4551, *Pittsfield.* Men only.
Eastover, 430 East St, tel: 637-0625, *Lenox.* Old mansion, now resort.
Blantyre Castle, Walker St, tel: 637-0475, *Lenox.* Scottish castle resort.
Cornell House, 197 Pittsfield Rd, tel: 637-0562, *Lenox.* Moderate inn.
Quincy Lodge, 19 Stockbridge Rd, tel: 637-9750, *Lenox.* Moderate; close to Tanglewood.

Red Lion Inn, Routes 7 and 102, tel: 298-5545, *Stockbridge.* Old big expensive inn, delightful to stay in.
Morgan House, 33 Main St, tel: 243-0181, *Lee.* Moderate-priced old inn.
The Dalton House, 955 Main St, tel: 684-3854, *Dalton.* Pleasant; moderate.
Wind Flower Inn, Routes 41 and 23, tel: 528-2720, *Great Barrington.* Moderate; with restaurant.
Mount Everett Youth Hostel, Rt 41, tel: 229-2043, *Sheffield.* Summer only; four miles outside of town; card required.
Ivanhoe Country House, Rt 41, tel: 229-2143, *Sheffield.* Moderate inn.
Jug End Inn, tel: 528-0434, *South Egremont.* Large, expensive resort complex.

**For more information on Massachusetts,** write to Massachusetts Department of Commerce Division of Tourism, 100 Cambridge Street, Boston, Mass. 02202. They can send you a brochure on campsites in the state as well. Hunters and fishermen should address their inquiries to the Massachusetts Division of Fisheries and Wildlife (same address as above).

# Vermont

'The Vermont Yankee is, one may say safely, the most impregnably Yankee of all Yankees.'

John Gunther

Perhaps the one thing that has done the most to make Vermont so unusual today is that it missed the physical and social disfigurement of the Industrial Revolution. Dairy farming, maple-sugaring and wood-working are still big industries in the isolated valleys of the Green Mountains. Native Vermonters can claim the purest Yankee pedigrees of any state in the Union; the largest minority, the French Canadians, have been so unassimilated as to continue to vote Democratic.

Bordered on one side by the Connecticut River and by Lake Champlain on the other, Vermont is one of our most mountainous states, with over a hundred alpine and nordic ski areas – Vermonters sometimes say it would be as big as Texas if ironed out flat. However, unlike the mountains of New Hampshire, the Green Mountains are fertile, tame and, as their name suggests, very, very green, complimented in intensity by a clear blue sky and bracingly fresh air. You can sense it, literally, the moment you cross the border into the state, save in March and April, Vermont's notorious 'mud season' which concludes 'ski season' with quicksand-like muck and mire in the backroads. When the mud runs the maple sap runs as well and maple-sugar houses stoke up their fires to boil the sweet, sticky goo and throw maple-on-snow parties with doughnuts, sour pickles and coffee.

Speaking of doughnuts, Vermonters are the country's connoisseurs of pastries. 'A Yankee is someone who eats pie for breakfast,' Robert Frost decreed, and Vermonters seem to like doughnuts for lunch and dinner as well. In many villages the centre of social life is the local doughnut diner, crowded at all hours of the day.

Although in recent years many 'outlanders' have settled in Vermont, seeking an escape from America's urban-suburban mayhem, the state has taken strenuous measures to keep the countryside from turning into a giant condominium development with its Land Capability and Development Act.

It is the state's simplicity of life that makes it so special; the understated Yankee sense of humour, the willingness to help out, the independent spirit and direct democracy of the citizenery are

QUEBEC
DERBY LINE
Jay Peak
JAY
NEWPORT
SWANTON
Isle La Mott
ST. ALBANS
FAIRFIELD
BROWNINGTON
Lake Willoughby
Grand Isle
CRAFTSBURY
Smugglers Notch
Mt. Mansfield
Lake Champlain
LYNDONVILLE
BURLINGTON
STONE
ST. JOHNSBURY
RICHMOND
CABOT
DANVILLE
SHELBURNE
Camels Hump
MONTPELIER
PEACHAM
PLAINFIELD
CEDAR BEACH
BARRE
NEW HAMPSHIRE
VERGENNES
WAITSFIELD
NORTHFIELD
Lincoln Gap
WEYBRIDGE
CHIMNEY POINT
91
MIDDLEBURY
BROOKFIELD
89
RIPTON
TUNBRIDGE
FAIRLEE
Green Mtn.
National Forest
STAFFORD
ORWELL
HUBBARDTON
WHITE RIVER JCT.
Lake Bomoseen
BOMOSEEN
WOODSTOCK
RUTLAND
4
CASTLETON
Killington Peak
POULTNEY
PLYMOUTH NOTCH
WINDSOR
7
N.Y.
WESTON
SPRING-
FIELD
11
PERU
MANCHESTER
VERMONT
BELLOWS FALLS
Green Mtn.
National Forest
mls
0
10
20
30
SHAFTSBURY
NEWFANE
Mt. Snow
9
BENNINGTON
BRATTLEBORO
WHITINGHAM
MASSACHUSETTS

only the vaguest of memories elsewhere in the country. Apart from the ski resorts, commercial and historical attractions are few; what visitors come for is that increasingly precious sense of what things would have been like if Jefferson's agrarian plan for the country had succeeded instead of Hamilton's mania for manufacturing. Someone once said that we may talk like Jeffersonians, but we always behave like Hamiltonians. In Vermont this doesn't seem true. As Bernard DeVoto once observed: 'There is no more Yankee than Polynesian in me, but when I go to Vermont I feel I am travelling toward my own place.'

## Getting Around Vermont

**By Air.** Burlington, Rutland and Montpelier are the major airports in the state. Burlington, the largest, is directly connected with over fifty cities in the United States and Canada. US Air, Delta, Air New England, Air North and Precision are the main carriers.

**By Train.** Amtrak's Montrealer from Montreal to New York and Washington passes through Vermont daily, stopping at St Albans, Essex Junction (Burlington), Waterbury, Montpelier Junction, White River Junction, Bellows Falls and Brattleboro. For schedule information in Vermont, tel: 1-(800)523-5720 (toll-free).

**By Ferry.** Billed as 'The Most Beautiful Ferry Crossings in North America', the Lake Champlain Ferries cross from Vermont to New York at three points: from Grand Isle to Plattsburgh, from Burlington to Port Kent, and from Charlotte to Essex in Adirondack Park. Only the ferry to Plattsburg runs all year round. For schedule information, write to Lake Champlain Transportation Company, King Street Dock, Burlington, VT 05401, or tel: 24 hours a day (802) 864-9804. In New York, call (518) 834-7960.

**By Bus.** The Vermont Transit Company covers the state, with connections on Greyhound to out of state locations. Besides local routes, Vermont Transit offers daily service to and from Logan Airport, express trips to Burlington from New York, Boston and Albany, as well as local connections from Montreal, Springfield, Portland, Bridgeport and Hartford. For information, call (802) 862-9671.

## History

Scholars now believe Vermont was inhabited as early as 2,000 BC by the Old Algonkins and the Adena people, who had a settlement now being excavated in Swanton. In the historical period it seems few Indians actually lived in the state, but used it as a sacred burial and hunting ground; a major trail from New York to Massachusetts passes through Vermont. Samuel de Champlain, the French explorer, was the first recorded white man to visit Vermont, at the behest of an Algonkin chief on the Ottawa River who asked his assistance in an expedition against the Iroquois. In the spring of 1609 Champlain and the Algonkins set out on the great lake that now bears the explorer's name, heading south to the area of Crown Point, where they met the Iroquois, who gravely outnumbered Champlain's troops. Things looked bad – then Champlain fired his arquebus and killed the Iroquois chief with a loud report. Amazed, the Iroquois fled. Some suggest this incident in the forest caused the antagonisms that led to the French and Indian War, the Iroquois never forgiving the French for Champlain's arquebus; but it was only the first of many such incidents, as the British and the Iroquois squabbled with the French and Algonkins in Canada over fur-trapping territories.

In 1741, Governor Benning Wentworth of New Hampshire began to sell land grants west of the Connecticut River, primarily to the Connecticut-born Ethan Allen and his brother Ira, who amassed over 12,000 acres. The colony of New York, which also claimed the land west of the Connecticut, protested at Governor Wentworth's land granting and took their case to the King, who decided in New York's favour in 1764. The New Hampshire settlers were outraged, particularly when New York decreed that they had to repurchase their land; by that time there were 131 towns in Vermont.

Enter Ethan Allen, one of the most extraordinary characters America has ever produced – in the words of Melville, 'a man of Patagonian stature'. Rather than submit to New York, he declared Vermont an independent Republic, to prevent, as he described, 'Women sobbing and lamenting, Children crying and Men pierced to the heart with sorrow and Indignation at the approaching tyranny of New York'. Allen organized the famous Green Mountain Boys, part militia, part gang, to keep the grasping New Yorkers at bay, while his brother Ira organized the government of the new Republic. The Constitution adopted in 1777 was the first to abolish slavery and to permit universal male suffrage. For fourteen years Vermont remained a Republic, with its own money, postal service and diplomatic relations with foreign states.

Meanwhile the Green Mountains Boys, by skirmish and Ethan Allen's eloquent bluster, harassed any New Yorker who set foot in Vermont. In 1774 New York passed the so-called 'Bloody Act', declaring that any Green Mountain Boy captured should be immediately executed. To 'the despotic fraternity of law-makers and law-breakers' Allen replied: 'Printed sentences of death will not kill us...' When news of Lexington and Concord reached him, Allen and the Green Mountain Boys soon found a new enemy to fight, and on 10 May 1775, they and Benedict Arnold crept up on the British and captured Fort Ticonderoga without firing a shot, and delivered one hundred much needed cannons to Washington.

Allen was later captured in an ill-fated attempt on Montreal and spent most of the war a prisoner. At the end of war, he returned to Vermont to continue the often comic-opera battle against New York and other states claimant on the Republic, while continuing to petition Congress for statehood. When Congress proved over and over again that it had no use for Vermont, Allen sought to change its mind by negotiating with British Canada. This gradually swayed the lawmakers, and Vermont became the fourteenth state in 1791, buying off New York's claim for $30,000. One of Allen's last achievements was a book of theology, of all things, *Reason, the Only Oracle of Man,* which made devout New England renounce him as a pagan.

Ethan Allen was only the first of famous iconoclasts produced in the bosom of Vermont's independent spirit; in 1839, in Putney, John Humphrey Noyes and his 'Perfectionists' founded the purest Communist community ever produced in the United States; he developed 'complex marriage' for the selective breeding of children, and was chased out of Vermont and various locales in New York before ending up in Oneida. Another son of Vermont, Joseph Smith, found the golden tablets and the Mormon church in Palmyra, New York. Brigham Young, his most famous follower, also hailed from Vermont.

Like the rest of New England, the first half of the 19th century in Vermont was a period of decline as thousands emigrated to the vast lands of the west. Like Connecticut, the state's sons were of an exceptional calibre: sixty went on to become the governors and eighty became college presidents, in other states. At the height of its population, 80% of Vermont was cleared for pasture and farmland; today 80% is forested, and only Wyoming has fewer people living within its borders.

What Vermonters may lack in quantity, they make up in quality; to wit: two Vermonters, Horace Greeley and Thaddeus Stevens, were leaders in the crusade to abolish slavery, and when the issue erupted into the Civil War, more Vermonters served per capita than any other state in the North. Recalling its days of independence, Vermont's legislature declared war on Germany on 11 September 1941 – two months before Pearl Harbor. Vermont was the first state to make provisions for a state university. In 1814 Emma Willard founded the country's first college for women at Middlebury; a sorority at the University of Vermont was the first in the country to admit a black student in 1946.

Vermont has its quirks: it has more cattle than people, and always elects its governors depending on what side of the mountain they come from (it alternates); it gave the country Calvin Coolidge, the most 'Yankee' of all our presidents; it was the first state to elect a Congressman while he was in jail (Matthew Lyon, imprisoned under the notorious Alien-Sedition Acts); and until recently refused any federal largess, even for flood control, though Vermont is one of the poorest states in the Union. It is also one of the most Republican – yet Burlington voters have recently elected a Jewish New York Socialist, Bernard Sanders, as mayor. Stubborn, individualistic and independent are the adjectives most often used to describe the Vermont character, but the attribute the visitor is most likely to encounter is neighbourliness, or 'helping out' as the locals would say. A true Vermonter, it has been said, when seeing your cow in the road, will not stop to ask you if you need help, but will go to work without a word.

## Southern Vermont (to Rutland)

Vermont's finest scenery, ski areas and culture are in the small towns and villages in the southern sector. Lovely **Bennington** in the southwest corner of the state is an appropriate place to begin; it was named in honour of New Hampshire governor, Benning Wentworth, for it was the first land he granted, in 1749, although no one settled there until 1761. Its landmark, a 306-ft stone monolith, is known as *The Bennington Battle Monument*, commemorating one of the big upsets of the Revolutionary War. Although the conflict actually took place in Hoosick, New York, nearby Bennington was the British goal, and Vermonters and New Hampshirites were the defenders, so Bennington had reaped the glory.

In the summer of 1777, General John ('Gentleman Johnny') Burgoyne's mission was to cut off New England from the other colonies, but with a supply line over 3,500 miles long, he needed provisions and horses. Learning that Bennington was a major supply depot for the Continentals, he sent 800 troops to seize what they could, and on 16 August they met General John Stark's ragtag militia. 'There are the Redcoats, and they are ours,' said the indomitable General, 'or this night Molly Stark sleeps a widow.' Together with Seth Warner, leading the Green Mountain Boys, he defeated the British and Hessians at their own redoubt, forcing them to flee. Their failure directly contributed to Burgoyne's defeat at Saratoga in October.

Today you can take an elevator to the top of the 1891 monument (open from April to October) for the exceptional views of the countryside. Near the monument a plaque marks the site of the *Catamount Tavern*, where Ethan Allen plotted the capture of Fort Ticonderoga. On West Main Street the excellent *Bennington Museum* houses the flag that flew in the Battle of Bennington, the oldest Stars and Stripes in the country; it also has an excellent collection of the renowed Bennington pottery and an old schoolhouse full of vintage Grandma Moses paintings (open March to November 9am-4.30pm; admission). In the nearby burial ground of the lovely *First Congregational Church* (1806), poet Robert Frost is buried among veterans of the Revolutionary War. His epitaph reads: 'I had a lover's quarrel with life'.

**North Bennington** is the home of innovative *Bennington College,* one of the most culturally progressive small colleges in America, and literally the most expensive. Near the college, don't miss 'The World's Largest Chair' – 19 ft high – in a furniture store parking lot. One of Vermont's few historic houses, the *Park McCullough House*, stands off Route 67A; an elaborate 35-room Victorian mansion which once belonged to Governor John McCullough, it still contains its original furnishings, including a tiny playhouse – a perfect replica of the larger house (open May to October, Monday to Friday 10am-4pm, Sundays 12pm-4pm; admission). South of Bennington is Vermont's only racecourse, the *Green Mountain Racetrack*, featuring pari-mutuel greyhound races; to the north, on East Road in **Shaftsbury**, Bennington Museum operates the *Peter Matteson Tavern* as a living colonial museum, with craft demonstrations (open 15 April to October, Tuesday to Saturday 9am-5pm, Sundays 1pm-5pm; admission).

Head north on Route 7, through **Arlington**, once home of Norman Rockwell and Vermont's most popular novelist, Dorothy Canfield Fisher, to the toll *Skyline Drive* that climbs to the summit of 3,816-ft Mount Equinox, tallest of the Taconic Range; the road is so steep that it closes in winter. Besides magnificent views, the Skyline Drive passes a 35-ton rocking boulder, a granite Carthusian Monastery, and a disappearing brook. The town of **Manchester** just north of Route 7 has been a resort ever since Lincoln's only son to survive childhood, Robert Todd, summered here with his mother and built *Hildene*, where his descendants lived until 1975. Located on Route 7 south of Manchester, it has many original furnishings, including an Aeolian Pipe Organ, played for visitors (open 23 May to 25 October, 10am-4pm; admission). Manchester itself is a fine old town, the home of the Orvis Company, one of the country's largest manufacturers of fishing equipment, on Route 7. The adjacent *Museum of American Fly Fishing* features such items as Winslow Homer and Herbert Hoover's fishing gear, antique rods and hand-tied flies (open 8am-5pm, 9am-5pm winter, closed holidays). The *Southern Vermont Art Center*, on West Road, has a permanent collection and a lovely sculpture garden (open June to October, Tuesday to Sunday 10am-5pm; admission).

East of Bennington, Route 9 climbs the Green Mountains to **Woodford**, the highest town in Vermont, then continues past several ski areas towards **Marlboro**, where the internationally acclaimed *Marlboro Music Festival,* under the direction of Rudolph Serkin, takes place every year (late June to mid August) on the campus of Marlboro college. (For concert schedules and ticket information write to the Marlboro Music Festival, 135 South 18 Street, Philadelphia, PA 19103; in June call Marlboro (802) 254-8163. Try to order tickets as early as possible.) A monument in **Whitingham** honours the great leader of Mormonism, Brigham Young, who was born there (Route 100 south).

**Brattleboro**, on the New Hampshire border, lies near the first English settlement in Vermont, Fort Dummer, established in 1724. The early settlement of the area, art, and Estey organs are the subjects of the *Brattleboro Museum and Art Center,* in an old railroad station on Vernon Street (open May to December, Tuesday to Sunday 1pm-4pm; donations). Route 30 leads north from here to **Dummerston**, where Rudyard Kipling built his home Naulahka in 1892. During his years in Vermont he wrote *The Jungle Book, Captains Courageous* and *Just So Stories*, and described his life in New England in *Letters of Travel.*

**Newfane,** north on Route 30, is considered by many to be the prettiest village in Vermont, with an elite summer colony that swears by it. North on Route 5 **Putney** is famous for Putney School and Senator George Aiken's *Wildflower Nurseries*, where wildflowers are cultivated and sold to home gardeners. One of the state's finest sugar houses, Harlow's, also on Route 5, lets visitors watch during maple season (March to April). **Bellows**

**Falls** north of Route 5 boasts of having the world's largest collection of steam locomotives in *Steamtown USA*; forty locomotives, steam train memorabilia, movies and a $1\frac{1}{4}$-hour trip on an antique train through several Vermont villages are a heady experience for a railroad maven (open weekends only, 29 May to 26 June and 11-26 September, with train trips at 11.35, 1.35 and 3.35; also open daily 27 June to 6 September and 27 September to 27 October; adults $5.50, children 2-11 $2.95). Hetty Green, 'The Witch of Wall Street', the richest woman in the world who lived on cold oatmeal and table scraps, lies in the cemetery of Immanuel Church in Bellows Falls.

To the west on Route 121 the tiny village of **Grafton** has been restored to its pristine, New England calendar appearance. West, in the Green Mountains, **Stratton** has winter sports and, in the summer, golf and art festivals. The Bromley resort to the north in **Peru** has an even more unusual summertime attraction: the world's longest alpine slide, 4,100 feet long, accessible via chairlift (open in good weather, 23 May to October, from 9.30am; admission).

**Danby,** north on Route 7 is where Helen and Scott Nearing, two teachers from New York City, moved in 1932 to become subsistence farmers. Their book *Living the Good Life*, a perennial favourite, chronicles the building of their house, their garden, their relations with neighbours and their attempt to keep culture alive in the backwoods – required reading for anyone contemplating a similar retreat from the rat race. Unfortunately for the Nearings, their paradise was encroached on by neighbouring ski resorts, and they moved to Maine. Two unique institutions have found their way to Danby: *The Peel Gallery* which displays and sells the works of sixty American artists at prices far below Soho's, and *Vermont Wineries*, which offer tastings of their unusual maple and rhubarb wines.

*Lake Bomoseen* has spawned two resort areas, **Hubbardton** and **Castleton**, the former the site of the *Hubbardton Battlefield and Museum*, where the only battle of the Revolution on Vermont soil took place, a prelude to the more important conflict at Bennington. On 7 July 1777, a foraging party sent by Burgoyne surprised Seth Warner and his Green Mountain Boys, fighting a confused battle for an hour before the Vermonters were forced to melt into the woods, and the British retreated to Ticonderoga, to meet later at Bennington. Near a monument on the field a newly built museum contains information and a diorama of the battle (open 15 May to 15 October, closed Mondays; donation).

Vermont's second largest town, **Rutland**, lies to the east, with its scenic backdrop of mountains and one of Vermont's finest publishing houses, Charles E. Tuttle and Co, who display rare books in their headquarters at 28 South Main Street. Also on South Main, the *Chaffee Art Museum* contains works by local and national artists in a fine old mansion (open Memorial Day to October, Monday to Saturday 11am-5pm, Sundays 1pm-4pm; free). Marble-quarrying **Proctor** nearby will tell you all you ever wanted to know about its main industry in the *Vermont Marble Exhibit* on 61 Main Street with films, displays, a collection of marble from all over the world, and a working sculptor (open 27 May to 15 October 9am-5.30pm; admission). Three miles from Proctor, on West Proctor Road, is the neo-Gothic *Wilson Castle* – according to its curious brochure, 'Haunted by silence, the slow workings of time leaving their mark upon the estate in many ways.' It is full of antiques from all over the world; added attractions are the Indian peacocks and Swiss Guards (open mid May to mid October 8am-6pm; admission).

Route 4 West leads to the *Killington Ski Area*, one of Vermont's best ski resorts in the winter, and, in the summer, home of the country's longest gondola rides ($3\frac{1}{2}$ miles) to the top of 4,241-ft Killington Mountain. From here you enjoy the same view that Reverend Samuel Peters had in 1763 when he gave the state 'a new name worthy of the Athenians and ancient Spartans; which new name is "Verd-Mont" in token that her mountains and hills shall be ever green and shall never die'. (The gondola, and the shorter chair-lift, are open daily from 29 June to 10 October, 10.30am-4.45pm, with sunset and evening rides on Wednesdays and Sundays; adults $4.50, children 6-12, $2.25 round-trip on the gondola.)

On the night of 3 August 1923, when news of Harding's death reached **Plymouth Notch** where Vice-President Calvin Coolidge was staying at his family homestead, his father, a public notary, got out the family Bible and swore him in as the 30th President of the United States. In 1956 Coolidge's son John donated the home to the state, furnished as it was that night; the recent renewal of conservative Republicanism has quadrupled the number of visitors to the birthplace of the man who uttered such aphorisms as 'The chief business of the American people is business' and 'The law that builds up the people is the law that builds up industry.' The *Calvin Coolidge Homestead* is open from Memorial Day to mid October 9.30am-5.30pm; admission. John Coolidge owns the *Plymouth Cheese Factory* nearby.

From here Route 100 heads south for Victorian **Weston**, where you can see a play in Vermont's oldest summer theatre, the *Weston Playhouse* (tel: 824-5288 for details), or pray with and purchase gifts from the Benedictines in the *Weston Priory*, an old farmhouse on Route 155.

**Windsor** on the Connecticut River may rightfully be called the birthplace of Vermont, for here in 1777 the representatives of the New Hampshire Grants met to adopt the Constitution of 'the Free and Independent State of Vermont' in a tavern. Just as they were about to sign the document, a messenger arrived with the news that Burgoyne's troops were in Hubbardton. Only a sudden storm prevented the Vermonters from rushing off to defend the new Republic, and the Constitution was duly signed. Today the *Old Constitution House* on North Main Street contains documents and other artifacts relating to the state (open late May to mid October, closed Mondays; admission). Lining Main Street are a number of fine old houses and the *American Precision Museum* and its collection of new and old inventions, photos and patent digests (open June to mid October 1pm-5pm; admission). The bridge crossing the Connecticut here, the *Windsor Covered Bridge*, is the longest covered bridge in America, built in 1866.

The country's first ski tow (1934) was built in **Woodstock**, to the north, an elegant old town, all lovingly restored. In the summer there are a number of festivals here, and major dog and horse shows. In nearby **Quechee,** the Ottauquechee River forms the *Quechee Gorge*, better known as Vermont's 'Grand Canyon', 165 feet deep.

**Restaurants.** *In Bennington:* Shirkshire**, 663 Main; Vermont Steak House*, 716 Main. *In Manchester:* Reluctant Panther***, West Road and Route 7; Colburn House**, Routes 11 and 30. *In Marlboro:* Silver Skates Inn**, Route 9. *In Brattleboro:* Country Kitchen**, Route 9. *In Bellows Falls:* Rita's*, lll Rockingham Road. *In Newfane:* Old Newfane Inn***, Route 30. *In Grafton:* Old Tavern***, Routes 121 & 35. *In Killington:* Killington Peak Restaurant***, at terminus of Gondola ride. *In Weston:* Vermont Country Store Restaurant*, Route 100. *In Windsor:* Top Hat**, Route 5. *In Woodstock Green:* Woodstock Inn***, on the Green.

## Northern Vermont

The state capital, tiny **Montpelier** is the centre of northern Vermont. On the banks of the Winooski river it fits Vermont well; the classically simple, gold-domed *Capitol*, topped with a statue of Ceres, goddess of agriculture, is set off by the green hills behind it. Built in 1859, it was one of the least costly capitol buildings in the country – not only are Vermonters frugal, but their elected officials may be the most honest of all the states. A Doric portico of Vermont granite graces the front of the structure; besides Vermont's legislature, when in session, it contains the usual tattered battle flags, etc. For some real Vermont memorabilia go to the Pavilion Buildings (originally a hotel) and the *Vermont Museum*, home of the state historical society (open Monday to Friday 8am-4.30pm, weekends in July/August 10am-5pm).

Some modest Vermont sprawl connects Montpelier and the larger town of **Barre** (pronounced 'Berry') a few miles away, where the biggest employer is the *Rock of Ages Granite Quarry*, the world's largest, in the nearby hamlet of Graniteville. The Visitors' Center here has a number of granite displays. Although they make other things out of granite besides memorials, it's hard to shake the feeling that you're in a tombstone showroom. However the view of the quarry is worth the trip, and from June to August, Monday to Friday, you can ride a special quarry train. (The Visitors' Center stays open May to October.) Just north of Barre in **Plainsfield,** *Goddard College* has very innovative learn-by-experience degree opportunities: south of Montpelier in Northfield, *Norwich University*, founded in 1819, is the country's oldest military college. **Brookfield**, south of US-89, has the country's last *floating bridge,* built over a pond after someone drowned one winter trying to drive their buggy across; now the bridge floats on 374 polyethylene barrels.

From **Duxbury** on Route 2 from Montpelier to Burlington you can see Vermont's most distinct mountain, aptly named *Camels Hump*. Here Route 100 intersects; to the north is Vermont's resort capital of **Stowe**, with its six mountains suitable for winter sports, including Vermont's highest, *Mount Mansfield* (4,393 ft). A four-passenger gondola will take you to the summit in the summer, as well as a toll road. An *Alpine Slide* will take you down. As its name suggests, **Smugglers Notch** below the mountain was once a highway of contraband to Canada. Golfing and theatre are among the summer activities, while all year round you can get into the hot-tub craze at the *Stowe Soaking Parlor* in the Stoware Mall.

South on Route 100, **Waitsfield** has the newly constructed *Bundy Art Gallery* with an international contemporary collection and a sculpture garden surrounded by woodlands (open 10am-5pm, Sundays 1pm-5pm, closed Tuesdays and holidays and in November; free). Some of Vermont's most striking scenery lies just south of here, in *Lincoln Gap* and at the *Moss Glen Falls*, both in the northern extension of Green Mountain National Forest.

Just east of Burlington, the small village of **Richmond** had five separate Christian sects in 1813 who decided that, instead of building five churches, they would pool their resources and build one for all – the result was the *Round Church Meetinghouse*, the only sixteen-sided church in the country.

**Burlington**, Vermont's largest city and only major industrial centre, once formed part of the Allen brothers' land grant. It boomed with the construction of the Champlain Canal, connecting the lake to the Hudson River and southern New York; at one time Burlington was the world's third largest lumber market, and many of its fine homes were the residences of lumber barons. When Charles Dickens passed through the area in the mid 19th century, he remarked that the steamboat *Burlington* on Lake Champlain was the most elegant in the world. Pleasant but dull, Burlington has several mementoes of Ethan and Ira Allen. On North Avenue stands the farmhouse that Ethan Allen built in 1785; he lies buried under a great monument in Greenmount Cemetery. Ira founded the *University of Vermont* here in 1791, where the *Fleming Museum* on Colchester Avenue has a diverse collection of art ranging from the pre-Columbian to American primitive to contemporary (open 9am-5pm, weekends 1pm-5pm; free).

The area's main attraction, however, lies just south on Lake Champlain. The vast *Shelburne Museum,* occupying 45 acres, has 35 buildings brought from all over New England, each filled with antiques that take a good day to see; collections include folk sculpture, early Delft, quilts, scrimshaw, Chippendale and Queen Anne furniture, pewter, toys, tools, Conestoga wagons, hats – and every child's favourite, the 220-ft Sidewheeler *Ticonderoga*, the last of its kind in the country (open 15 May to 15 October, 9am-5pm; adults $5, children 6-16 $2.50).

**Weybridge** saw the development of the first uniquely American horse breed, the Morgan Horse. Here the *University of Vermont Morgan Horse Farm,* a National Historic Site, has sixty descendants of the powerful Justin Morgan, a rare case of one animal producing a whole new breed. The Morgan farm has tours of the stables, and an audiovisual presentation on the horse's development (open May to October 9am-4pm; admission).

*Middlebury College* is an excellent undergraduate school in a pretty town; here the *Johnson Gallery* features temporary art exhibits, and the *Egbert Starr Library* has Robert Frost memorabilia. Robert Frost spent his last years in **Ripton,** where he began the famous Bread Loaf Writers Conference in 1921. You can visit his three-room farmhouse – ask directions in Ripton. Middlebury's *Sheldon Museum* at 1 Park Street has a wide variety of objects and furnishings from the 19th century (open June to mid October, 10am-5pm, closed Sundays; admission).

US-89 leads north from Burlington into Quebec, passing by way of **St Albans**, site of the Vermont Maple Festival.

From *Swanton* and the *Missisquoi National Wildlife Refuge* (4,800 acres on Lake Champlain) you can cross the bridge to Alburg and *Isle La Motte*, site of Vermont's first settlement when in 1666 the French built Fort Ste Anne.

East of here stretch the three counties that form Vermont's Northeast Kingdom, a sparsely populated region of hills, lakes and picturesque villages. Several of these are right on the Canadian border, like Beebe Plain and Derby Line, where there are people who sleep in the United States but eat dinner in Canada. Vermont's northernmost ski area, 'the Crown of Vermont', *Jay Peak* (3,870 feet) has an aerial tram to the top in summer and fall, taking sixty passengers at a time. Pretty *Montgomery Center* just to the south has six covered bridges. Many lovely lakes surround the Brownington area; the most beautiful, *Lake Willoughby,* was formed by a glacier; it measures 600 ft in depth and is surrounded by hills.

**Lyndonville** further south produces Vermont's strangest export, half of which they sell in California. Called Bag Balm, its original purpose was to relieve sore cow udders; today joggers rub it on their feet, sailors apply it to protect themselves from salt spray, people put it on squeaky machines. **St Johnsbury**, the largest town in the area, stands at the junction of three rivers and has made its living producing scales ever since resident Thaddeus Fairbanks invented the platform scale here in 1830. Members of the Fairbanks family built the town's two cultural institutions, the *Fairbanks Museum of Natural History* (83 Main Street) with push-button physical science displays and a large collection of birds from all over the world (9am-4.30pm; free), and the *St Johnsbury Athenaeum* at Routes 2 and 5, built in 1871 by John Davis Hatch. The paintings inside are the work of the Hudson River School and other American artists, the most impressive of them being 'The Domes of Yosemite' by Albert Bierstadt (open Monday to Friday 10am-8pm, Tuesday to Thursday 10am-5pm, Saturdays 1pm-2pm; free). The world's largest maple candy factory here sponsors the *Maple Grove Maple Museum,* with movies, sugaring exhibits and factory tours (open June to October 8am-5pm, weekends 9am-5pm; free).

**Danville,** seven miles west, is worth visiting for its robber-proof bank, the *Caledonia National Bank of Danville*, last robbed in 1934. Confidence runs high; Danville has 1,500 inhabitants but the bank has 6,000 customers. **Peachem's** church (south of Danville) is considered the prettiest in Vermont. New England's largest producer of cheddar cheese and butter, **Cabot**, lies to the west.

**Restaurants.** *In Montpelier:* Tavern Motor Inn**, 100 State. *In Barre:* Country House*, 276 N. Main Street. *In Brookfield:* Fork Shop**, by Floating Bridge. *In Stowe:* The Lodge, at Smugglers Notch***, Route 108; Green Mountain Inn**, Main Street. *In Waitsfield:* Millhouse Gallery***, Route 100. *In Burlington:* Park**, 139 Main Street; Chez Dufais*, 185 Pearl Street. *In Vergennes:* Painter's Tavern***, on the Green. *In Middlebury:* The Dog Team**, US-7; Middlebury Inn**, US-7. *In St Albans:* Charlie Vermont**, 3 Federal Street. *In Newport:* Frank & Pierre's***, 45 Main Street. *In St Johnsbury:* Aime's*, US-2 & Route 18; Lincoln Inn**, 20 Hastings Street.

## Annual Events

**February:** Winter Carnival and Snow Bowl, *Middlebury.*
**March to April:** Maple sugaring demonstrations throughout the state.
**April:** Apple Blossom Cotillion, *Springfield.*
**June:** Summer Solstice Festival, *Springfield;* Vermont Morgan Horse Show, *Essex Junction*; Vermont Dairy Festival, *Enosburg Falls.*
**June to September:** Killington Playhouse performances, *Killington.*
**Late June to August:** Marlboro Music Festival, *Marlboro.*
**July:** Antique Flivvers and Flyers, Sugarbush Airport, *Warren;* Cracker Barrel Bazaar, *Newbury;* Connecticut Valley Fair, *Bradford;* Old Time Fiddlers' Contest, *Craftsbury.*
**July to August:** Festival of Vermont Crafts, *Middlebury;* Champlain Shakespeare Festival, *Burlington*; Mt Mansfield Summer Playhouse, *Stowe.*
**August:** Bennington Battle Days, *Bennington;* Old Time Fiddlers' Contest, *Chelsea*; Green Mountain Horse Show and Dressage Competition, *Woodstock;* Scottish Festival, *Quechee.*
**September:** Vermont State Fair, *Rutland*; World's Fair, *Tunbridge;* Dowsers' Convention, *Dansville;* Old Time Fiddlers' Contest, *Barre;* Banjo Contest, *Craftsbury;* Antique and Classic Auto Show, *Bennington.*
**October:** Fall Foliage Festival, *Northeast Kingdom;* Apple Pie Festival, *Dummerston Center;* Fall Festival, *Montpelier*; Octoberfest, *Stowe.*
**November:** Wild Game Supper, *Bradford*; Craft Fair, *Jericho.*

## **Accommodation in Vermont** (area code: 802)

*(Note that there are free shelters every few miles on the Long Trail for hikers crossing Vermont.)*

**Southern Vermont**
Paradise Motor Inn, 141 Main St, tel: 442-8351, *Bennington.* Moderate; near museum.
Colonial Guest House, Orchard Rd and Rt 7, tel: 442-2263, *Bennington.* Inexpensive old farmhouse.
Inn at Manchester, Rt 7, tel: 363-1793, *Manchester.* Moderate; good restaurant.
Wilburton Inn, River Rd, tel: 362-2500, *Manchester.* Deluxe; old private estate, restaurant.
Kandahar Lodge, Rt 30 & Rt 11, tel: 824-5531, *Manchester.* Near 3 ski areas; expensive.
Hidden Lake Lodge, tel: 254-2770, *Marlboro.* Moderate to expensive; near Music Festival and Hogback Mountain ski area.
Dalem's Chalet, 16 South St, tel: 254-4323, *Brattleboro.* Moderate; restaurant.
Molly Stark Motel, Rt 9, tel: 254-2440, *Brattleboro.* Inexpensive.
Inn at Sawmill Farm, Rt 100, tel: 464-8131, *West Dover.* very expensive; many sports, near Mount Snow ski areas.
Snow Lake Lodge, Rt 100, tel: 464-3333, *Mount Snow.* Expensive; resort hotel.
The White House Inn, Rt 9, tel: 464-2135, *Wilmington.* Elegant, fairly dear, ski touring centre.
The Hayes House, tel: 843-2461, *Grafton.* Small, inexpensive inn.
Blue Gentian, tel: 824-5908, *Londonberry.* Expensive lodge near ski lifts of Magic Mountain.
The Londonberry Inn, Rt 100, *Londonberry.* Near ski areas and summer recreation; moderately expensive rooms, but inexpensive bunks with breakfast.
Johnny Seesaw's, tel: 824-5533, *Peru* (near Bromley). Moderate; family-oriented lodgings.
Tag's Motel, Rt 4A, tel: 468-5505, *Castleton.* Moderate.
Country Squire Motel, US-7B and Rt 103, tel: 773-3805, *Rutland.* Inexpensive.
Summit Lodge, US-4, tel: 422-3535, *Killington.* Deluxe; resort lodge.

*There are 90 lodges within a 25-mile radius of Killington Mountain, all covered under a central reservations bureau: 422-3711. Ski conditions are given toll-free in the Northeast outside of Vermont: (800)451-4301.*

Farmbrook Motel, Rt 100A, tel: 672-3621, *Plymouth.* Inex-

pensive.
New England Inn, Rt 4, tel: 457-9804, *Woodstock*. Inexpensive; Victorian inn.
Wolpert's Mountain Inn Motel, Rt 5, tel: 674-5565, *Windsor*. Inexpensive; fine views.
The Inn at Weston, Rt 100, tel: 824-5804, *Weston*. Moderate; breakfast included.
The Darling Family Inn, Rt 100, tel: 824-3223, *Weston*. Moderate; with breakfast, near ski areas.

**Northern Vermont**
Montpelier Tavern Motor Inn, 100 State St, tel: 223-5252, *Montpelier*. Moderate; near capitol.
Arnholm's Motel, US-302, *Barre* (between Barre and Montpelier). Only six rooms but charming, with many antiques. Inexpensive.
The Hollow Motel, 278 S. Main, tel: 479-9313, *Barre*. Moderate; breakfast.
Green Trails Country Inn, tel: 276-3412, *Brookfield* (by Floating Bridge). Moderate to expensive; historic building.
Whitetail Corners Guest house, tel: 889-5565, 3 miles out of *Tunbridge*. Inexpensive; with breakfast.
Hollywood Motel & Cottages, Rt 5, tel: 333-4471, *Fairlee* (1 mile north of town). Moderate.

*Like Killington, Stowe has an area association to call for information or reservations, toll-free (800)451-5100, or in Vermont 253-7321.*

Stowehof Inn, Edson Hill Rd, tel: 253-8500, *Stowe*. Deluxe Alpine ski resort.
The Inn at the Mountain, Rt 108, tel: 253-7311, *Stowe* (at Smuggler's Notch). Deluxe.
Trapp Family Lodge, Luce Hill, tel: 253-8511, *Stowe*. Fairly dear lodgings with the von Trapps of 'Sound of Music' fame.
Spruce Pond Inn, Rt 100, tel: 253-4828, *Stowe*. Moderate.
Tucker Hill Lodge, Rt 17, tel: 496-3983, *Waitsfield*. Moderate; near Mad River Glen and Sugarbush ski areas.
Sugarbush Inn, Rt 100, tel: 583-2301, *Warren*. Deluxe resort.
Knoll Farm Country Inn, Bragg Hill, tel: 496-3939, *Waitsfield*. Small old-fashioned guest farm with extraordinary views. Reservations a must.

*There are many other lodges, motels and inns in the Sugarbush area; call the Central Vermont Chamber of Commerce 229-4619 for more listings.*

Radisson Burlington Hotel, Burlington Square, tel: 658-6500, *Burlington*. Large, expensive downtown hotel.

Hotel Huntington, St Paul & Main St, *Burlington*. Inexpensive central hotel.

YWCA, 278 Main St, tel: 862-7520, *Burlington*. Inexpensive dormitories; women only.

T-Bird Motel, Rt 7, tel: 985-5663, *Shelburne*. Inexpensive; near museum.

Middlebury Inn, Rt 7, tel: 388-4961, *Middlebury*. Moderately priced old inn near college.

Maple Manor Motel, Rt 7, tel: 388-2193, *Middlebury*. Inexpensive.

Charlotte-Ellen Villa, 229 N. Main St, tel: 524-3602, *St Albans*. Very inexpensive.

Royle Swan's Motel, Rt 7, tel: 868-2010, *Swanton*. Inexpensive; restaurant.

Alpine Haven Chalets & Waldhof Lodge, tel: 326-4567, *Montgomery Center*. Expensive resort, near Mount Jay ski slopes.

Village Motel, tel: 988-2888, *North Troy*. Inexpensive; near Jay Peak area.

Bay View Motel, Rt 5, tel: 334-6543, *Newport*. Inexpensive; restaurant.

Echo Ledge Farm, Rt 2, tel: 748-4750, *East St Johnsbury*. Inexpensive accommodation on farm.

Aime's Motel, Route 2 & 18, tel: 748-3194, *St Johnsbury*. Moderate.

**More detailed information** on subjects like antiques, maple-sugar houses, covered bridges, inns and ski facilities may be had by writing to The Vermont Travel Division, 61 Elm Street, Montpelier, VT 05602 (tel: 828-3236).

# New Hampshire

'She's one of the two best states in the Union,' wrote New England poet, Robert Frost; 'Vermont's the other.' Wedged together, our 43rd and 44th largest states (New Hampshire is exactly 200 square miles smaller) are occasionally known as the Twin Sisters. In many ways they do have much in common. Vermont originally belonged to New Hampshire and both states have beautiful scenery, similar calendar-picture small towns, ski resorts, maple-sugaring, summer colonies of artsy people, and Yankee Republican philosophies. Today both their economies depend on tourism – New Hampshire more than any state in New England. However, they do have their differences.

Compared to Vermont's placid Green Mountains, the White Mountains of New Hampshire tower rocky and rugged, the highest range on the East Coast. Down their granite slopes rush the streams that form the Merrimack River, one of the key sources of water power of the early Industrial Revolution in America. Numerous mills, among them Manchester's Amoskeag, the world's largest, sprang up on its banks in New Hampshire and Massachusetts.

Unlike Vermont, industry in this state attracted a large influx of foreign workers – French Canadians, Irish, Poles and Greeks, who diluted New Hampshire's once pure English-Yankee stock. Today New Hampshire has twice as many people as Vermont; it was the only state east of the Mississippi to increase its population by more than 20% over the last ten years. Although the old mills have all closed, new industries have taken their place, lured by a unique lack of state sales or state income tax.

New Hampshire may rightfully claim to be the most democratic of the fifty states. It declared its independence from Britain seven months before the other colonies, and wrote into its state constitution the Right of Revolution. It gave American democracy its Demosthenes, Daniel Webster, who according to Stephen Benet's story, could out-argue the Devil himself. Not only do its citizens continue to participate in Town Meetings, New England's version of direct democracy; they also elect the third largest legislative body in the English-speaking world to represent them – 400 Congressmen for 870,000 people. Every four years it holds the first Presidential Primary in the country, on which hopeful candidates spend an incredible amount of time and money, visiting tiny villages and personally telephoning wavering voters. Every four years, the wee town of Dixville Notch

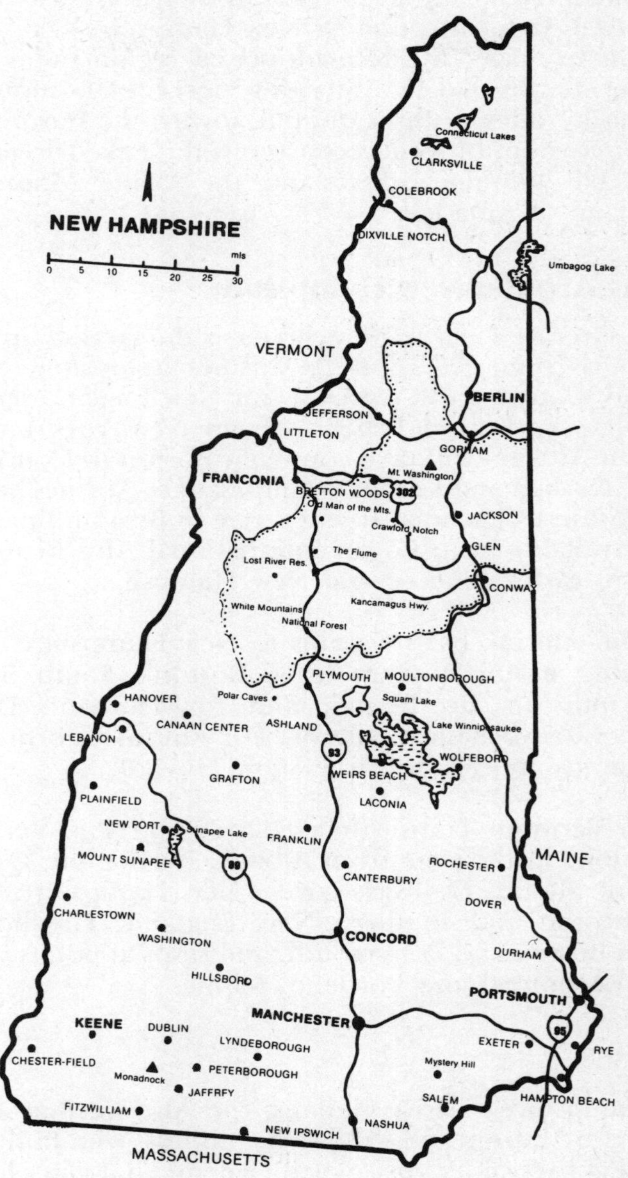
NEW HAMPSHIRE
mls
0
5
10
15
20
25
30
Connecticut Lakes
CLARKSVILLE
COLEBROOK
DIXVILLE NOTCH
Umbagog Lake
VERMONT
BERLIN
JEFFERSON
LITTLETON
GORHAM
Mt. Washington
FRANCONIA
BRETTON WOODS
302
Old Man of the Mts.
JACKSON
Crawford Notch
GLEN
The Flume
Lost River Res.
CONWAY
Kancamagus Hwy.
White Mountains
National Forest
PLYMOUTH
MOULTONBOROUGH
Polar Caves
Squam Lake
HANOVER
CANAAN CENTER
ASHLAND
Lake Winnipesaukee
LEBANON
93
WOLFEBORO
WEIRS BEACH
GRAFTON
PLAINFIELD
LACONIA
NEW PORT
Sunapee Lake
FRANKLIN
MOUNT SUNAPEE
89
MAINE
ROCHESTER
CANTERBURY
DOVER
CHARLESTOWN
CONCORD
WASHINGTON
DURHAM
HILLSBORO
PORTSMOUTH
MANCHESTER
KEENE
DUBLIN
95
LYNDEBOROUGH
EXETER
RYE
CHESTER-FIELD
Mystery Hill
Monadnock
PETERBOROUGH
JAFFREY
SALEM
HAMPTON BEACH
FITZWILLIAM
NASHUA
NEW IPSWICH
MASSACHUSETTS

in the north of the state manages to call in its twenty or so votes before any other place in the nation, which the media circus considers an important barometer of the national vote.

Despite its small size, New Hampshire has six distinct regions: the **Coastal Area**, surrounding New Hampshire's eighteen miles of ocean frontage; the **Monadnock**, a region quite similar to Vermont, dominated by America's most literary mountain; the **Merrimack Valley**, with its old mill towns; the **Dartmouth-Lake Sunapee** Region, of scenic recreation; the **Lake District**, around giant Lake Winnipesaukee; and the **White Mountains**, the Switzerland of America.

## Getting Around New Hampshire

**By Air.** Grenier Field in Manchester is the largest airport in the state; it is connected by Delta airlines to Boston, New York, Portland, Detroit and Cleveland. Air New England serves Keene from New York, and Lebanon from New York and Boston. Precision Airways will take you from Boston to Concord, Manchester, Nashua and Keene; Winnipesaukee Airlines has a service from Boston to Laconia. If you arrive in Boston, limousine service is available from Logan International Airport to points in southern, eastern and central New Hampshire.

**By Train.** Amtrak has no trains to New Hampshire, but direct connecting motor coaches leave Boston's South Station for Portsmouth on Greyhound, and for Durham, Dover and Rochester on Michaud Trailways. For Amtrak information from New Hampshire, tel: toll-free 800-523-5720.

**By Bus.** Vermont Transit (tel: (802) 295-3011 in Vermont) has connections in the state from Albany, Burlington, Quebec and Portland, Maine. Trailways covers New Hampshire from New York, Boston and southern New England; Greyhound runs between Boston and Portsmouth, and stops at points in the state between Montreal and Portland, Maine.

## History

New Hampshire's native Indians, the Abnaki, may have been preceded by Europeans – the Celts, no less, who built an astronomical observatory in North Salem, not far from New Hampshire's sea coast. Radio carbon-testing has dated the site as far back as 2,000 BC, but most archaeologists want nothing to do with Mystery Hill, as it is known, or any of the other non-Indian prehistoric sites in America: there are just too many questions and loose ends for a reputation to get snagged on. Until the scientific community reaches a consensus on its date and origins, you will have to visit Mystery Hill and judge for yourself (see 'The Coastal Region').

The first historical European settlement took place in 1623, at Odiorne's Point on the coast, and applied itself to fishing and trading. The new colony grew slowly, and in 1641 Massachusetts annexed it, although even this failed to attract more settlers because no one was sure to whom the land belonged, owing to a number of conflicting land grants and claims. By 1679 New Hampshire had only 209 eligible voters, but Robert Mason, heir to the original landowner, got the King to declare it a separate province, all the better to remove squatters. This failed; even back then the People's Assembly had too strong a voice to let Mason have his own way. He eventually sold it in disgust, and it changed hands a number of times before the King finally appointed a royal governor, Benning Wentworth, in 1741. Wentworth complicated matters further by granting land right and left on disputed territory after taking 500 acres for himself each time. When he granted lands west of Connecticut River, New York, which claimed the territory, formally complained to the King and Wentworth was forced to resign.

During Wentworth's reign, Major Robert Rogers and his Rangers became a New Hampshire legend in their battles against the Indians; Eleazar Wheelock founded Dartmouth College for the Indians; but perhaps most famously, Wentworth married his serving maid. Although this caused a terrible scandal at the time, it would only be an historical footnote if Longfellow hadn't written a poem about it in his *Tales of a Wayside Inn*.

Benning Wentworth was replaced by his nephew John Wentworth in 1766. The younger Wentworth restored his family's good name and was quite popular, although as the years went by he found it increasingly difficult to combine the interests of the King with the interests of his constituents. In 1774 he managed to keep the citizens of Portsmouth from dumping the King's tea into the harbour, even though he sympathized with their anger over the tea tax. Finally, when British ships took over the harbour and intercepted supply cargoes to Portsmouth, Governor Wentworth withdrew (August 1775). A local congress adopted a constitution for the colony in January 1776, in effect declaring its independence from Britain.

During the Revolutionary War Portsmouth became an important shipbuilding port, its most famous vessel, the *Ranger*, commanded by John Paul Jones. It also built the 74-gun *America* in 1782, at the time the largest ship ever made in America, and given by Congress to the French government in gratitude for its assistance in the war. Some of the ships built in Portsmouth became privateering vessels, and the port grew extremely wealthy with their prizes. The War of 1812 seemed like another windfall, until Portsmouth suffered a devastating fire in 1813; one of the homes burnt down belonged to a young lawyer named Daniel Webster, soon to make legal history in the Dartmouth College case of 1818, in which he convinced the Supreme Court that private and public corporations should be protected from federal interference. Meanwhile New Hampshire's economy shifted focus from the coast to the Merrimack River. Manchester became known for its great textile mills, and Concord for its Concord coaches, reputedly the sturdiest stagecoach ever built: it could float and take the roughest roads, even in Africa. By the mid 19th century, manufacturing industries employed over half the people in the state.

The Slavery Compromise of 1850 was engineered by New Hampshire's Daniel Webster and supported by President Franklin Pierce of New Hampshire, elected in 1852. New Hampshire's wavering position on slavery angered the rest of abolitionist New England, and Emerson was moved to write:

> The God who made New Hampshire
> Taunted the lofty land with little men–
> Small bat and wren.

However, once the Civil War began, New Hampshire responded by sending ten per cent of its entire population to aid the Union.

Ever since then, the state has been a bulwark of the Republican party and the one state-wide paper, the *Manchester Union Leader*, is the party's most conservative voice.

## The Coastal Region – Merrimack Valley and Monadnock

New Hampshire may have an extremely short coast, but it makes the most of it. Near the Massachusetts line, the country's most protested nuclear reactor *Seabrook* looms on the horizon. State parks and beaches line the rest of the waterfront; Hampton Beach, Great Boars and Little Boars Head are the most popular of the latter. At *Odiorne Point State Park* at Rye a stone monument commemorates the first settlers in New Hampshire. Just beyond is **New Castle**, a pleasant small town with New Hampshire's poshest resort hotel, Wentworth-by-the-Sea, in operation since 1874.

'Strawbery Banke', named for its fields of wild strawberries in 1630, lost its picturesque name for **Portsmouth** in 1653. It grew slowly to become the largest town in 18th-century New Hampshire, exporting masts and millions of feet of lumber to Great Britain and building ships for the Royal Navy. Elegant homes were constructed to accommodate the newly wealthy; most were burned in the fire of 1813, from which Portsmouth never really recovered. Although America's various wars since then revived its use as a port, the old neighbourhood fell into such decline that urban renewal slated it for destruction in the 1950s. A group of local citizens had an alternative proposal, an American first: instead of tearing down the old port, why not use the urban renewal money to rehabilitate it? The government agreed, and today *Stawbery Banke* is operated by a non-profit corporation. It consists of 35 buildings, almost all open to the public as museums, gift shops, craft demonstrations and galleries (open May to October 9.30am-5pm; $3.50, children 6-16 $1).

North along the Piscataque River, Market Street leads to the *Viking Dock* of the New Hampshire Port Authority from where you can take a cruise of Portsmouth harbour or the Isles of Shoals (see 'Maine'), or go on a whale-watching expedition. (For information tel: Viking Cruises 224-2525 in New Hampshire, or toll-free out of state 1-(800) 258-3608.)

Outside of Stawbery Banke, Portsmouth has a slew of historic houses, including the *John Paul Jones House* (State and Middle Streets) where Jones lived for a year during the Revolution, supervising the construction of the *America*, 'the most lingering and disagreeable service' he was charged with during the war. In the end, he didn't even get to sail the great vessel before Congress gave it to France. Today the house is the headquarters of the Portsmouth Historical Society, and contains a wide variety of local historical artifacts (open 15 May to 1 October, Monday to Saturday 10am-5pm; admission). Three impressive Georgian mansions survived the great fire: The *Wentworth-Gardner House* (1760) on Mechanic Street, an almost perfect example of the genre; the *Warner MacPheadris House* (1716) at 150 Daniel Street, a beautifully proportioned mansion on the National Historic Register; and the *Moffatt-Ladd House and Garden* (1763) at 154 Market Street, once occupied by William Whipple, Signer of the Declaration of Independence, and particularly noted for its grand stairway. All are open to the public for modest admission.

South of Portsmouth on Route 101, **Exeter** is the home of America's most elite prep school, the *Phillips Exeter Academy*; it was also the birthplace of Daniel Chester French, one of the country's greatest sculptors – the *War Memorial* in town was his handiwork. One of New Hampshire's four original towns, Exeter began as a lumbering centre. Its first sawmill, *Gilman Garrison*, built in 1650 as a house-fort for protection from the Indians, may be visited at 12 Water Street (open summer: Tuesday/Thursday/Sunday 1-5). In the early 18th century the British chopped down the tallest and straightest trees in the area for the King's Navy with total disregard for property rights, thereby inciting a 'tree-party' of Exeter men dressed up by Indians who sank the British agents' boat and chased them back to Portsmouth. Today Exeter's stately elms fear neither the Indians nor the British, but the gypsy moth caterpillar. These are the plague of New England; in 1981 there were so many of them that their slippery bodies on the tracks stopped the trains.

From Exeter Route 111 will take you to the wee hamlet of **North Salem** and the most fascinating attraction in the state: the oldest buildings in the United States, 'America's Stonehenge' – *Mystery Hill*. Of the 300 prehistoric stone cellars and huts located in New England, Mystery Hill is by far the most important, apparently serving as a religious centre for a megalithic culture 4,000 years ago. The first white settlers to encounter the strange stone ruins probably thought the Indians had made them, if they thought about them at all. Jonathon Pattee built his home on top of some the structures and sold half the stone to the city of Lawrence for sewers (1823-49). His house was later burned down and the site remained abandoned until William Goodwin purchased it in the 1930s. Goodwin believed the ruins were the work of Irish Culdee monks, and 'reconstructed' the site according to his beliefs, which few accepted. In 1958 the present owner and founder of the New England Antiquities Research Association, Robert Stone, opened the site to the public.

Carbon-dating, the style of the hand-cut standing stones and walls, some questionable inscriptions, the primitive stone tools discovered on the site – all point to a megalithic culture of around 2,000 BC, similar to the Iberian-Celtic civilization of the period. The centre of the complex, from where most of the stones were quarried, has carefully carved drains, wells and stone buildings, the largest of which is 'the Oracle Chamber' with its 'Speaking Tube' connected to the 4½-ton grooved 'Sacrificial Table'. Similar structures and sacred crystals, discovered at the bottom of the wells, have been noted at other megalithic sites, but the clincher that Mystery Hill is the real thing is its astronomical observatory; fortunately, the Lawrence sewer men left us the great standing stones in the outer walls. You can easily sight the various alignments from the *Astronomical Viewing Platform*, a recent structure replacing the original that was destroyed by the diligent Mr Goodwin. The stones, covering some fifteen acres, pinpoint astronomical events of 1,500 BC including the position of the old pole star Thuban and the exact location of the sunrise on the summer solstice 3,500 years ago. You can visit Mystery Hill and find out the latest mind-boggling discoveries from April to November on weekends, 10am-4pm, and daily from May to 31 October 9.30am-5pm; admission $4.

Route 111 meanders towards the Massachusetts border past Salem's *Canobie Lake Park* with rides, cruises and other entertainment in the summer, and *Benson's Wild Animal Farm* in Hudson with 500 exotic fauna, trained animal shows, midway rides, a garden maze, etc (open mid April to mid October, 10am-5pm; admission). Children will also enjoy the special *Children's Museum* in the *Arts and Science Center* in **Nashua**, a large industrial city on the other side of the Merrimack. Besides the Children's Museum, there are changing exhibits at the Center, located at 14 Court Street (open daily expect at lunch hour, closed Mondays and summer Sundays; admission).

Just north of here on Route 3 you can tour the *Anheuser-Busch Brewery* in **Merrimack** with free samples of brew, or just take in the *Busch Clydesdale Hamlet* where the famous horses with the furry feet live when not filming commercials; even when the Clydesdales are on tour, two remain in the hamlet (all open daily except Mondays from 1 October to 1 June, with brewery tours from 9.30am-3.30pm; free).

New Hampshire's largest city, **Manchester**, was called Derryfield and was a typical New England town when Samuel Blodgett arrived on the scene in 1793; by 1807 he had built a canal around the falls in the river and proclaimed: 'As the country increases in population we must have manufactures, and here, at my canal, will be a manufacturing town that shall be the Manchester of America.' Three years later the Amoskeag Manufacturing Company was formed, manufacturing locomotives, fire engines and paper, as well as textiles. The first mill workers came from rural New England; after the Civil War French Canadians, Irish and other Europeans formed almost 90% of the workforce. Amoskeag did its best to keep them from unionizing by providing a wide range of benefits – everything except higher wages and a less than 54-hour working week.

In 1927 the world's largest mill began to self-destruct, liquidating its cash reserves; in 1922 and 1933 employees walked out, the Depression sharply curtailed business and a flood in 1936 caused heavy damage. Under somewhat suspicious circumstances Amoskeag shut down, to the advantage of bondholders but causing the loss of 82,000 jobs in Manchester.

Manchester has recovered from this devastating blow; today the Amoskeag buildings house over a hundred different firms. Among its various cultural institutions are the *Manchester Historic Association* at Amherst and Pine, with a large collection of decorative arts and historical artifacts (open Tuesday to Friday 9am-4pm, Saturdays 10am-4pm; free), and the *Currier Gallery of Art*, at 192 Orange Street, containing European and American art and New England furnishings and crafts (open Tuesday to Saturday 10am-4pm, Sundays 2pm-5pm; free).

**Bow**, north along the Merrimack, was the birthplace of Mary Baker Eddy, founder of the Christian Science Church. She lived many years in **Concord**, the state capital, a quiet town that pays court to the *State House* on the Main Square. John Gunther in his *Inside USA* called it 'the ugliest state capitol I ever saw', and he saw them all. Although some of the atrocities there in the 1940s have since been purged, Concord still isn't much. However, the people in the Visitors' Center of the State House are very friendly and will answer any questions you may have about New Hampshire. The *New Hampshire Historical Society* at 30 Park Street features, among its rooms of New Hampshire historical memorabilia and decorative arts, an original Concord Coach (Monday to Friday 9am-4.30pm; free). The *Pierce Manse*, at 14 Penacook Street, was the home of Franklin Pierce, fourteenth President of the United States and, by all accounts, the most dashing. Located in Concord's Historic District, it contains items from the President's life (open from June to Labor Day, closed weekends and holidays; admission).

To the north, **Canterbury** had one of the nation's very last Shaker colonies, surviving into the 1960s – it was founded in 1792. Today you can tour *Shaker Village* (Shaker Road, off Route 106) with its interesting Museum of Inventions, Industries and Craftsmanship of the busy Shakers (open 23 May to 14 October, closed Sunday and Monday; admission).

The southwestern corner of New Hampshire has a number of ski areas, lakes, and one of New Hampshire's two famous mountains – *Monadnock,* the towering 3,165-ft landmark of this picturesque region, located southeast of Keene. Its name, a geographical term referring to its stubborn resistance to erosion, continues to inspire American writers and musicians and artists who make their summer homes in the area, most famously in Peterborough's *MacDowell Colony.* Founded by Marian MacDowell, widow of composer Edward, the Colony consists of 25 studios that guarantee peace and privacy. Open to the public are the MacDowell Log Cabin and gravesite, and the Colony library with exhibits.

**Jaffrey** to the south hosts the *Monadnock Music Festival* every summer, as well as the Amos Fortune Forums every Friday evening in the summer. Amos Fortune, buried in the 1775 *Old Meeting House* cemetery, was according to his epitaph: 'Born free in Africa. A slave in America, he purchased liberty, professed Christianity, lived reputedly, and died hopefully Nov. 17 1801. At 91.' In his will he left sums to the church and to the establishment of a public school. Also buried here is novelist Willa Cather. South of Jaffrey, signs in **Rindge** direct you to the *Cathdral of the Pines*, a national memorial to men and women who died in America's wars, featuring the Altar of the Nation, made from stones brought from the four corners of the globe.

In May, the *Curtis Dogwood Reservation* in Wilton is a riot of blossoms. West of Rindge the pretty village of **Fitzwilliam** lies in the shadow of Little Monadnock and the *Rhododendron State Park* where acres of rhododendrons bloom in July.

Route 32 leads north from here to **Keene**, the largest town in the area, one of the country's first manufacturers of glass and pottery. You can see some of the famed Keene Glass and Hampshire Pottery in the *Colony House* at 104 West Street. Other exhibits include locally manufactured toys and antiques (open May to mid October 10am-4.30pm, closed Mondays; admission). The *Antique Carriage and Sleigh Museum*, on the bank of the Connecticut River in **West Chesterfield** (Route 9), contains a diverse, interesting collection of pre-automobile vehicles (open May to mid October; admission).

**Restaurants.** *In Portsmith:* Yoken's**, Route 1; Red Lion**, 2470 Lafayette Road. *In Rye:* Joseph's Rye of the Rocks***, 1505 Ocean Boulevard. *In Exeter:* Exeter Inn***, 90 Front Street. *In Nashua:* The Chart House**, 1 Nashua Drive. *In Merrimack:* The Hannah Jack Tavern**, D. W. Highway. *In Manchester:* The Hanover House***, 897 Hanover; China Dragon**. *In Antrim:* Maplehurst Inn***, Route 202. *In Milford:* Hayward Farms**, Route 101 A. *In Peterborough:* Ridan**, Route 202 N. *In Keene:* Henry David's***, 81 Main Street.

## Dartmouth-Lake Sunapee, the Lakes District and White Mountains

**Lake Sunapee,** the resort centre of southwest New Hampshire, lies at the foot of *Mount Sunapee* in a state park of the same name; in the summer you can take a gondola to its 2,743-ft summit (daily from mid June to Labor Day; admission) for the lovely panorama, or swim at *Mount Sunapee State Beach*, one of the finest in the state, or take a cruise out of *Sunapee Harbor* on the *Mount*

*Sunapee II* (daily departures at 10 and 2.30 from late June to Labor Day; tel: 763-4030). In the winter there are ski areas at Mount Sunapee and nearby at *King Ridge* and *Ragged Mountain.*

The southern extension of Mount Sunapee State Park, *Pillsbury State Park* recalls the New Hampshirite who immigrated to Minneapolis to found a flour empire; **Washington** just south of it, named back in December of 1776, has been called 'the most pristine village' in the state. **Newport**, just west of Lake Sunapee, is a fine old town noted for its 1822 *Congregational Church* and near it, on the Common, the *Clock Museum* with five centuries of timepieces and other collectables (open summer only, 9am-4pm, Sundays 1pm-4pm; admission).

North along the Connecticut at **Cornish** a summer art colony was begun by Augustus Saint-Gaudens in 1885, which soon attracted many of the artistic leaders of the late Gilded Age, like fairy-tale illustrator Maxfield Parrish, novelist Winston Churchill, Herbert Croly and Finley Peter Dunne. Today the *Saint-Gaudens National Historic Site* pays homage to one of America's greatest sculptors, who created some of his best work here from the time he bought the house until his death here in 1907. Today visitors may tour his home, gardens and reconstructed studio where some 300 examples of his work are on display (located on Route 12A, open May to October 8.30am-5pm; admission).

**Hanover**, home of Ivy League *Dartmouth College*, is north along the Connecticut. Chartered in 1769 by King George III as an Indian college (the Indians didn't stay long), Dartmouth's lovely campus has several sites worth visiting, most famously the 1962 *Hopkins Center*, in itself the major cultural arena north of Boston, with two theatres featuring year-round performances of the Dartmouth Players, a concert hall, several art galleries with changing exhibits, studios, a sculpture garden and, in July, the 'Celebration Northeast' of traditional performing arts – fiddling, clogging, story-telling, etc. (The Center is open daily, 11am-4pm and 7pm-10pm.) The *Dartmouth College Museum* on College Street contains natural science and anthropology collections from all over the world (open Monday to Saturday 9am-5pm, Sundays 2pm-5pm; free), and in the *Baker Memorial Library* you can see Orozco's famed murals.

East of Hanover rock-hounds won't want to miss the *Ruggles Mine* in **Grafton** (Route 4), the oldest mica, uranium, feldspar and beryl mine in the United States, first dug in 1803. The road leads up to Isinglass Mountain where visitors can pocket free samples – after paying $2.50 admission fee. There is also an exhibit on regional minerology (open daily from June to mid October).

The main feature of the Lakes District, **Lake Winnipesaukee** was named by the Indians in honour of a marriage between a maiden and a chief of warring tribes. After the ceremony the newlyweds sailed across the lake in their canoe, making the dark churning waters grow calm and sparkling; the Indians believed it a good omen, and henceforth called the lake Winnipesaukee, 'The Smile of the Great Spirit'. Today summer resorts and activities line its uneven shores, best enjoyed on a cruise on one of the ships of the *Winnipesaukee Flagship Corp* (tel: 366-5531) departing from Weirs Beach, Wolfeboro, Center Harbor, Alton Bay and Meredith. Lake Winnipesaukee is surrounded by hills; at **Gilford** a ski area and Alpine Slide at *Alpine Ridge* overlook the lake and White Mountains. (The slide is open from mid June to mid October.) For the new 'Aquaboggan' water slide you need your bathing suit. *Funspot* at nearby **Weirs Beach** has such features as an Indian Village, Storybook Forest, Go-Karts, 350 electronic games, pony rides, Paco's Tacos, etc, etc, rather like the pleasure land for naughty boys in Pinocchio (open all year round from 10am).

**Laconia**, just to the south, hosts the World Sled Dog Championships every February. **Plymouth**, to the north, saw the beginning of two careers, Daniel Webster as a lawyer and Robert Frost as a poet – Frost taught at what is now Plymouth State College. The *Polar Caves* in West Plymouth (Route 25) are the big attraction here; an ancient glacier knocked the side of Mount Haycock off into a dramatic pile of granite boulders that form the caves. Inside you can see fluorescently lit minerals and native plant life, and outside the Rock Garden of the Giants (open 17 May to 13 October, 9am-5pm; admission).

To **Moultonborough** on the north shore of Lake Winnipesaukee came midget millionaire Thomas Gustave Plant in the first decade of this century to build a castle like his idol Napoleon, high on a lava outcropping of the Ossipee Mountains. It cost him $7 million, and the result may be seen in a truly magnificent setting, with views of up to 75 miles – hence the name *Castle in the Clouds*. The house contains Plant's Napoleon collection, but what most people come for are the 6,000-acre grounds with very scenic riding trails and waterfalls (open May to October daily 9am-6pm; admission).

On the eastern shore of Lake Winnipesaukee, **Wolfeboro's** most popular attraction is the *Wolfeboro Railroad Company's* trains that make a lovely 2-hour, 24-mile round trip journey to Wakefield and Sanbornville, where you can board as well. (Trains run from 23 May to 18 October; tel: 366-5531 for schedule.) From Wolfeboro take Routes 28 and 16 north to *West*

*Ossipee* and the *Whittier Gondola*. The summit of Mount Whittier, named for the poet who summered near here, affords fabulous views (gondolas run weekends all year round, daily from mid June to mid October), but even more fabulous are those from atop Mount Cranmore (4,895 ft.) in *North Conway*, attainable via skimobile. The skimobile, a local innovation built in 1938, operates from May to October. In summer the mountain attracts intrepid hang-gliders, who compete in August. The *Conway Scenic Railway* on Route 16 offers a tamer way to see the White Mountains, via steam locomotive; the round trip takes one hour (tel: 356-5251 for schedule).

**Glen**, north on Route 16, has two very popular commercial attractions: *Story Land*, an imaginative amusement park for children (open from mid June to Labor Day, 9am-6pm), and its more recent relative, *Heritage New Hampshire*, which attempts to bring the state's history alive via life-sized dioramas and Sensurround trickery (open from Memorial Day to mid October 9am-6pm; admission). Glen is at a major crossroads in *White Mountain National Forest*, dominated by the Presidential Range and the highest peak in the northeast, *Mount Washington* (6,288 ft). From Indian times to Nathaniel Hawthorne, these majestic mountains – older than the Rockies – have garnered many legends; by the end of the 19th century this 'Switzerland of America's' natural attractions – the Old Man of the Mountains, the Flume, the Connecticut Lakes – were well known among the resort set. Anthony Trollope passed through them on his American visit, believing them to be 'inhabited either by Mormons, Indians, or simply black bears' but instead finding hotels on every bit of level land; several of these remain, including the famous Bretton Woods, where the World Monetary Conference was held in 1944. (Visitors today can receive detailed information on skiing, snowmobiling, canoeing, swimming etc, by writing to the White Mountains Region Association, Lancasterm, NH 03584.)

Route 16 north of Glen leads to **Jackson**, site of three alpine ski areas and the *Wildcat Mountain Gondola* which takes you up to Mount Washington's next door neighbour (operates summer only, from Memorial Day to mid October, 9.30am-5.30pm). This, one of the oldest gondolas in the country, is on the other side of *Pinkham Notch*, past Glen Ellis Falls. From Glen House begins the toll automobile road to the summit of *Mount Washington;* built in the 19th century P. T. Barnum called the drive 'the Second Greatest Show on Earth'. The mountain stands out almost overbearingly above the others in the Presidential Range and affords really unforgettable views; Captain John

Smith noticed it while exploring the coast, and named it in 1614 'the Twinkling Mountain of Angososico'. The road and the Cog Railway (Route 302) to the summit are open only from May to October as weather permits. This is important, as the summit of Mount Washington has the worst weather in the Continental United States, with a mean temperature of 27° and a recorded wind speed of 231 mph – the highest wind ever recorded (April 1934). Arctic flowers grow in the permafrost in the *Alpine Garden* on the upper slopes of the mountain. (The fee for driving up Mount Washington is $8 per car and $2 per passenger. If you don't care to drive, a stage service operates to take you to the summit from 8am to 4.30pm; $9 per person, $4.50 for children 5-13.)

Route 16 continues north to **Berlin**, a town of unusual smells, a pretty Russian Orthodox Church on the hillside, and home of the country's first ski club, which built the *Nansen Ski Jump* just north of town.

Route 302 from Glen passes through **Crawford Notch** beneath Mount Washington. About halfway through the White Mountains a place called *Willey House* recalls a spooky occurrence that Nathaniel Hawthorne fictionalized in 'The Ambitious Guest' of his *Twice-Told Tales*; on 28 August 1826 the Willey family, who operated an inn in the Notch, heard the roar of a landslide approaching the house and fled to safer ground. Rescuers later found the house standing intact, as the Willeys had left it, and the bodies of the family buried in rubble a short distance away – a ridge had diverted the landslide just above the house. North of here, in an elegant old hotel in **Bretton Woods,** the World Bank was organized, the dollar became the international exchange currency, and the price of gold was set after the war at the Monetary Fund Conference. Today it is a major alpine and cross-country ski area, very near the Base Station of the *Mount Washington Cog Railway*. Built in 1866 and funded by the New Hampshire legislature, it climbs 3½ miles to the top of the mountain – the world's first mountain-climbing railroad, with grades averaging 25%, its steepest grade 34.4% on the trestle called Jacob's Ladder; the cog engines are tilted to compensate for the incline. The railway has operated every year except during the Great War and has never had an accident. (The train runs at weekends from Memorial Day to 26 June, daily through Labor Day, less frequently until 12 October. Trains generally run every hour, and passengers are advised to come early in the day to avoid long waits in line. A round trip will set you back $10, children 6-12, $5).

At *Twin Mountain* you can either continue on Route 302 to

Littleton or take Route 3 southwards for **Franconia Notch**, the western pass through the White Mountains. Here the main site is the **Old Man of the Mountains**, the great stone profile in the mountain immortalized by Hawthorne in his story 'The Great Stone Face'. The Old Man was formed 200 million years ago, but in recent years the state has had to lend a hand in preserving it from erosion. Very nearby is the entrance to the *Cannon Mountain Aerial Tramway*, the oldest in the country, with new 80-passenger cars that take you to the top of 4,200-ft Cannon Mountain where you can see as far away as the Adirondacks of New York (open 23 May to 18 October; admission). Further south Mother Nature has created more wonders: **The Basin**, a glacier-formed granite pothole 20 ft in diameter, and **The Flume**, an 800-ft abyss by Mount Liberty, with walls as high as 70 ft and no more than 20 ft apart, which visitors stroll through on a boardwalk to a waterfall (open 23 May to 18 October; admission).

Further south, in **Lincoln** the visitor encounters *Clarke's Trading Post* with train rides through a covered bridge, a haunted house and trained bears high on perches. At Lincoln the *Kancamagus Highway* (Route 112) cuts across the mountains to Conway (see above), a scenic route that passes by *Loon Mountain*, where yet another gondola ride will take you to the top (open mid June to mid October); here you can ski on the grass in the summer. To the west, Route 112 leads to the lovely *Lost River Reservation*, named for the river that appears and disappears among the boulders in Lost River Gorge. A boardwalk follows the river's scenic antics down the gorge and through caves (admission); there is also a free nature garden with 300 species of flora and an ecological museum (all open May to October, 9am-5.30pm).

Commander of the Union balloon force in the Civil War, scientist and inventor Thaddeus S. C. Lowe was born in **Jefferson**, just north of White Mountain National Forest. Today the town has been given over to tourism, with such attractions as *Six Gun City* (Route 2), a Wild West amusement park and show, and *Santa's Village*, also on Route 2, with deer, macaws, rides, and Christmas in July. In the former luxury hotel, the Waumbek Inn, the new *Waumbek Arts Center* (Route 2) sponsors a seven-week White Mountains Festival of the Arts in July and August, featuring nationally known artists and performers (for a schedule, write to them at Box 145, Jefferson, NH 03583, or tel: 586-4322).

From here Route 3 follows the course of the Connecticut River northwards to **Columbia**, with a very pretty covered bridge spanning the Connecticut, and **Colebrook**, with the Oblate Fathers' *Shrine of our Lady of Grace* on manicured grounds; to the east Route 26 heads for tiny **Dixville Notch**, famous for getting its election returns in first and for its Wilderness Ski Area. Further north the country is wild, the towns frontier-like. During the 1820s and '30s, the inhabitants of this area, disgusted by the border conflict with Canada, formed themselves into the 'Independent Republic of Indian Stream', with **Pittsburg** as the capital and residence of its president. **Clarksville** is dead on the 45th parallel, halfway between the Equator and North Pole. A plaque in the town informs you that a line from here, through the centre of the earth, would emerge in the Indian Ocean 982 miles from Perth, Australia.

**Restaurants.** *In Mount Sunapee:* Gary's*, Route 103. *In Newport:* Old Brick Hearth Steak House**, Routes 11 and 103. *In New London:* Pleasant Lake Inn***, N. Pleasant Street. *In Charlestown:* Trolley Stop**, Main Street. *In Lebanon:* Landers***, Route 120. *In Hanover:* The Hanover Inn*** and Peter Christian's Tavern**, both near the Green. *In Plymouth:* Candelight Travelers**, US-3. *In Ashland:* The Common Man***, Route 93. *In Gilford:* King's Grant Inn**, Routes 11B and 11C. *In Wolfeboro:* Wolfeboro Inn**, Route 109. *In Laconia:* Hickory Stick Farm**. *In North Conway:* The Eating House**, Route 16. *In Pinkham Notch:* Dana Place Inn*, Route 16. *In Gorham:* Saladino's*. *In Bretton Woods:* Darby's Tavern**. *In Franconia:* The Horse & Hound Inn***, Wells Road. *In Littleton:* Emilio's**. *In Dixville Notch:* The Balsams***, Route 26.

## Annual Events in New Hampshire

**Easter:** Sunrise Service, *Cathedral of the Pines*.
**April to October Sundays:** Antique Fair at *Amherst*.
**Mid June:** Rock Swap & Mineral Tours, *Gilsum,* north of Keene.
**June to August:** Barnstormers' Theater, *Tamworth*. New Hampshire's oldest summer theatre (tel: 323-8600 for information).
**1-15 July:** Rhododendron blossom season, *Fitzwilliam*.
**4 July:** Celebrations and fireworks at *Weirs Beach* and *Keene*.
**Mid July:** Annual performance of the Old Homestead Play, *Swanzey*.
**Late July:** Regional Craftsmen's Fair, *Canaan;* also, Volvo International Tennis Tournament, Mount Cranmore, *North Conway*.
**10 July to August:** Summer Fair, Waumbek Center, *Jefferson*.
**Early August:** Craftsmen's Fair, Mount Sunapee State, *Newbury;* Monadnock Antique Show, *Peterborough;* Epsom Old Home Day Weekend, *Epsom;* also White Mountains Old Time & Blue Grass Festival, in *West Ossipee*.

**Late August:** Lakes Region Fine Arts & Crafts Festival, *Meredith*; Antique Show, *Milford;* State Fair, *Plymouth.*
**Labor Day:** Celebration at *Francestown.*
**Early September:** Antique Show, *Milford;* Air Show, *Lebanon.*
**Mid September:** Ceres Street Invitational Golf Tourney, *Portsmouth*, golf tournament through the streets and restaurants; also Ralifans Day, *Conway Scenic Railway;* and Gathering of the Scottish Clans, *Mount Loon.*
**Late September:** Oktoberfest, *Keene.*
**Early October:** Fall Foliage Tours, *Monadnock Region;* also Fall Foliage Festival at *Warner.*
**First Weekend of October:** Firemen's Parade & Muster, *Keene.*
**Mid November:** Christmas Craft Fairs at *Canaan* and Strawbery Banke, *Portsmouth.*
**27 November to 3 January weekends:** Christmas Illumination at La Salette Shrine, *Enfield.*

## **Accommodation in New Hampshire** (area code: 603)

**Southern New Hampshire**
Ashworth By the Sea, 295 Ocean Blvd, tel: 926-6762, *Hampton Beach.* Expensive resort, fine restaurant.
Windjammer Motel, 935 Ocean Blvd, tel: 962-2500, *Hampton Beach.* Fairly moderately priced; near beach.
Inn at Christian Shore, 335 Maplewood, tel: 431-6770, *Portsmouth.* In 1800 house, moderate, breakfast included.
Wentworth-by-the-Sea, New Castle Island, tel: 436-3100, *Portsmouth.* Deluxe old resort recently redone.
Hoyt's Motor Court, 891 Ocean Blvd, tel: 436-5350, *Rye.* Moderate to expensive; housekeeping cottages, great views, near beach.
Randall Hostel, University of New Hampshire, tel: 862-2120, *Durham.* Youth hostel members only, reservations encouraged.
The Exeter Inn, 90 Front St, tel: 772-5901, *Exeter.* Expensive old classic.
Rancho Motor Lodge, 234 N. Broadway, tel: 898-2268, *Salem.* Moderate; near Mystery Hill.
Green Ride Motor Lodge, D. W. Hway, tel: 888-2500, *Nashua.* Moderate; with restaurant.
Susse Chalet Motor Lodge, 2 Progress Ave, tel: 889-4151, *Nashua.* Inexpensive chain.
YMCA, 30 Mechanic St, tel: 623-3558, *Manchester.* Men only, inexpensive.
Queen City Motor Inn, 140 Queen City Ave, tel: 622-6444, *Manchester.* Moderate.

Brick Tower Motor Inn, 414 S. Main St, tel: 224-9565, *Concord.* Modern, with restaurant; moderate.
YMCA, 15 N. State St, tel: 224-5351. *Concord.* Men only.
The Willows Inn, Rt 101, tel: 924-3746, *Petersborough.* Moderate to expensive.
Sharon Studio Barn, tel: 924-6928, *Petersborough.* Inexpensive dorm or room accommodation; open mid May to mid October, call first.
Woodbound Inn, Woodbound Rd, tel: 532-8341, *Jaffrey.* Golf course, skiing, winter sports; expensive.
Winding Brook Lodge, Park Ave, tel: 352-3111, *Keene.* Moderate; excellent restaurant, pool.
Doyle House, Keen State Colle, tel: 352-1909, *Keene.* Summer youth hostel, card required.
Yankee Traveler Motel, Rt 12, tel: 357-0044, *Keene.* Inexpensive.
John Hancock Inn, Main St, tel: 525-3318, *Hancock.* Moderate inn, since 1789.

**Northern New Hampshire**

The Inn at Sunapee, Burkehaven Rd, tel: 763-4444, *Sunapee.* Moderate; spacious grounds, restaurant.
Hide-Away Lodge, Twin Lake Villa Rd, tel: 526-4861, *New London.* Inexpensive; fine country inn with good restaurant, near sports.
Pleasant Lake Inn, N. Pleasant St, tel: 526-6271, *New London.* Moderate; near skiing.
Hilltop Motel, Routes 11 and 103, tel: 863-3456, *Newport.* Moderate.
The Hanover Inn, Main & East Wheelock, tel: 643-4300, *Hanover* (near Dartmouth). Expensive.
Indian Shutters Inn, Old Claremont Rd, tel: 826-4445, *Charlestown.* Inexpensive small inn from 1791.
Candlelite Travelers, Rt 3, tel: 536-2330, *Plymouth.* Moderate to expensive.
Pilgrim Motel & Cottages, Rt 3, tel: 536-1319, *Plymouth.* Inexpensive.
Little Holland Court, Routes 3 and 175, tel: 968-4434, *Ashland.* Moderate cabins with many sports.
Christmas Island Resort, Rt 3, tel: 366-4378, *Laconia.* Expensive; on Lake Winnipesaukee.
Lord Hampshire Resort, Rt 3, tel: 524-4331, *Laconia.* Moderate to expensive; private; lovely view.
Lakeside Hotel, Lakeside Ave, tel: 366-4662, *Weirs.* Inexpensive; private beach.
Pick Point Lodge & Cottages, Rt 109, tel: 569-1338, *Wolfeboro.*

Expensive; on lake, sports.

Allen A. Resort, Rt 28, tel: 569-1700, *Wolfeboro*. Deluxe resort, beach, entertainment.

Wabanaki Lodge, tel: 323-8536, *West Ossipee*. Very rustic (no electricity) cottages, beach, trails, etc.

Matterhorn Motor Lodge, Rt 25, tel: 253-4314, *Moultonborough*. Moderate to expensive; between White Mountains and Lake Winnipesaukee.

Darby Field Inn, Bald Hill, tel: 447-5919, *Conway*. Moderate; fine dining, lovely views.

The Bernerhof Inn, Rt 302, tel: 383-4414, *Glen*. Bed and breakfast; inexpensive.

Dana Place Inn, Pinkham Notch Rd, tel: 383-6822, *Jackson*. Moderate; fine restaurant.

Thorn Hill Lodge, tel: 383-4242, *Jackson*. Facing Mount Washington; expensive; good dining.

Wildcat Inn, tel: 383-4245, *Jackson*. Charming inn, moderate, views.

Mount Washington Hotel, tel: 278-1000, *Bretton Woods*. Elegant old resort, tennis, summer only.

Grand View Lodge, Rt 3, tel: 846-5731, *Twin Mountain*. Moderate old inn, winter sports.

Lovett's Inn, Routes 18 & 141, tel: 823-7761, *Franconia*. Expensive; gourmet restaurant.

Raynor's Motor Ledge, Routes 18 &142, tel: 823-5651, *Franconia*. Moderate.

Mount Liberty Motel & Cabins, tel: 745-2288, *Lincoln*. Inexpensive to moderate.

Jack O'Lantern Resort, Rt 3, tel: 745-8121, *Woodstock*. Deluxe resort.

Kancamagus Motor Lodge, Kancamagus Hway, tel: 745-3365, *Lincoln*. Moderate.

The Inn at Loon Mountain, Kancamagus Hway, tel: 745-8111, *Lincoln*. Expensive resort.

Beal House Inn, 247 Main, tel: 444-2661, *Littleton*. Inexpensive; furnished with antiques.

Redwood Motel, Rt 26, tel: 237-5211, *Colebrook*. Inexpensive; with dining.

The Balsams, Rt 26, tel: 255-3400, *Dixville Notch*. Hightly rated deluxe resort.

**For more information on New Hampshire**, with lists of campsites, winter sports, maple sugar houses, etc, write to the Office of Vacation Travel, Department of Tourism, State House, Box 856, Concord, NH 03301, or tel: 603-271-2666.

# Maine

> 'Ayuh, the tourists all say they come for the scenery, but I don't understand how. You can't see nawthin' 'cause there's so many trees in the way.'
>
> Overheard in a Bangor laundromat

The state of Maine is only 200 square miles smaller than the rest of New England combined – its northernmost county, potato-growing Aroostook, is larger than both Connecticut and Rhode Island. Forests cover 87% of the state; paper companies own 52% of the land and bring Maine its greatest revenue, after tourism. Maine leads the nation in toothpick production, also in blueberries and sardines; it has its very own cat, the Maine Coon cat, said to have originated in China and mated with a raccoon. Its glacier-furrowed, jagged, rockbound coast zigzags for 3,500 miles, adorned with over a thousand islands. This is 'Down East', named by sailors who noticed how the southwesterly winds pushed them along the coast 'down wind to the east'. Today it is Maine's prime tourist attraction, scenically magnificent, and nursery of the best lobster in the Atlantic.

The tremendous growth of the sunbelt in America has had a reciprocal reaction in the northeast corner of the country. With extremely variable seasons and a small-town, homespun way of life, Maine, New Hampshire and Vermont have become the fastest growing states east of the Mississippi in the past fifty years, and this, according to most newcomers, has something to do with the quality of life in these old Yankee strongholds. The reasons for choosing one over the other are personal; would-be 'Mainiacs' hanker after a salty breeze and a bracing climate, and would probably agree with Booth Tarkington, who said, 'To my mind Maine is the most beautiful state we have in this country, but even more appealing is its homeliness.'

Despite all the well-educated newcomers, Maine's per capita income is the lowest in New England and 43rd in the nation. For all the people on the coast or in the ski resorts that cater to the tourist trade, there are others scratching a living from oft-times marginal land. Interestingly though, the more outside influences invade Maine, the more the natives pride themselves on resisting change. Maine has been out of the mainstream of American life for so long that it has formed an individual, shrewd, humorous and genuine character, devoid of flattery. There's a strong feeling of state pride, flying of the state flag, and schooling the children

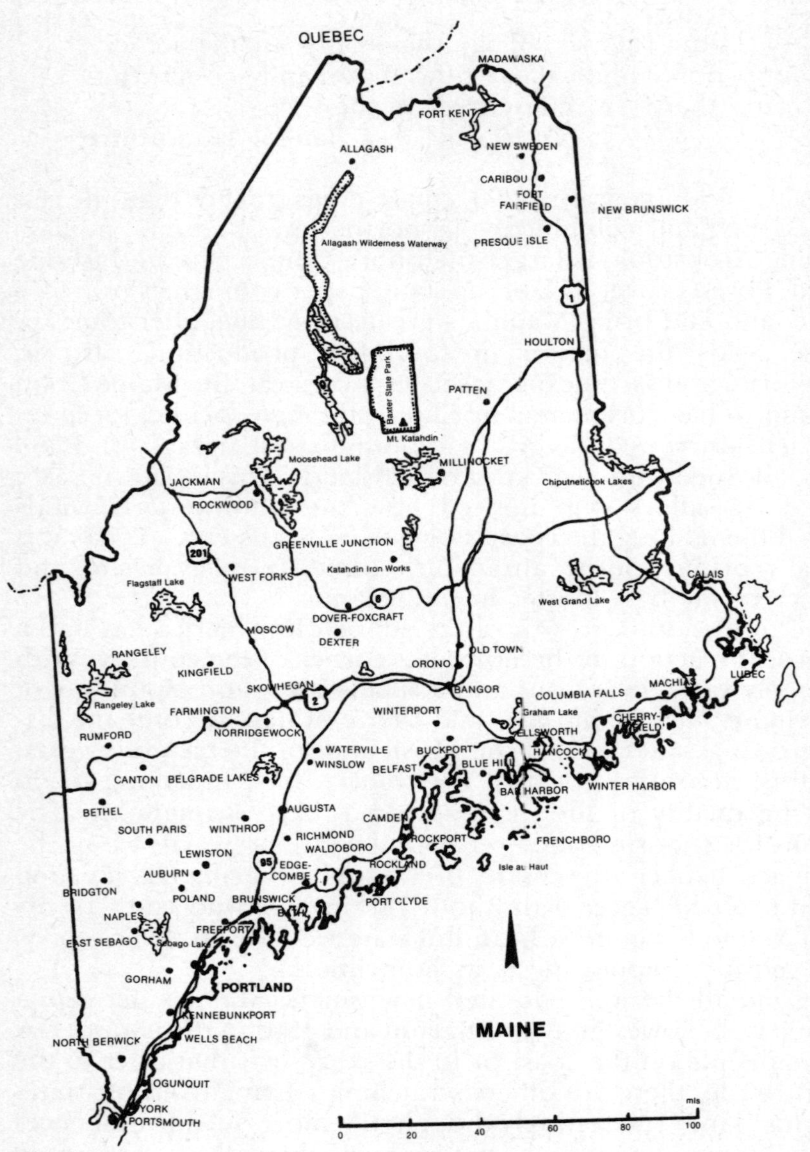
QUEBEC
MADAWASKA
FORT KENT
NEW SWEDEN
ALLAGASH
CARIBOU
FORT FAIRFIELD
NEW BRUNSWICK
PRESQUE ISLE
Allagash Wilderness Waterway
1
HOULTON
Baxter State Park
PATTEN
Mt. Katahdin
Moosehead Lake
MILLINOCKET
Chiputneticook Lakes
JACKMAN
ROCKWOOD
GREENVILLE JUNCTION
201
WEST FORKS
Katahdin Iron Works
Flagstaff Lake
CALAIS
6
West Grand Lake
DOVER-FOXCRAFT
MOSCOW
DEXTER
OLD TOWN
RANGELEY
KINGFIELD
ORONO
LUBEC
MACHIAS
SKOWHEGAN
2
BANGOR
COLUMBIA FALLS
Rangeley Lake
FARMINGTON
WINTERPORT
Graham Lake
CHERRY-FIELD
NORRIDGEWOCK
ELLSWORTH
RUMFORD
WATERVILLE
BUCKPORT
HANCOCK
WINSLOW
BELFAST
BLUE HILL
CANTON
BELGRADE LAKES
BAR HARBOR
WINTER HARBOR
BETHEL
AUGUSTA
CAMDEN
SOUTH PARIS
WINTHROP
RICHMOND
ROCKPORT
FRENCHBORO
WALDOBORO
LEWISTON
95
EDGE-COMBE
ROCKLAND
Isle au Haut
AUBURN
1
BRIDGTON
POLAND
BRUNSWICK
PORT CLYDE
NAPLES
FREEPORT
EAST SEBAGO
GORHAM
PORTLAND
KENNEBUNKPORT
MAINE
NORTH BERWICK
WELLS BEACH
OGUNQUIT
YORK
PORTSMOUTH
mls
0
20
40
60
80
100

in Maine history, all very removed from the 'vacationland' slogan on Down East licence plates.

Rural Maine has its own dialect of 'Yankee talk'; at its best it is colourful, rich in metaphor, and all but incomprehensible to the untrained ear. Natives are not as taciturn as their reputation would have it. They disdain small talk; try it, and all you may get in response is an 'ayuh' (yes) or more likely 'daow' (no). When the rest of America may say 'okay' a Mainer will say 'elegant'. If an old fisherman says your new yacht is 'the finest kind of pork', take it as a compliment. The state capital is properly pronounced 'Auguster', while Boston's most famous college is 'Hahvud', except in Aroostook County where it is 'Harrvarrd'. Expressions deemed obscene anywhere else in the US have been rendered harmless here through constant use; grizzled old men call each other 'deah' and lobsters are 'spiders'. If you need a dictionary, pick up a copy of *How to Talk Yankee* by Gerald E. Lewis, available in many Maine bookstores.

Maine is a state for outdoor activity par excellence, if only to sit on a hard-packed beach or stroll along a cliff path. For those who prefer something more vigorous, write to the following: Maine Windjammer Association (Box 317T, Rockport, ME 04856) for descriptions of eleven different schooner cruises up the coast; Kennebec Dories (P.O. Box 1, West Forks, ME 04985) or Northern Whitewater Expeditions Inc. (P.O. Box 100, The Forks, ME 04985) for whitewater raft or dory trips on the Kennebec, Penobscot, upper Hudson or Dead Rivers; Sunrise County Canoe Expeditions Inc. (Cathance Lake, Grove Post Office, ME 04638) for all manner of canoe journeys in northern Maine and Labrador, some of which can be combined with hunting or fishing; Maine Guides Association (Box 27A, Winterport, ME 04496) for a complete list of canoe guides. If stalking the great Maine moose is your dream, you'll have to make friends with a resident who has one of the two hundred annual moose permits. For smaller game, write to the Maine Fish and Game Department (State Office Building, Augusta, ME 04330) for information and a licence. Camping in Maine's thirty-one State Parks is available on a first-come first-served basis, except for Baxter State Park where reservations are required. Write to the Maine Publicity Bureau (97 Winthrop Street, Hallowell, ME 04247) for listings. For a listing of private campgrounds, write to Maine Campground Owners Association (North Fryeburg, tel: ME 04058), and for Acadia camping write to Acadia National Park Headquarters (Route 1, Box 1, Bar Harbor, ME 04609). For listings of primitive campsites, maps, trails, fishing and hunting in northern Maine, write to North Maine Woods (P.O. Box 382,

Ashland, ME 04732).

## Getting Around Maine

**By Air.** Major airports in the state are located in Augusta, Bangor, Portland, Bar Harbor, Lewiston, Waterville, Rockland and Presque Isle, and are connected to Boston and New York on Air New England (tel: 800-225-3900 toll-free for information), and the intrastate line – which also serves New England airports and Quebec City – Bar Harbor Airlines (tel: 800-432-7854). Delta flies from other states to Portland and Bangor. Taxi airservice is available to sportsmen and others to Maine's more remote corners.

**By Train.** Although there are no trains up the Maine coast, Greyhound and Michaud Trailways have connecting motor coach services to Old Orchard Beach, Portland, Brunswick, Belfast, Lewiston, Augusta, Bangor and Bar Harbor, and to Sanford and Springvale from the Amtrak station in Boston. VIA Rail Canada's line from Montreal to Halifax passes through northern Maine, with several stops between Jackman and Vanceboro.

**By Ferry.** Two large auto ferries take passengers to Yarmouth, Nova Scotia, from Portland (Prince of Fundy Cruises, P.O. Box 4216, Portland, ME 04101; tel: 207-775-5616) and from Bar Harbor (CN Marine, Bar Harbor, ME 04609; tel: 800-432-7344) in the summer. From Portland the trip is overnight; both cruises have gambling facilities while ships are in international waters.

Service to most of Maine's islands is by the State of Maine (for schedules, write to Department of Transportation Ferry Service, P.O. Box 646, Rockland, ME 04841; tel: 594-5543). State ferries operate between Rockland and Vinalhaven, Bass Harbor and Swans Island, Rockland and North Haven, and Lincolnville and Isleboro. Service to the Casco Bay Islands departs from Portland (Casco Bay Lines, Custom House Wharf, Portland, ME 04101; tel: 774-7871) with limited car-ferry service; from Port Clyde to Monhegan Island on Monhegan-Thomaston Boat Line (tel: 372-8848 for information) and from Boothbay Harbor to Monhegan (tel: 633-3244) and summer excursions from New Harbor to Monhegan (tel: 799-1091). Many of these ferries only run in the summer; if you plan a trip in July or August, it's always safest to make a reservation. The Isles of Shoals may be reached by ferry from Portsmouth, New Hampshire, for summer excursions.

**By Bus.** Maine is served by both Greyhound and Michaud Trailways, from Boston to Portland and Sanford. A daily bus leaves Bangor for points in Northern Maine between Fort Kent; from Bangor a daily bus also goes to the Maritime Provinces and eastern Maine on US–1 down to Portland. Bangor and Portland are the main departure points for Augusta and points inland. (Greyhound's terminal in Portland is at 950 Congress Street, tel: 772-6587; Trailways is at 169 High Street, tel: 773-5400.)

## History

Throughout much of its early history, Maine was a bone of contention between the French and English. Both sent explorers along the coast in the 16th century – John Cabot for Britain and Giovanni de Verrazzano for the French – but neither power made much of its discoveries until the early 17th century. In 1604 the French, led by Pierre du Guast and Samuel de Champlain, founded the first colony on Maine Territory, on Dochet's Island, but after half of the seventy colonists died during the first winter, the colony removed to Port Royal, Nova Scotia. The French nevertheless left the name Maine behind, after the province in France.

That same year five Indians (most of Maine's Indians belonged to the Abnaki tribe, of the Algonkin family) played an involuntary role in the English settlement of their native land, when they were kidnapped and taken to England, with the object of teaching them English. When their host, Sir John Popham, heard their tales of great forests and furs, he sent a group of colonists to the Sagadahoc Peninsula. Again, a bitter winter caused many of the Popham colonists to go home; the rest followed shortly thereafter. French Jesuits had the next move in 1613, when they founded the first mission for Indians east of California on Mount Desert Island, but British Captain Samuel Argall chased them off the following year. The 'shock troops of Christ' were never ones to give up easily, and they returned in later years, most famously Father Sebastian Rale, who lived with the Indians for thirty years and learned their language before being murdered in 1724 during the French and Indian Wars.

In 1614 Captain John Smith explored and mapped the coast of Maine, and in 1622 the Council for New England granted 'The Province of Maine' to John Mason and Sir Ferdinando Gorges, including all land between the Merrimack and the Kennebec; by 1677 Massachusetts had gobbled it up. Meanwhile the French had settled in east of the Penobscot, led by one Baron de St Castine. When the British under Governor Andros captured

French forts in the area, the Baron struck back along the coast, beginning the second French and Indian War (1688). By the turn of the century most of the English settlements had been abandoned but the French and the Indians had reached the peak of their strength. The English returned to Maine, and the French were pushed further back, until 1760 and the surrender of Canada.

In 1775 Maine saw action on three fronts. In Machias, citizens sailed a small boat up to the British man-of-war *Margaretta* and captured it with their pistols in one of the first, if not the first, naval battles of the Revolution. In the autumn, Benedict Arnold and 1,000 troops hiked from Fort Popham on the Kennebec to Quebec through the wilderness – the few who survived failed in their mission to take the city; on 18 October the British bombarded Portland from the sea and levelled it. The British occupied Maine from 1779 to 1783 and during the War of 1812 until 1814, when the eastern border between Canada and Maine was drawn. In 1819 Maine became independent of Massachusetts and a year later, a state.

Maine entered the Union in 1820 as part of the Missouri Compromise, engineered by Southern Senators in the face of a wakening abolitionist mood in the North. Maine was allowed to become a state only on condition that Missouri be a slave state and that from henceforth slavery be legal south of 36° 30′. Mainers were not too happy about their unwitting role in institutionalizing slavery; to compensate, some citizens like Neal Dow took upon themselves the role of moral uplifters. Maine passed a Prohibition Law in 1846. Abolitionists began to hold lectures a month after Maine became a state; under the influence of Massachusetts editor William Lloyd Garrison, Maine developed into one of the most militant states demanding the end of slavery. In Brunswick, Harriet Beecher Stowe had the vision that led to her writing *Uncle Tom's Cabin,* an indirect cause of the Civil War.

Maine also fought its own peculiar war with Canada over its northeast boundary, the so-called Aroostook War. Lumber interests were at the root of the quarrel, which began in 1827 when someone raised the Stars and Stripes in the disputed territory. In the 1830s Fort Kent and Fort Fairfield were built to defend Maine's claims, and in 1839 men were being drafted to serve in what seemed certain to escalate into a real shooting war, if President Van Buren hadn't sent General Winfield Scott ('Old Fuss and Feathers') to mediate. Finally Daniel Webster and Lord Ashburton wrote the treaty settling the dispute in 1842.

The soul of modern Maine, similar to states in the west, is

divided, with the tourist industry and environmentalists on one hand, and on the other, the logging interests, potential drillers for oil on the Georges Bank, and promotors of creating jobs through industry. So far the state has managed to strike a compromise between the two, as in the 94-mile Allagash Wilderness Waterway, where within 500 feet of one another, loggers harvest timber and canoeists enjoy near-pristine views along the river.

## West of the Kennebec River

Southwestern Maine, with the state's metropolis, Portland, sandy shores, lakes, wilderness, agriculture, and part of the White Mountain National Forest, is the most populous sector of the state, and bears the heaviest tourist traffic as well.

Right on the New Hampshire—Maine border are the nine rocky little **Isles of Shoals**, named by fishermen for their rich fishing grounds. Discovered by John Smith during his coastal explorations, they have such picturesque names as Smutty Nose, Malaga and Appledore, the latter of which had one of the most popular hotels of the 19th century, attracting the great literati of the era. Up to 300 ships used to dock at these wee isles, their holds full of mackerel; today they are strange and haunted. In the summer there are cruises to the isles from Portsmouth, New Hampshire.

**York**, incorporated as Gorgeana in 1642, lies near the extreme southwest corner of Maine and looks the part of the oldest chartered city in America. Its structures mainly date from 1692, the year the Indians attacked and massacred fifty inhabitants; the *Old Gaol,* built in 1719 as the King's Prison for the Province of Maine, is one of the oldest public buildings still standing in English America. Its dungeons and collection of decorative arts are its main attraction (open mid June to September, Mondays to Saturdays 10.30am-5pm, Sundays 1.30pm-5pm, admission; located at Lindsay Road and York Street, Route 1-A). Next door, the *Emerson-Wilcox House,* a 1742 structure that has served as a post office, tavern, general store and dwelling during its career, displays more decorative arts (particularly crewelwork) and historical artifacts (same hours as the Gaol, combined admission available). At the bottom of Lindsay, on the York river, the *John Hancock Warehouse,* once owned by the 'Prince of Smugglers', is the only surviving commercial building of colonial York; today it houses ancient ship models (open in summer 10.30am-5pm, Sundays 1.30pm-5pm). A replica of *Sewall's Bridge,* the innovative pile drawbridge built in 1761, spans the river near here. **York**

**old churches, the First Anglican, built in 1736. North of York village are two other 'Yorks': York Beach** and **Cape Neddick,** both with fine sandy beaches.

Artsy **Ogunquit,** an upper class haven to the north, has several institutions, most famously the *Ogunquit Playhouse* on Route 1 and John Lane, a highly rated summer theatre (tel: 646-5511 for play information). The *Museum of Art of Ogunquit* on the harbour is devoted to contemporary American art (July to Labor Day, Mondays to Saturdays 10.30am-5pm, Sundays 1.30-5pm, free); and the *Barn Gallery* on Bourne's Lane and Shore Road has a permanent collection and changing exhibits of American artists, some for sale (open mid June to mid September, 10am-5pm, Sundays 2pm-5pm; free). *Perkin's Cove* is connected to the town's beautiful beach via electric trolley; take it, because there will be no parking place at the Cove, once a tiny fishing village, now crammed full of art galleries and restaurants, and in the middle, a pedestrian drawbridge. Watch for signs to Ogunquit's *Marginal Way,* a wonderfully scenic cliff walk over the beach.

Inland, **South Berwick** claims to be the oldest permanent English settlement in Maine (1631) and site of the country's first sawmill. Maine's favourite novelist, Sarah Orne Jewett, lived here (1774); her residence at 101 Portland Street is now the *Sarah Orne Jewett Memorial,* with fine furnishings (open June to September, Tuesday/Thursday/Saturday/Sunday 1pm-5pm, May weekends only; admission). One of her novels, *The Tory Lover,* had the *Hamilton House* (1787) as its setting. Built by a wealthy merchant and since restored in almost every detail, it is an exceptional historic house (open same hours as Jewett Memorial, admission; located on Vaughan's Lane).

**Wells,** back on the shore, has inexpensive family accommodation and a fine beach; **Kennebunk** and **Kennebunkport** have become popular destinations for their unusual, ornate 19th-century homes, like the *Wedding Cake House* on Route 35, and for sundry seasonal attractions like the Boon Island Boat Race and National Dump Week, when the National Trash Pile Trophy is awarded to the town in America most deserving of the title 'dump' and a lucky girl is crowned 'Miss Dumpy'. Kenneth Roberts, author of *Northwest Passage,* was born here, and the *Kennebunkport Historical Society* on North Street has an exhibit on his life and that of the town (open July and August, Tuesday to Thursday 1pm-4pm, Saturdays 10am-12am; Tuesdays 1pm-4pm in June and September; free). Billed as 'the world's largest electric railway exhibit', the *Seashore Trolley Museum* on Log Cabin Road features a hundred old trolleys from around the world, transport (open mid June to Labor Day, 10am-6pm; Labor Day to October weekends 12am-5pm; admission).

Route 9 passes the picturesque fishing village-summer colony at **Cape Porpoise,** named by Captain John Smith for the playful creatures he saw there, and **Goose Rocks Beach,** another summer colony towards **Old Orchard Beach,** a long stretch of sand much favoured by Canadians and teenagers, sometimes known as 'Maine's Coney Island', with hot dogs, amusements, etc; the Ocean Pier, destroyed in a great storm in February 1978, is being rebuilt.

Back on the coast, the strange, marshy *Prouts Neck Bird Sanctuary* was a gift to the town of Scarborough from Charles Homer, in memory of his brother Winslow, who used to live in the village at the tip of the peninsula. Here also are two state beaches, Crescent and Scarborough, while the eastern coast of *Cape Elizabeth* is strewn with giant rocks, particularly at *Two Lights State Park*. As lighthouses go, however, the most famous is the *Portland Head Light,* visible from Two Lights in good weather. George Washington ordered it built in 1791, one of four he had constructed on the Atlantic coast. It is the only one never rebuilt.

**Portland** is Maine's largest city, cultural and commercial centre; it is a bustling, prosperous, trendy city, so attractive to young professionals in particular that housing vacancies average about one per cent. Scenically situated on Casco Bay, it has the state's finest architecture, much of it rehabilitated during the past twenty years. Portland's motto, *Resurgam* (I shall rise again), is particularly apt. It has had as many ups and downs as names; when originally settled in 1632, it was called Machigonne, then Casco, then Falmouth, then, after the Revolution, Portland. It prospered in the fur trade until the Indians wiped it out in 1675; it was rebuilt only to be decimated again by the Indians and French in 1690. With the fall of Quebec (1759) Portland rose once more, exporting lumber and masts to England, rapidly becoming so important – and so Revolutionary – that a British naval squadron saw fit to bombard it for twelve hours from the sea. In 1776 for the duration of the war the city remained empty; by 1820, however, it had revived again, this time in the lumber-molasses trade with the West Indies, and after the Embargo of 1807, as a port and shipbuilding centre. With 13,000 inhabitants, it was the largest city in Maine and its first state capital. It became a terminus for railroads in eastern Canada and one of that country's principal ports for sending goods to Europe. A firecracker on Commercial Street on 4 July 1866 caused a fire that destroyed central Portland, leaving 10,000 homeless. Again the city arose, in a grand Victorian guise; decline set in again after World War II and particularly after the St Lawrence Seaway opened in 1959, taking over Portland's Canadian business. The city's renewal today may be traced primarily to its location; it is the only place 'Down East' with real urban amenities, yet still convenient for shore, mountain, forest and lake.

Your first stop in Portland should be the *Greater Portland Chamber of Commerce* at 142 Free Street to pick up their free informative guides to the city's historic neighbourhoods. One of these neighbourhoods is *Old Port Exchange* on the waterfront; it was the first place to be settled in the 17th century, but as it was also the first place to suffer in the 1775 bombardment and the Great Fire, all the fine brick commercial buildings date from after 1866. Exchange and Commercial streets are its main thoroughfares; today trendy restaurants, clubs and shops occupy the restored area. Notice the *trompe l'oeil mural* on a brick wall at the corner of Exchange and Middle Streets. Take Fore Street down to the waterfront's Eastern Promenade and *Fort Allen Park,* with views of the Casco Bay Islands (sometimes known as the 'Calendar Islands from the claim that there are 365 of them – 28 within the Portland city limits). *Fort Gorges* in the harbour, a hexagonal granite fortess, was built in the 19th century, abandoned after the Civil War, and is open today to anyone who wants to sail to it. Cruises to the islands run all day in the summer on Casco Bay Lines (see 'Getting There').

From here, take Congress Street up Munjoy Hill to the *Portland Observatory,* an 82-ft wooden tower built in 1807 to signal and watch for approaching ships. Today you can climb its creaking steps for an unexcelled view of the city, Casco Bay and even the White Mountains (June to Labor Day, 10am-8pm). Continuing on Congress, past the granite City Hall – inspired by New York City's elegant building and housing the beautiful Kotzschmar organ – you'll come to the *Maine Historical Society,* located in the *Wadsworth-Longfellow House* (487 Congress), where poet Henry Wadsworth Longfellow grew up and wrote his first poems. Built by Longfellow's grandfather in 1785, it is the oldest brick building in Portland, and contains furnishings and family memorabilia, manuscripts and a pretty garden (guided tours June to September, Monday to Friday 9.30am-4.30pm; admission). Further on, at Congress and State stands the famous statue of the poet by Franklin Simmons in *Longfellow Square.* Many fine homes line the State Street area, fashionable in the 19th century and untouched by the 1866 fire. One of the most recent is the *Victoria Mansion* (1863), an Italian Villa-style pile at 109 Danforth Street, featuring seven Carrara marble fireplaces, a flying staircase of mahogany, and furnishings made especially for the house (open mid June to October, Tuesday to Saturday 10.30am-4.30pm, admission). The *Portland Museum of Art* is nearby at 111 High Street; it owns the adjacent 1800 Sweat mansion (decorative arts) and has a large number of European and American paintings, particularly Winslow Homers, the State of Maine collection, and 16th-century Belgian tapestries (open Tuesday to Saturday 10am-5pm, Sundays 2pm-5pm; admission to Sweat House).

The coast northeast of Portland is wildly indented, with inlets and offshore islets. **Falmouth,** just north, took the name that Portland rejected; today it has the headquarters of the *Maine Audubon Society,* 118 Old Route 1, in a building devoted to energy conservation and alternative energy sources, explained by various displays (open Monday to Saturday). The Audubon Society operates a Wildlife Sanctuary nearby in **Freeport,** on Lower Mast Landing Road. If you're in Freeport at 4 in the morning and need some fishing tackle or a backpack right away, don't despair; L. L. Bean, the Sears-Roebuck of the outdoorsy set, has a retail store on Route 1, open 24 hours a day all year long. Freeport has an even more unusual attraction off Route 1: the *Desert of Maine.* This appeared one day in the 19th century, first as a patch of sand, which grew and grew until today it covers many acres. Geologists believe the sand was packed into a crater during the last Ice Age, and as the land was eroded, the lid on it grew thinner and thinner until at last the sand burst through. Today it engulfs 70-ft pine trees as the dunes shift back and forth.

Nearby **Brunswick** is the home of Maine's most famous college, *Bowdoin* (chartered 1794), the alma mater of Nathaniel Hawthorne, Franklin Pierce, Henry W. Longfellow, and Arctic explorers Admiral Robert Peary and his assistant, Donald B. MacMillan; the latter two are the subject of the *Peary—MacMillan Arctic Museum* in Hubbard Hall on campus, with polar mementoes, equipment, photos and glass slides (open Tuesday to Saturday 10am-5pm, Sundays 2pm-5pm, in summer also open 7am-8.30pm; free). Bowdoin's excellent *Museum of Art* in the Walker Art Building has a Stuart portrait of Jefferson and other early American portraits, as well as collections of European masters and Winslow Homer (open same hours as Arctic Museum; free).

Bowdoin College's *First Parish Church* and chapel were designed by Richard Upjohn; the church was the inspiration for a scene in *Uncle Tom's Cabin,* which Harriet Beecher Stowe, wife of a Bowdoin professor, wrote while living in Brunswick (today her house is a motel). *Brunswick Summer Playhouse* presents Broadway musicals in the summer on the Bowdoin campus (for information tel: 725-8769).

Two narrow peninsulas jut into the sea south of Brunswick; Route 123 leads to the *Harpswells,* haunted in the 19th century by a phantom ship that inspired Whittier's 'The Dead Ship of Harpswell'. Off the coast here, *Eagle Island* was the home of Admiral Peary, first to reach the North Pole. His house, with interpretative panels on his expeditions, is open 20 June to Labor Day, but you'll have to sail there to see it. The other peninsula may be reached via Route 24. At its tip is a bridge across to Orr's Island and from here another bridge – 'the world's only cribstone bridge' of honeycombed granite blocks – links Orr's to *Bailey Island,* a trip worth making for its marvellous views of Casco Bay.

**Bath,** at the junction of the Kennebec and Androscoggin Rivers, a protected twelve miles from the sea, has launched more than 5,000 ships in its shipbuilding career and still builds steel-hulled vessels today. From its yards came some of America's most notable vessels, like the *Wyoming*, a six-masted schooner and the largest wooden ship the country ever produced, and the *USS O'Bannon* of World War II fame. The history of Bath, at one time the greatest shipbuilding town in the country, is portrayed in the fascinating *Bath Marine Museum* that spans four locations in town: the Sewell Mansion at 903 Washington Street, with 31 rooms of marine memorabilia; the Winter Street Center, with displays on regional maritime history, in a Gothic Revival Church; the Apprentice Shop, where trainees learn how boats were built in previous centuries; and, on the other side of the Kennebec, the Percy and Small Shipyard (connected by a boat in the summer), the only surviving shipyard in America to have built wooden ships (open 20 May to 22 October 10am-5pm; admission $3.50, children $1.25). The town of Bath itself has many fine houses, particularly along Washington Street, where many wealthy shipbuilders once lived.

From Moosehead Lake 150 miles away the Kennebec River flows into the sea at **Phippsburg**, named for Sir William Phipps, Royal Governor of Massachusetts during the Salem Witch trials, a position he earned by capturing Port Royal during an Indian war. The first attempt by the English to settle the New World, the *Popham Colony* (1607) has recently been excavated near Popham Beach on Hoss-Ketch Point, marked by a plaque; the colonists gave up and returned after the first winter, disheartened by the death of their president, Sir George Popham. Before they left, however, they had built America's first transatlantic trading vessel, *The Virginia*, presaging the region's major industry; there is a model of it in the Bath Marine Museum. Granite *Fort Popham* nearby defended the Kennebec River, the last (1861) of several forts on the site. It was here that Benedict Arnold and his company began their long trek to Quebec, a journey the modern adventurer can follow on the *Benedict Arnold Trail,* marked at various points by interpretative plaques.

The *Western Lakes* region of Maine, on the map, looks as international as the United Nations; towns are named Mexico, Sweden, Poland, Norway, Peru, Wales, Carthage, etc. *Sebago Lake,* Maine's second largest, is a half-hour's drive from Portland and a popular resort area with its sandy beaches and water sports. On the western shore of Sebago Lake, the *Jones Study Gallery* in Douglas Hill has a notable collection of antique china and glass, and marvellous views of the lake. From **Naples** north of the lake the *Songo River Queen,* a replica of an old paddle-wheeler, takes summer cruises on the Songo and on Long Lake, one of a chain of lakes north of Sebago Lake. The Sabbathday Lake Shaker colony, America's oldest religious community, not far from the old resort town of **Poland Spring** operates the *Shaker Museum* (Route 26). The brothers and sisters offer walking tours of their old village; the museum contains Shaker furniture, tools and art (open 30 May to Labor Day, Tuesday to Saturday 10am-4.30pm; admission). In Poland Spring itself you can see the State of Maine building from the Chicago World's Fair of 1893, as well as visit the source of the famous bottled water. The twin manufacturing cities of **Auburn** and **Lewiston** on the Androscoggin together form Maine's second largest metropolis. Lewiston is dominated by the granite towers of *St Peter and St Paul,* the largest church in Maine. At Bates College in Lewiston the *Treat Gallery* has a notable collection by Maine artist Marsden Hartley, while the *Stanton Museum* contains an excellent ornithological collection.

Lincoln's vice-president, Hannibal Hamlin, was born in **Paris,** a pretty community north of Route 26; next to his boyhood home on Paris Hill, the Old Court House has become the *Hamlin Memorial Hall,* featuring Hamlin memorabilia, primitive American art and Oxford County minerals (open Tuesday to Saturday 10am-4pm, winter Tuesday to Friday 3pm-5pm, Saturdays 9am-2pm; free). A larger collection of Maine minerals is on display at *Perham's Maine Mineral Store Museum* (Routes 26 and 219); here collectors can learn about open quarries in the area (open 9am-5pm, Sundays 2pm-5pm; free). **Bryant Pond,** north of Route 26, is one of the last two places in the country served by magneto (hand-crank) telephones, serving 512 customers. You can visit the Bryant Pond Telephone Company and watch operators run the old switchboards (open daily 9am-5pm).

operators run the old switchboards (open daily 9am-5pm).

**Bethel,** further along on Route 26, is the gateway to the *White Mountain National Forest,* which Maine shares with New Hampshire. Maine's loveliest covered bridge may be seen just to the north at **Newry;** the *Penacook Falls* on the Androscoggin River at **Rumford** are most spectacular. In **Andover** you can tour the *Comsat Satellite Earth Station* to learn about satellite communications (Memorial Day to Labor Day 9am-5pm). Further north, Rangely and the **Rangely Lakes** have been a holiday destination for the adventurous ever since a narrow-gauge railway used to bring guests up to the grand old hotels. Still a sportsman's paradise, at 2,000 feet in altitude refreshing even at the height of summer, Rangely is near forty trout-filled lakes, the Appalachian Trail, and the Carrassett Valley ski area at *Sugerloaf Mountain.*

**Restaurants.** All along the coast of Maine you'll find lobster pounds where you can choose your crustacean, watch him boil, and eat him in a rustic setting with drawn butter and clam chowder. Some are surprisingly inexpensive, others are quite elaborate, like Cape Neddick Lobster Pound***, Shore Road, in *York.* York is also the place to go for another Down East speciality, the clambake, featuring steamed lobsters, clams, corn on the cob, baked onions, potatoes and blueberry cake, at Bill Foster's Downeast Clam Bakes**, Route 1A, served July to Labor Day, Wednesday to Saturday at 7pm (advance reservations necessary: tel: 363-3282). Other restaurants are listed below. *In Ogunquit:* Whistling Oyster***, Shore Road; Ogunquit Lobster Pound**, Route 1; Barbara Dean's**, Shore Road. *In Kennebunkport:* Olde Grist Mill***, Mill Lane; Seacrest Inn**, Ocean Avenue. *In Kennebunk:* The Kennebunk Inn***, Route 1. *In Saco:* Three Thieves Inn, 63 Storer Road. *In Old Orchard Beach:* Kate's on the Pier**. *In Portland:* Boone's***, 6 Custom House Wharf; Hollow Reed***, 334 Fore Street; Cap'n Newick's Lobster House*, 740 Broadway. *In Freeport:* J. L. Gabbiano**. *In Brunswick:* Stowe House***, 63 Federal Street. *In Auburn:* No Tomatoes***, 36 Court Street. *In Bailey Island:* Cook's Lobster House**. *In Bethel:* Bethel Inn***. *In Bridgton:* Switzer Stubli**, Ridge Road. *In Kingfield:* Le Papillon***, Route 27, by Sugar Loaf. *In Rangely:* Rangely Inn**, Main Street.

## The Coast Northeast of the Kennebec River

As you cross the Kennebec, Route 127 dives south for the very pictureqe fishing village of **Five Islands** and the sandy beach at

*Reid State Park.* US-1 continues to **Wiscasset** on the Sheepscot River, a larger but equally picturesque town of sea captains' mansions. For many years, in the 18th century, Wiscasset was the busiest port east of Boston; the melancholy hulks of two four-masted schooners in the harbour provide a constant reminder of the days when Wiscasset played host to two exiles, Louis Philippe and Talleyrand. Marie Antoinette's luggage sailed to North Edgecomb, across the river, but she wasn't able to escape with it. Today Wiscasset has made a name for itself with its worms, which it supplies to fishermen across the country. On Federal Street the old Lincoln County Jail and jailer's house form part of the *Lincoln County Museum,* which features Maine crafts (open mid June to Labor Day, Monday to Saturday 10am-5pm, Sundays 12.30pm-5pm; admission). The *Maine Art Gallery* on Warren Street specializes in paintings by the state's artists (open all year round). The most fun, however, is *The Musical Wonder House,* in an elegant sea captain's house at 18 High Street. Six rooms are filled with musical instruments and music boxes that play for you on the guided tour – singing birds, mechanical dolls, player pianos, gramophones, etc. (open June to Labor Day, Monday to Saturday 10am-5pm, Sundays 1pm-5pm; admission $4.00).

On the other side of the Sheepscot River (home to a family of seals), **Head Tide** was the *birthplace of poet Edwin Arlington Robinson* in 1869. His home, on Route 194, one of fourteen buildings in the hamlet, has recently been opened to the public (July to Labor Day, Wednesday and Sunday 2pm-4pm; free). **Alna,** next to it, boasts one of Maine's loveliest churches, the *Old Alna Meetinghouse* (1789), with box pews and an hourglass pulpit fitted with a 'pulpit leveller' for short preachers (July and August, Wednesday and Sunday 2pm-4pm).

The *Boothbays,* south of Edgecomb, are a major summertime destination for thousands, centred in scenic **Boothbay Harbor,** with shops, restaurants, art galleries, Windjammer Days (mid July) and cruises along the coast, the most popular being the Cabbage Island Clambake, with boat fare and dinner included in the price. On 100 Commercial Street the *Sherman Zwicker* (1942), one of the few remaining dory fishing boats, has been converted into the *Grand Banks Schooner Museum* with tours of the boat and films on dory fishing on the Grand Banks (mid June to mid October 9am-5pm; admission). On Corey Lane, the *Boothbay Theater Museum* in Boothbay has a unique collection of theatrical memorabilia from the 18th century on, including posters, playbills, costumes, and actress glass, located in a 1784 home (open mid June to mid October, Monday to Saturday 10am-4pm by reservation only: tel: 633-4536).

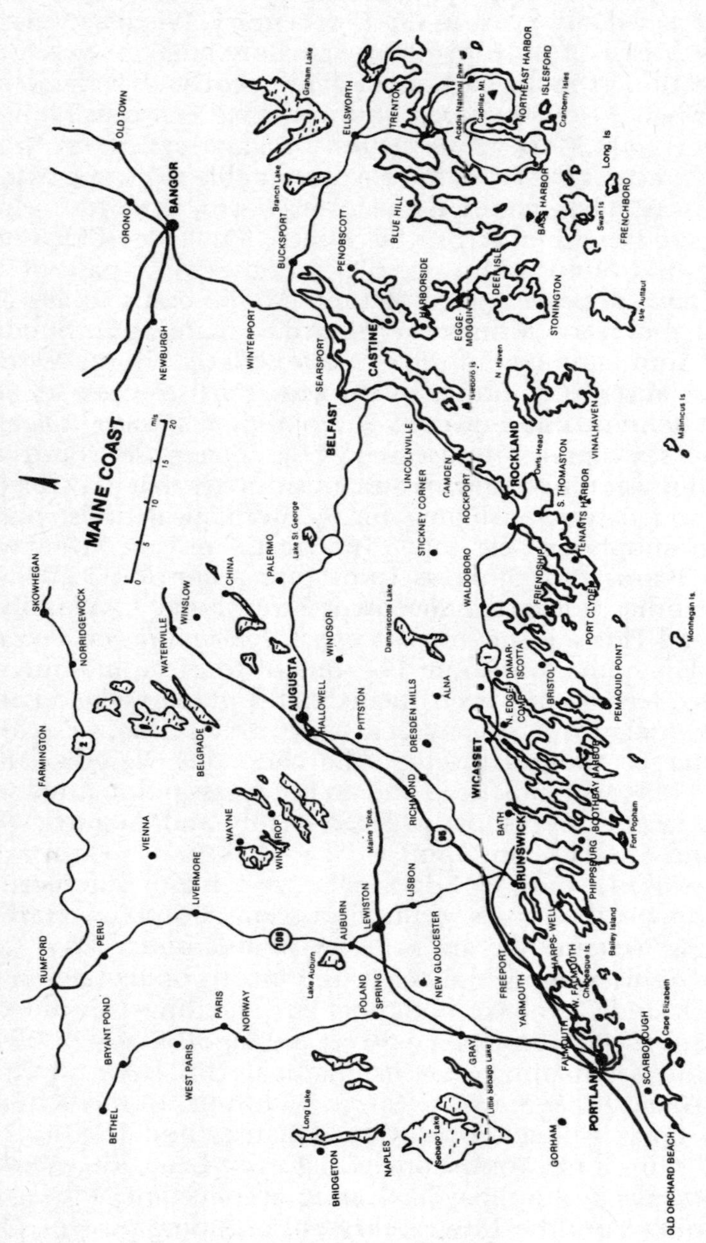
MAINE COAST
0 5 10 15 20 mls
BANGOR
OLD TOWN
ORONO
NEWBURGH
WINTERPORT
BUCKSPORT
Branch Lake
Graham Lake
ELLSWORTH
TRENTON
Acadia National Park
Cadillac Mt.
NORTHEAST HARBOR
ISLESFORD
Cranberry Isles
Long Is
BASS HARBOR
Swan Is
FRENCHBORO
BLUE HILL
PENOBSCOTT
HARBORSIDE
EGGE-MOGGIN
DEER ISLE
STONINGTON
SEARSPORT
CASTINE
BELFAST
N. Haven
ROCKLAND
VINALHAVEN
Matinicus Is.
Owls Head
S. THOMASTON
TENANTS HARBOR
LINCOLNVILLE
CAMDEN
ROCKPORT
STICKNEY CORNER
Lake St George
PALERMO
CHINA
WINSLOW
WATERVILLE
SKOWHEGAN
NORRIDGEWOCK
FARMINGTON
2
WINDSOR
Damariscotta Lake
WALDOBORO
FRIENDSHIP
PORT CLYDE
Monnegan Is.
DAMAR-ISCOTTA
1
BRISTOL
PEMAQUID POINT
N. EDGECOMB
AUGUSTA
HALLOWELL
PITTSTON
DRESDEN MILLS
ALNA
WICASSET
BOOTHBAY HARBOR
BELGRADE
WAYNE
WINTHROP
VIENNA
Maine Tpke.
RICHMOND
95
BATH
BRUNSWICK
PHIPPSBURG
Fort Popham
LISBON
LEWISTON
AUBURN
108
LIVERMORE
PERU
RUMFORD
BRYANT POND
BETHEL
WEST PARIS
PARIS
NORWAY
POLAND SPRING
Lake Auburn
NEW GLOUCESTER
FREEPORT
HARPS-WELL
Bailey Island
W. FALMOUTH
Chebeague Is.
YARMOUTH
FALMOUTH
Cape Elizabeth
SCARBOROUGH
PORTLAND
GRAY
Little Sebago Lake
Sebago Lake
Long Lake
NAPLES
BRIDGETON
GORHAM
OLD ORCHARD BEACH

**Damariscotta,** on the river of the same name, is the centre of an area well known to Maine historians and archaeologists. Along the river by Newcastle the ancient *Damariscotta Shell Heaps* were left by generations of prehistoric diners. The oldest Catholic church in New England, the 1808 *St Patrick's* is in Newcastle; Damariscotta's oldest house, the *Chapman-Hall House,* dating from 1754, contains period furnishing, an 18th-century rose garden and figureheads carved in the town (open mid June to Labor Day, Tuesday to Sunday 1pm-5pm). Route 130 south from Damariscotta leads to the *Ancient Pemaquid Restoration,* an early 17th-century trading post discovered in 1965. While digging up the site, archaeologists found a large number of Indian artifacts as well as a strange skeleton in armour, believed to be a Viking. A museum adjacent to the site houses many of the finds (open 30 May to Labor Day, 10am-6pm). At the end of Route 130 stands Maine's most dramatic lighthouse at the tip of the Pemaquid peninsula, located high over the sea on an unusual stratified rock formation. From the lighthouse you can see Christmas Cove, named by John Cabot who spent the holiday there in 1614.

**Waldoboro,** at the head of Muscongus Bay, was settled by German immigrants, who built a particularly fine Lutheran church, the *Old German Church* on Bremen Road (open to visitors in July and August). One of the state's most popular sloop races takes place every July in **Friendship,** south of Waldoboro, celebrating the renowned sloop made in town. The *Friendship Museum* at Route 220 and Martin's Point Road has memorabilia and historical data regarding the Friendship sloop (July to Labor Day, Monday to Saturday 12pm-5pm, Sunday 2pm-5pm). Andrew Wyeth aficionados will want to visit nearby **Cushing**, the artist's summer home and subject of several of his paintings. **Thomastown,** a town of elegant homes, was a busy port and ship building centre in the 19th century; here General Henry Knox chose to build his mansion *Montpelier* in 1793. Knocked down in the 19th century for a railroad, a replica from the architect's drawings was built in 1931 on High Street; many of the furnishings, however, are from the original house (open 30 May to 1 November 10am-5pm). On the peninsula extending south of Thomaston is **Port Clyde,** sardine capital of Maine, where you can take the ferry to *Monhegan Island* with its awesome cliffs, a long established summer colony. In **Owls Head,** by South Thomaston, the exceptional *Owls Head Transportation Museum* not only has the displays of antique autos and bi-planes one expects in a transportation museum but on summer weekends they actually run. A rally of antique vehicles takes place here the second weekend of August (on Route 73, open 27 May to 7 October 10am-4pm; admission). Also on Route 23 stands another of Maine's scenic lighthouses, the *Owls Head Light,* now surrounded by a small state park.

Nearby is **Rockland,** commercial hub of the mid coast, lobster distribution centre, ferry terminus to several points, and host of Maine's greatest seafood festival for five days in early August, complete with 'King Neptune and his Court of the Sea' and 'The crowning of Maine's Seagoddess'. In quieter times Rockland was the birthplace of Edna St Vincent Millay, the poetess with the poetic name. The *William A. Farnsworth Library and Art Museum* at 19 Elm Street features among its 18th–20th-century collection the paintings of three generations of Wyeths: N.C., Andrew, and James (open Monday to Saturday 10am-5pm, Sundays 1pm-5pm, closed Monday in winter; free). At 169 Camden Street, *Ureneff's Sunken Garden of Tuberous Begonias* is a pretty place, with a brook and over sixty varieties of begonias (July to September till 5pm; free). From Rockland the ferry trip is about 1½ hours to **Vinalhaven,** the largest of the Penobscot Bay islands, a fishing centre also known for its granite quarries. Lodging, food and shopping are all available here, but not at neighbouring **North Haven,** which has only one small shop. Another Rockland ferry sails to tiny **Matinicus,** with two beaches and a guesthouse.

**Rockport** and **Camden,** north along the coast, are two old fishing villages, now popular destinations for their lovely bay views, art galleries, summer concerts and pretty architecture, evoking for many what they like best about Maine. Yachtsmen call at their ports during cruises on the island-studded bay; sit by the harbour and you'll see all kinds of craft, from schooners to Chinese junks. Camden distinguishes itself with a small waterfall right on the harbour, and iron baskets filled with flowers along the streets. Rockport is the summer home of Andre the seal, who migrates to the harbour every year from Boston; his enthusiasm for overturning lobster dories has forced authorities to keep him in a big pen, where he performs for visitors every afternoon. Rockport's Opera House hosts cultural events throughout the year, most famously the Bay Chamber Concerts on summer Thursdays. Blueberry-growing **Lincolnville,** on the other side of Camden Hills State Park, is the point of departure for **Isleboro,** a beautiful island with tourist accommodation and beaches.

Route 1 leads to **Searsport,** Maine's second largest deep water port, from where one out of ten merchant marine captains came in the late 19th century. Their portraits, all 284 of them, line the walls in the *Penobscot Marine Museum* on Church Street. Other exhibits in the museum include whaling and marine artifacts, items from the China trade and navigational instruments spread out in three sea captains' homes and the old town hall (open 24 May to 15 October, Monday to Saturday 9.30am-5pm, Sunday 1pm-5pm; admission). Modern Searsport claims to be 'the antiques capital of Maine' for its numerous shops lining Route 1.

**Fort Knox,** guarding the mouth of the Penobscot River, was built in 1844 during the Aroostook War. Of all Maine's coastal fortifications, Fort Knox, made of solid granite from nearby Mount Waldo, is the largest and most elaborate, with underground passageways which you will need a flashlight to explore (open 30 May to Labor Day, 10am-6pm).

South of Bucksport across the mighty Penobscot extends the *Nasket Peninsula,* a beautiful unspoiled section of the coast, home of writers like E. B. White. The Blue Hill, a feature of the landscape in the northern part of the peninsula, is often as blue as the blueberries that grow on its slopes; from its summit the views of Mount Desert Island are spectacular. **Castine** on the western side of the peninsula is named for the Baron de St Castin, who occupied the settlement for thirty years and built the first fort at *Fort George;* during the Revolution the British occupied Castine to ensure a supply of lumber for their shipbuilding yards in Nova Scotia. The Massachusetts Board of War sent nineteen ships of war to dislodge them in 1779, under Commodore Richard Saltonstall, Brigadier General Peleg Wadsworth (grandfather of H. W. Longfellow) and Paul Revere. It was an unmitigated disaster for the Americans; not only did they fail to take Castine but they were forced to burn their ships to prevent capture. Later in the War of 1812 the English occupied it and several other key positions east of the Penobscot; Massachusetts seeming indifference to Maine's plight intensified calls for separation. Today Fort George on Route 166 is being excavated, and there are plans for its reconstruction. In history-conscious Castine itself (it has over a hundred historical markers) the *Wilson Museum* on Perkins Street houses a large collection of prehistoric implements from North and South America, rocks and minerals and local artifacts.

**Harborside,** by the Holbrook Island Sanctuary, has become the informal capital of organic gardening ever since Scott and Helen Nearing moved here from Vermont. Admirers of their book *Living the Good Life* have imitated their experiment in subsistence farming in many parts of rural Maine. From the quiet port of **Stonington** further south you can take the mail boat to beautiful **Isle au Haut,** with its two villages and sections of Acadia National Park.

On the east coast of the peninsula the major town is **Blue Hill,** home of a remarkable Renaissance man, Reverend Jonathan Fisher, the first pastor of the Blue Hills church as well as scientist, furniture-maker, linguist, surveyor, artist and inventor. Examples of his handiwork may be seen in the 1814 *Parson Fisher House* on Main Street (open July to mid September, Tuesday to Friday 2pm-5pm, Saturday 10am-12 noon). The wonderful view of Mount Desert from Blue Hill and the pottery workshops in town are other attractions here.

**Ellsworth,** 'the gateway to Acadia National Park', has two sites to detain the visitor. The *Stanwood Wildlife Foundation Museum* (Route 3) is a memorial to Cordelia J. Stanwood, pioneer ornithologist and photographer; exhibits include family treasures, mounted birds, etc. and adjacent is a forty-acre bird sanctuary (open 15 June to 15 October, 10am-4pm). The 1826 *Colonel Black Mansion* on West Main Street is an elaborate home with many fine details, imported woods and valuable antiques, a formal garden and a carriage house full of antique vehicles (open June to 15 October, Monday to Saturday 10am-5pm; admission).

Lovely **Mount Desert Island,** named by Samuel de Champlain 'Ile des Monts Deserts' for the bare rocky summits of its mountains, lies south of Ellsworth, connected by a bridge to the mainland. Some 32,000 acres of the island are occupied by *Acadia National Park,* the only national park on the east coast north of Florida, its name recalling its early French heritage when explorers and Jesuit missionaries called it 'Acadie'. Within it tower several mountains over a thousand feet high, the tallest on the Atlantic seaboard. **Bar Harbor,** once the Newport of Maine with enormous summer 'cottages' for the wealthy, is the tourist centre of Mount Desert Island but what the Great Depression didn't destroy the Great Fire of 1947 did. Since rebuilt, Bar Harbor is a pleasant if somewhat commercial town, and very crowded in the summer. The history of the town is relived at the *Bar Harbor Historical Society* (34 Mount Desert Street) with photographs and old hotel registers (open mid June to mid September, Monday to Saturday 1pm-4pm, Wednesday and Friday 10am-2pm; free). Just outside of town on Route 3, the world's largest research centre of genetic disorders, the *Jackson Laboratory,* offers lectures and films (mid June to mid September, Tuesday/Wednesday/Friday at 3pm; free admission).

Acadia National Park sponsors nature walks, campfire outings and boat trips with the rangers (inquire at Park Headquarters on Route 3 or write to Naturalist Program, Acadia National Park, Box 1, Bar Harbor, ME 04609). Highlights of a driving, biking or walking tour of the park include a drive to the top of *Cadillac*

*Mountain* (1,532 ft) for some truly wonderful views. From its summit early birds can claim to be the first in the United States to see the sun on that particular day. Near the Jackson Laboratory, at the Sieur de Mont Spring is the *Robert Abbe Museum*, with a large collection of Stone Age relics (open June to September). Nearby are the *Wild Gardens of Acadia,* with 300 species of local flora, and further south *Old Thunder Hole,* where the tide literally booms on stormy days, and the adjacent sandy beach where you can swim. By Jordan Pond begins one of the numerous carriage paths in the park built by John D. Rockefeller, who donated a third of the park acreage to the public. Here the Jordon Pond House serves tea and popovers in a scenic setting. Route 3 continues to *Somes Sound,* a fjord that divides Mount Desert into two peninsulas. From **Northeast Harbor,** a small village at the mouth of the fjord, you can take the ferry to the Cranberry Islands; on Little Cranberry Island the *Isleford Museum* documents the early settling of the Acadia area. On the western side of Mount Desert, the villages of **Southwest** and **Bass Harbor** (ferries to Swan Island and Frenchboro) have scarcely been touched by the great flow of tourists, but continue to earn their livelihood from the sea.

East of here the coast is often referred to as 'way down east'. **Hancock** on Route 1 hosts the annual Monteux Memorial Festival, at the conductors' summer school in town. A turn off near here affords a magnificent view of Frenchman Bay and Mount Desert. *Schoodic Point,* at the tip of the Gouldsboro Peninsula, is part of Acadia National Park; here the surf rages against pink granite ledges. Winter Harbor and Corea on the peninsula are typical fishing villages. Route 1 continues northeast to **Cherryfield,** 'Blueberry and salmon fishing capital of New England', and to **Columbia Falls,** where a local society maintains the unusual *Ruggles House,* just off Route 1. Built in 1818 for a judge, the house contains intricate carvings done over a three-year period by a penknife-wielding craftsman, and a flying staircase; the furnishings are original or were donated (open June to 15 October, Monday to Saturday 9.30am-4.30pm, Sunday 12pm-4pm; admission).

**Machias** is a leading contender for the honour of having fought the first naval battle of the Revolution. On 11 June 1775, the captain of the British man-of-war *Margaretta* insulted Machias by taking down its Liberty Pole, then firing upon the town after an abortive attempt by the local citizenry to capture him. The next day, armed with fowling pieces and pitchforks, forty men sailed after the British ship in a tiny sloop, boarded her, mortally wounded the captain, and won the prize. The British wounded were taken to *Burnham Tavern* at Main and Free

Streets, believed to be the oldest building in Eastern Maine, containing artifacts relating to the capture of the *Margaretta* (open mid June to Labor Day, Monday to Friday 10am-5pm, Saturday 10am-3pm; admission). *Quoddy Head State Park* is at Maine's easternmost extremity, where the tides are so great that a number of projects have been proposed to harness them for hydroelectric power. **Lubec,** to the north, vies with Cadillac Mountain as the first place in America to see the sun every morning. Just across the Canadian border from Lubec in New Brunswick good Democrats and other fans of F.D.R. won't want to miss *Roosevelt Campobello International Park* on Campobello Island, former summer home of the New Deal president. Set in 2,600 acres, the house contains its original furnishings (late May to mid October 9am-5pm; free). Inland much of the land belongs to the *Moosehorn National Wildlife Refuge*. **Calais,** in the St Croix valley, is the easternmost point of entry into mainland Canada.

**Restaurants.** *In Boothbay:* Fisherman's Wharf***, 42 Commercial Street; Blue Ship**, Foot Bridge; Rocktide**, 45 Atlantic. *In North Edgecomb:* Muddy Rudder***. *In Waldoboro:* Moody's*, Route 1. *In Rockland:* The Dry Dock**, on the Pier; the Salad Patch**, 310 Main Street. *In Rockport:* Sail Loft***. *In Camden:* Whitehall Inn***, High Street; Bay View Street Garage**. *In Lincolnville Beach:* The Lobster Pound**, Route 1. *In Searsport:* Yardarm***, Route 1; Lobster Shack*, Trudy Road. *In Bucksport:* Jed Prouty Tavern**, 52 Main Street. *In Stonington:* The Fisherman's Friend*, School Street. *In Little Deer Isle:* Eaton's Lobster Pool**. *In Isleboro:* Isleboro Inn**. *In Bar Harbor:* Testa's**, Main Street; Il Giardino***, 27 Cottage Street; Town Farm**, Kennebec Place; Fisherman's Landing*, West Street. *In Southwest Harbor:* Sou'weste*, Clark Point Road. *In Hancock:* The Crocker Country Inn***. *In Isleford:* Isleford Dock**. *In Winter Harbor:* Fisherman's Inn**. *In Cherryfield:* Eagle's Nest*, Stillwater Road. *In Machias:* Jennie's**, Route 1. *In Calais:* Wickachee Inn**, 282 Main Street.

## Inland

**Upper Kennebec Valley.** Some state capitals give you the feeling that state government isn't all that important. Although **Augusta,** a sleepy town if there ever was one, is reputedly controlled by the lobbies of the big paper companies and Central Maine Power, the casual visitor will certainly find no evidence of anything insidious in Charles Bulfinch's *State House,* a classic of state capitol buildings, constructed of Hallowell granite. Next to it, *Maine State Museum* has a wide-ranging collection of Maine historical artifacts, natural history and changing exhibits (open Monday to Friday 8am-5pm, weekends 1pm-4pm; free). Also on State Street you can visit the *Blaine House,* former house of Speaker of the House and one-time Presidential candidate, and presently the residence of the governor of Maine; inside are some of the original Blaine furnishings and the silver from the battleship *Maine* (open Monday to Friday 2pm-3.30pm; free). Augusta is surrounded by three chains of lakes: the China Lakes to the east, the Belgrade Lakes to the north and the Winthrop Lakes to the west. All have excellent fishing, swimming and canoeing.

**Hallowell,** just down river from Augusta, has been declared a National Historical District for its many fine preserved homes dating back to the town's shipbuilding days. Today Hallowell sports many antique shops and the *Harlow Gallery* (160 Water Street), the Kennebec Valley Art Association's gallery of permanent and temporary exhibitions. The *Arnold Expedition Historical Society,* south of Route 27 in **Pittston,** contains items from that ill-fated venture, along with a series of explanatory panels (open June to September 10am-4pm; admission).

**Waterville** can be reached via the *Waterville—Winslow Two Cent Bridge,* the last toll footbridge in America, although free at the moment. Waterville's *Redington Museum* (64 Silver Street) has a large collection of old photographs, Indian relics, and a complete 19th-century apothecary (open 15 May to 29 September, Tuesday to Saturday 2pm-6pm; admission). Further upriver, **Skowhegan** was the home of Margaret Chase Smith, the country's first woman senator, who served for four terms and became famous for standing up to Senator McCarthy. Also in Skowhegan is the state's oldest summer theatre, the *Lakewood Theater* (tel: 474-3331 for information). The Jesuit missionary Father Sebastian Rale preached to the Indians in nearby **Norridgewock,** and was held in high esteem. In 1724 the town was destroyed and Rale killed by a force from Massachusetts, who suspected him of planning French raids on English settlements. A mural of the massacre and Father Rale's own collection of Indian artifacts are on display in the *Norridgewock Historic Museum and Indian Village* on Route 2 in Oosoola Park (open 19 April to 15 October, by appointment: tel: 872-8797).

North of here the Upper Kennebec is whitewater raft territory as it spills out of *Moosehead Lake,* Maine's largest. Around it on the state highway map many of the roads are marked private; unless noted to the contrary, these roads belong to the paper companies and may be used by the public. Moosehead Lake, forty miles long and twenty miles wide, is famous for its fishing; fishermen catch more fish over five pounds here than in any other lake in the country. Bears can often be seen scrounging in the town dump of **Rockwood** on Route 15, the closest settlement to remarkable *Mount Kineo,* a solid flint escarpment rising a sheer 700 feet out of the lake. Indian tools made of Mount Kineo flint have been found all over eastern America. Campsites for canoeists, hikers and hunters dot the shores of Moosehead Lake, and there are motels in Rockwood, Jackman, to the west, and **Greenville.** From here, as well as from Millinocket and Lincoln, you can hire a float plane to lift you into the north woods, as far from civilization as you care to go.

From Moosehead Route 15 leads south to **Dover-Foxcroft,** the largest town in the region. Once two towns, Dover-Foxcroft is the centre of summer activity on *Sebac Lake,* formerly the home of Maine's land-locked salmon. From Brownville Junction to the east, go north five miles on Route 11 to the gravel road marked 'K.I.' for the *Katahdin Iron Works,* a busy mine and smelting mill established in 1843 and producing 2,000 tons of iron annually for fifty years. The charcoal kiln and blast furnace have been restored (open 30 May to Labor Day 10am-6pm).

**The Penobscot.** From 1830 to 1850, **Bangor,** the largest city on the Penobscot River, was the centre of a great lumber boom, the terminus of enormous log-runs down the river every spring. In the 19th century speculation in Maine's north woods, shipbuilding and the ice trade gave Bangor a frantic, wheeling-and-dealing, frontier atmosphere like no other city in Maine. Today the names of Bangor's two largest department stores, Sleeper's and Freeze's, tell only part of the story; the city may no longer be the lumber shipping capital of the world, but it is the commercial hub of northern and eastern Maine. Locals claim that Paul Bunyon, the great lumberjack of American folklore, was born in Bangor the day the city was incorporated in 1834, an event commemorated by a 31-ft-tall statue of Paul beside the Municipal Auditorium. Old Bangor is also remembered in the *Bangor Historical Society* at 159 Union Street (open Monday to Friday 10am-4pm). North of Bangor in **Orono** is the main campus of the University of Maine. In South Stevens Hall, the *University of Maine Anthropology Museum* houses exhibits from all over the world, with a special section on prehistoric Maine (open Monday to Friday 9am-3.30pm; free). On the other bank of the Penobscot, **Old Town** is the site of a Penobscot Indian Reservation and, on Indian Island, the *Penobscot National Historical*

*Society* with the history of the Indians, artifacts and photos (open 12pm-8pm; free).

Newsprint-manufacturing **Millinocket,** at the source of the Penobscot, is the last town before *Baxter State Park,* dominated by Maine's tallest peak, Mount Katahdin, almost exactly a mile high. Mount Katahdin marks the northern terminus of the Appalachian Trail; around it are a number of primitive campsites which you will need a reservation to use. The park is named in honour of Governor Percival P. Baxter, who purchased the land and gave it to the people of Maine when the legislature continuously refused to act on his proposal to designate it public land. Since 1930 the state has added to Baxter's original gift and the park today covers over 200,000 acres; deer, bear and moose are common sights. (For information, rules and a map of Baxter, stop at Park Headquarters, 64 Balsam Drive, Millinocket, ME 04462. Write to them as early as possible for camping reservations – 1 January is not too early.)

**Aroostook County. Patten,** a crossroad-town north of Millinocket, is another good base for Baxter and canoe trips on a number of Maine's 5,147 rivers. Patten's *Lumbermen's Museum* covers the history of the lumber industry in Maine, with dioramas, tools, models and log-hauling vehicles from the past (open 20 May to 1 November, Tuesday to Saturday 9am-4pm, Sunday 1pm-6pm; free). At the end of the Maine turnpike, **Houlton** is one of the fleshpots of vast spud-carpeted Aroostook County (often referred to in Maine as 'The County'), with a population of about 9,000. The prettiest times to visit Aroostook are in July, when thousands of acres of potatoes are in bloom, and during the fall foliage season. Houlton's *Aroostook Historical and Art Museum,* at 109 Main Street, contains exhibits on the county's history (open June to September, Monday to Friday 10am-5pm).

A hundred miles north of Houlton are a number of potato towns in the St John valley, with the largest, **Caribou,** in the centre. Here, at 393 Main Street, the *Nylander Museum* contains fossils, botanical collections, shells and Indian items (open 15 March to 1 December, Monday to Friday 1pm-4pm; free). **New Sweden,** northwest of Caribou, recalls its heritage in the *New Sweden Historical Museum,* off Route 161 (open June to August, Monday to Saturday 8.30am-4.30pm, Sunday 2pm-5pm), with crafts made by early Swedish settlers. The New Swedes whoop it up on Midsummer's Day in a festival that attracts thousands.

*Acadian Village* on Route 1 in **Van Buren** consists of sixteen buildings tracing the history of Acadian contributions and culture in Maine from 1785 to 1900 (open 15 June to 15 September, Monday to Saturday 10am-5pm, Sunday 12pm-5pm; admission). More on the Acadians can be seen in the *Tante Blanche Museum* and *Acadian Cross Historic Shrine* in **Madawaska,** the northernmost town on the East Coast. The shrine marks the landing site of the first Acadians in the valley (open 8 June to Labor Day, Monday to Friday 9.30am-4.30pm, Sunday 1.30pm-4.30pm; free). West along the St John River, *Fort Kent* was the second blockhouse built during the Aroostook War (1840); the *Fort Kent Memorial* off Route 1 is the original wooden structure, housing historical items pertaining to that bloodless conflict and logging memorabilia (open Memorial Day to Labor Day, from 9am until sunset).

From Fort Kent Route 161 follows the St John River to the town of **Allagash,** the terminus of the *Allagash Wilderness Waterway,* a 92-mile-long stretch of water and forest famous among canoeists and fishermen, wild and remote and yet supervised by park rangers with whom visitors must register. Highlights are the 40-ft Allagash Falls and the abandoned locomotives of the Eagle Lake and Umbazooksus Railroad that used to haul lumber between the two lakes. (For more information on Allagash, write to the Bureau of Parks and Recreation, Maine Department of Conservation, State House Station 19, Augusta, ME 04333.)

**Restaurants.** *In Augusta:* Hazel Green's***, 349 Water Street. *In Waterville:* Silent Woman**, Kennedy Memorial Drive. *In Skowhegan:* Whittemore's**, Route 201. *In Rockwood:* Mystic Moon**. *In Greenville:* Greenville Inn**. *In Bangor:* Cityside***, 277 State Street; Pilot's Grill**. *In Houlton:* Ivey's***, Bangor Road. *In Patten:* Shin Pond House*. *In Dover-Foxcroft:* Blethen House Inn**.

## Annual Events in Maine

**March:** 30-mile dog-sled race, *Rangely.*
**Last week in March:** Exhibition of Maine artisans, *Wiscasset.*
**Mid April:** National Open Canoe Championships, Lower Dead River.
**Third week in June:** Acadian Festival, *Madawaska;* also Antique Auto Parade and Show, *Bar Harbor.*
**Last week in June:** Schooner Days and Chicken Barbeque, *Camden* and *Rockport.*
**July to August:** Bay Chamber Concert Series, every Thursday at 8pm, *Rockport.*
**4 July:** World's Fastest Lobster Boat Race, *Jonesport.*

**First week of July:** Windjammer Days, *Boothbay Harbor;* also Dump Week in *Kennebunkport,* with Giant Trash Parade.
**Mid July:** Dulcimer Festival, *Bar Harbor;* Belfast Bay Festival, *Belfast;* Maine Potato Blossom Festival, *Fort Fairfield;* Maine Quilt show and sale, *Augusta;* Clam Festival, *Yarmouth;* Acadian Scottish Festival, *Trenton.*
**End of July:** Friendship Sloop Days, *Friendship;* Bean Hole Bean Festival, *Oxford.*
**End of July to beginning of August:** Maine Seafoods Festival, *Rockland.*
**All of August:** Maine Festival of the Arts, Bowdoin College, *Brunswick.*
**Beginning of August:** Bangor State Fair, *Bangor;* Tuna Tournament, *Boothbay Harbor;* International Festival, *Calais.*
**Second week in August:** Aroostook County Firemen's Muster, *Van Buren;* Lobster Festival, *Winter Harbor;* Monhegan Island Yacht Race, *Falmouth;* Indian Festival, Point Pleasant Reservation, *Eastport;* Summer Arts Fair, *Bar Harbor.*
**Mid August:** Skowhegan State Fair, *Skowhegan;* Blueberry Festival, in *Machias* and *Winslow.*
**End of August:** Union Fair, *Union;* Log Day Festival, *Skowhegan.*
**Beginning of September:** Blue Grass Festival, *Brunswick;* Potato Feast, *Houlton.*
**End of September to October:** Fall Foliage Festival, *Rangely* and *Boothbay.*
**Mid October:** Lobster Festival, *Bass Harbor.*
**Beginning of December:** Christmas Parade, tree lighting, etc. *Bethel.*

## Accommodation in Maine (area code: 207)

### West of the Kennebec River

Stack Neck Inn, 135 Stage Neck Road, tel: 363-3850, *York Harbor.* Expensive resort.
Sands Motel, Ocean Avenue, tel: 363-2211, *York Beach.* Moderate.
The Cliff House, Bald Head Cliff, tel: 646-5124, *Ogunquit.* Expensive; south of town, views.
Sparhawk Resort Motel, Shore Road, tel: 646-5562, *Ogunquit.* Expensive; on sea, good restaurant.
Riverside Motel, Shore Road, tel: 646-2741, *Ogunquit.* Moderate; by Perkin's Cove.
Admiral's Loft Guest House, 97 Main Street, tel: 646-5496, *Ogunquit.* Inexpensive; in old Victorian mansion.

Seagull Motot Inn, US-1, tel: 646-7062, *Wells*. Moderate; family resort.

The Kennebunk Inn, Route 1, tel: 985-3351, *Kennebunk*. Moderate; old inn.

Nonantum Hotel, Ocean Avenue, tel: 967-3338, *Kennebunkport*. Deluxe; grand old hotel.

The Colony, Ocean Avenue, tel: 967-3331, *Kennebunkport*. Fine resort hotel.

Tides Inn by the Sea, Goose Rocks Beach, tel: 967-3757, *Kennebunkport*. Casual but fairly dear beach inn.

Diplomat, E. Grand Avenue, tel: 934-4621, *Old Orchard Beach*. Deluxe; private beach.

Gull Motel, 89 W. Grand, tel: 934-4321, *Old Orchard Beach*. Moderate to expensive; near beach.

Windsor Cabins, Ocean Park Road, *Old Orchard Beach*. Inexpensive.

Executive Inn, 645 Congress Street, tel: 775-5411, *Portland*. Expensive downtown hotel.

YWCA, 87 Spring Street, tel: 772-1906, *Portland*. Inexpensive; women only.

YMCA, 70 Forest Street, tel: 773-1736, *Portland*. Men only.

The Buoy Motel, US-1, tel: 781-3145, *Falmouth*. Moderate.

Eagle Motel, US-1, tel: 865-3371, *Freeport*. Moderate.

Maineline Motel, 133 Pleasant, tel: 725-8761, *Brunswick*. Moderate.

Stowe House Motor Inn, 63 Federal Street, tel: 725-5543, *Brunswick*. Expensive; in Harriet Beecher Stowe's former residence.

Baily Island Motel, Route 24, tel: 833-2886, *Bailey Island*. Moderate.

Flamingo Inn, 1243 Lisbon Street, tel: 784-2351, *Lewiston*. Inexpensive.

YMCA, 62 Turner Street, tel: 784-7222, *Auburn*. Men only; cheap.

Aimhi Lodge, tel: 892-6538, *South Windham* (on Little Sebago Lake). Expensive.

Chute Homestead Cottages, tel: 693-6425, *Naples* (on Sebago Lake). Moderate to expensive cottages on the lake.

Sunday River Inn, tel: 824-2410, *Bethel*. Ski resort centre.

Saddlebrook Lake Lodge, tel: 864-5501, *Rangely*. Expensive resort.

The Rangely Inn, Main Street, tel: 864-3341, *Rangely*. Expensive.

Tarry-A-While Resort, Highland Lake, tel: 647-2522, *Bridgton*. Moderately expensive lodging, many activities.

The Winters Inn, Route 27, tel: 265-5421, *Kingfield*. Expensive, by Sugarloaft ski area.

**North Coast**

Whitfield Motel and Cabins, US-1, tel: 882-7137, *Wiscasset*. Moderate.
Spruce Point Inn, Atlantic Avenue, tel: 633-4152, *Boothbay Harbor*. Deluxe resort.
Fishermen's Wharf Inn, 42 Commercial Street, tel: 633-5090, *Boothbay Harbor*. Expensive; located downtown.
Thistle Inn, tel: 633-3541, *Boothbay Harbor*. Moderate; good dining.
Moody's, Route 1, tel: 832-5362, *Waldoboro*. Moderate; good food, view.
The East Wind, tel: 372-8800, *Tenants Harbor*. Moderate; near Port Clyde.
Trade Winds, 303 Main Street, tel: 596-6661, *Rockland*. Fairly expensive; overlooking harbour.
Glen Cove Motel, US-1, tel: 594-4062, *Rockland*. Inexpensive.
Newcastle Inn, tel: 563-5685, *Newcastle*. Old inn on the Damariscotta River; moderate.
Samoset, Waldo Road, tel: 594-2511, *Rockport*. Expensive resort.
Windjammer Motor Inn, US-1, tel: 236-8351, *Rockport*. Moderate.
Camden Harbor Inn, 83 Bayview, tel: 236-4200, *Camden*. Expensive but charming. Folk music, restaurant.
Whitehall Inn, 52 High Street, tel: 236-3391, *Camden*. Expensive old hotel.
Camden Hills Motor Lodge, Route 1, tel: 236-8478, *Camden*. Moderate; overlooking sea.
Surprise Hotel and Cabins, Route 1, *Camden*. Inexpensive.
Snow Hill Lodge, US-1, tel: 236-3452, *Lincolnville*. Moderate; fine view.
Colonial Gables, Motel and Cottages, Searsport Avenue, tel: 338-4000, *Belfast*. Moderate to expensive; private beach.
Wonder View Cottages, Seasport Avenue, tel: 338-1455, *Belfast*. Inexpensive.
Yardarm Motel, E. Main Street, tel: 548-2404, *Searsport*. Moderate; views.
Jed Prouty Motel, 52 Main Street, tel: 469-3113, *Bucksport*. Moderate; historic inn.
The Pentagoet Inn, tel: 326-8616, *Castine*. Expensive; in Victorian mansion.
Blue Hill Inn, tel: 374-2844, *Blue Hill*. Moderately expensive old inn.

Isleboro Inn, Gilkey Harbor, *Isleboro*. Moderate; island inn.
The Captain's Quarters Inn, Main Street, tel: 367-2420, *Stonington*. Moderate; on harbour.
Twilight Motel, US-1, tel: 667-8165, *Ellsworth*. Moderate.
Bar Harbor Motor Inn, Newport Drive, tel: 288-5169, *Bar Harbor*. Deluxe.
Bluenose, Eden Street, tel: 288-3733, *Bar Harbor*. Expensive; fine views.
Frenchman's Bay Motel, Eden Street, tel: 288-3321, *Bar Harbor*. Moderate to expensive.
Cadillac Motor Inn, 366 Main Street, tel: 288-3831, *Bar Harbor*. Moderate.
Wonder View Motor Lodge, Eden Street, tel: 288-3358, *Bar Harbor*. Expensive; lovely views.
Manor House Inn, 106 West Street, tel: 288-3759, *Bar Harbor*. Moderate.
McKay Cottages, 243 Main Street, *Bar Harbor*. Inexpensive.
YMCA, 36 Mount Desert Street, tel: 288-5008, *Bar Harbor*. Women only; cheap.
Kimball Terrace Inn, Huntington Road, tel: 276-3383, *Northeast Harbor* (on Mount Desert Island). Expensive.
Harbor Light Tourist Home, Main Street, tel: 244-3835, *Southwest Harbor* (on Mount Desert Island). Charming and inexpensive.
Crocker House, tel: 422-6806, *Hancock Point*. Expensive old inn, fine dining.
Harbor Hill, tel: 963-8872, *Winter Harbor*. Expensive; homey.
Ocean Spray Cottages, Sunset Point, tel: 483-2780, *Harrington*. Two-bedroom cottages on the water, moderate to expensive.
The Bluebird Motel, US-1, tel: 255-3332, *Machias*. Moderate.
The Eastland Motel, by the airport, tel: 733-5501, *Lubec*. Moderate.
International Motel, Main Street, tel: 454-7515, *Calais*. Moderate.

**Inland**

The Senator Inn, Western Avenue, tel: 622-5804, *Augusta*. Moderate to expensive.
YMCA, 33 Winthrop Street, tel: 622-6391, *Augusta*. Men only; cheap.
Holiday Inn, 375 Upper Main Street, tel: 873-0111, *Waterville*. Expensive chain.
Breezy Acres, US-201, tel: 474-2703, *Skowhegan*. Moderate.
Somerset Motor Lodge, US-201, tel: 474-2227, *Skowhegan*.

Moderate; sports.

Squaw Mountain Lodge, tel: 695-2272, *Greenville*. Four-season recreation; expensive; on Moosehead Lake.

Chalet Moosehead, tel: 695-2950, *Greenville*. Efficiencies; free canoes; moderately expensive.

Moosehead Motel, tel: 534-7703, *Rockwood*. On Moosehead Lake, great views; expensive.

The Birches, tel: 534-7305, *Rockwood*. Log cabins, ski-touring centre, moderate to expensive.

McIver's Lakeshore Cottages, tel: 534-7702, *Rockwood*. On lake; moderate.

Attean Lake Resort, tel: 668-3792, *Jackman*. Expensive log cabins; food.

Wildwood Lakeside Cabins, Bigwood Lake, *Jackman*. Inexpensive.

Blethen House Inn, tel: 564-2481, *Dover-Foxcroft*. Downtown location; inexpensive.

Big Lake Hostel, Stanhope Mill Road, tel: 794-8200, *Lincoln*. Open 15 May to 15 October; hostel card required.

King Henry's Motor Inn, Route 89, tel: 493-3311, *Caribou*. Moderate; restaurant.

Rock's Motel, Main Street, tel: 834-3133, *Fort Kent*. Moderate.

Northern Lights, Route 1, tel: 764-4441, *Presque Isle*. Moderate.

Gateway Motel, tel: 728-3318, *Madawaska*. Moderate.

Ivey's, Route 2A, tel: 532-2236, *Houlton*. Moderate; restaurant; dancing.

**For more information about Maine,** write to the Maine Publicity Bureau, 97 Winthrop Street, Hallowell, ME 04347.

# Selected Reading


Alderman, Clifford L., *Gathering Storm: The Story of the Green Mountain Boys,* Messner, 1970.

Alper, M. Victor, *America's Freedom Trail,* MacMillan, 1976.

Bearse, Ray (ed.), *Vermont, A Guide to the Green Mountain State,* Houghton Mifflin, 1966.

Borland, Hal, *A Place to Begin: The New England Experience,* Sierra Club, 1976.

Boston Society of Architects, *Architecture Boston,* Barre, 1976.

Bradford, William, *Of Plymouth Plantation* (1650), Modern Library, 1967.

Bremer, Francis, *The Puritan Experiment,* St Martins, 1976.

Brown, Richard, *Massachusetts,* Norton, 1978.

Clark, Charles, *Maine, A History,* Norton, 1977.

Dicken, Charles, *American Notes,* Fawcett, 1961.

Drake, Samuel Adams, *A Book of New England Legends and Folklore,* Tuttle 1981.

Federal Writers Project, *Connecticut, A New Guide,* Houghton Mifflin, 1938.

Gunther, John, *Inside USA,* Harper & Brothers, 1947.

Hadlin, Oscar, *Boston's Immigrants,* Belknap, 1979.

Hill, Ralph Nading, *Yankee Kingdom: Vermont and New Hampshire,* Harper & Row, 1973.

Hoyt, Edwin, *Nantucket, The Life of an Island,* Greene, 1978.

James, Henry, *The American Scene,* Indiana, 1968.

Jones, Howard, and Jones, B., *The Voices of Boston,* Atlantic, 1975.

Kipling, Rudyard, *American Notes,* Standard, 1930.

McBride, Stewart, *Boston in Color,* Hastings, 1977.

McLoughlin, William G. *Rhode Island, A Bicentennial History,* Norton 1978.

McMaster, John Bach, *The Political Depravity of the Founding Fathers,* Noonday Press, 1964.

Morison, E. F., *New Hampshire*, Norton, 1976.

Needham, Walter, *A Book of Country Things,* Funk and Wagnalls, 1965.

O'Connor, Thomas, *Bibles, Brahmins and Bosses,* Boston Public Library 1976.

Rich, Louise, D., *The Coast of Maine,* Crowell, 1975.

Roth, David, *Connecticut,* Norton, 1979.

Sarmiento, Domingo, *Travels in the United States in 1847,* Princeton, 1970.

Snow, Edward R., *The Romance of Casco Bay,* Dodd Mead, 1975.

Steinberg, S., and McGuigan, C., *Rhode Island,* Rhode Island Bicentennial Foundation, 1976.

Thoreau, Henry David, *A Week on the Concord and Merrimac Rivers,* Princeton, 1980.

Thoreau, Henry David, *Cape Cod* (1855), Heritage, 1968.

Tree, Christina, *Massachusetts,* The Countryman Press, 1981.

Tunnard, C., and Reed, H. H., *American Skyline,* Houghton Mifflin, 1956.

Whitehall, Walter M., *Massachusetts from the Berkshires to the Cape,* Viking, 1977.

Wissler, Clark, *Indians of the United States,* Doubleday, 1966.

Yeadon, David, *Hidden Corners of New England,* Funks & Wagnalls, 1976.

# INDEX OF PLACE-NAMES

## by Frederick Smyth

Principal references are in **bold type**